HUMANITIES AND THE COMPUTER

HUMANITIES AND THE COMPUTER
New Directions

Edited by
DAVID S. MIALL

CLARENDON PRESS · OXFORD
1990

Oxford University Press, Walton Street, Oxford OX2 6DP

Oxford New York Toronto
Delhi Bombay Calcutta Madras Karachi
Petaling Jaya Singapore Hong Kong Tokyo
Nairobi Dar es Salaam Cape Town
Melbourne Auckland
and associated companies in
Berlin Ibadan

Oxford is a trade mark of Oxford University Press

Published in the United States
by Oxford University Press, New York

British Library Cataloguing in Publication Data
Humanities and the computer: new directions.
1. Humanities. Applications of computer systems
I. Miall, David S
001.3'028'5
ISBN 0–19–824244–1

Library of Congress Cataloging in Publicaton Data
Data available

Printed Great Britain
by Biddles Ltd,
Guildford and King's Lynn

Contents

List of Figures

Notes on the Contributors

David A. Bantz is the Director of Humanities Computing at Dartmouth College, Hanover, New Hampshire

Alison Black is a Research Fellow in the Department of Typography and Graphic Communication, University of Reading

John Cooper is employed on the CTI Project of the Oxford University Computing Service

Paul Davis is Principal Lecturer in Music Science in the Music Division, Ealing College of Higher Education

Peter Denley is Lecturer in History at Queen Mary and Westfield College, London

Alan Dyer is Senior Lecturer in Psychology and Art in the Department of Art and Design, Coventry Polytechnic

Jo Freedman is a CTI Project Programmer at the Oxford University Computing Service

Edward A. Friedman is a Professor of Management at Stevens Institute of Technology, Hoboken, New Jersey

Charles Henry is Assistant Director for the Division of Humanities and History, The Libraries, Columbia University

Susan Hockey is the Director of CTI at the Centre for Literature and Linguistic Studies, Oxford University

Frank Knowles is Professor of Modern Languages at Aston University, Birmingham

Agnes Kukulska-Hulme is Lecturer in French in the Department of Modern Languages, Aston University, Birmingham

Roger Martlew is a Lecturer in the Department of Archaeology, University of Leicester

James E. McClellan III is Professor of the Humanities at Stevens Institute of Technology, Hoboken, New Jersey

David S. Miall is Principal Lecturer in English at the College of St. Paul and St Mary, Cheltenham, and an Affiliate Professor of Psychology at the Centre for the Advanced Study of Theoretical Psychology, University of Alberta

Kate Milner is an Associate Lecturer in Information Technology at Barnet College, London

Nicholas J. Morgan is a Lecturer in the Department of Scottish History, University of Glasgow

Brendan O'Flaherty is a Research Assistant in the Department of Archaeology, University of Southampton

Sebastian Rahtz is a Lecturer in Computer Science in the Department of Electronics and Computer Science, University of Southampton

Felicity Rash is a Lecturer in the Department of German, Queen Mary and Westfield College, London

Julian Richards is a Lecturer in the Department of Archaeology, University of York

Arthur Shapiro is a Professor of Management at Stevens Institute of Technology, Hoboken, New Jersey

Stephen Shennan is a Lecturer in the Department of Archaeology, University of Southampton

John M. Slatin is Director of the Computer Research Laboratory, Department of English, University of Texas at Austin

Arthur Stutt is a Research Fellow in the Department of Archaeology, University of Southampton

Richard H. Trainor is a Lecturer in the Department of Economic History, University of Glasgow

R. A. Young is a Lecturer in the Department of Philosophy, University of Dundee

1

Introduction

David S. Miall

1 Overview

The primary purpose of this book is to examine the role of computers in the Humanities, with a predominant focus on new developments in higher education. But a number of issues beyond those involved in teaching and learning are also discussed: these range from the current situation of higher education (university management, funding, the relation of teaching and research) to the models of mind which lie behind the increasing use of computers in the Humanities. In this introductory chapter I review briefly some of the salient issues which are raised in the chapters that follow; this will serve to chart the directions in which Humanities computing seems to be developing or is likely to develop in the near future. By tracing here the high ground of the arguments that the authors present in their various chapters, I hope to highlight not only the significant role that computers are destined to play in the Humanities, but also the role that the Humanities can play in the development of computing.

Given that the book deals with a field undergoing rapid development, it might be thought that the cover should reach you stamped with a 'sell-by' (or 'eat-by') date. This would be the case if it were limited solely to describing current hardware and software applications. But the book is distinctive for dealing extensively with the principles raised by the use of computers in Humanities disciplines: how the Humanities are conceptualized, what models of human thought and communication they embody, and questions about the nature of learning—all of which seem likely to remain significant areas of debate for some time to come. In particular, the introduction of computer methods is requiring us to define, perhaps redefine, what we understand by the Humanities and how they should be taught.

The status of the Humanities in an increasingly technological world is currently being subjected to urgent questioning, particularly in the U.S.A. (eg., Bloom, 1987; Hirsch, 1987). In this context it is opportune that the development of computing and its associated sciences has reached a level at which serious computer-based models of Humanities thinking can now be envisaged. There is a historical irony here which future generations may come to appreciate: just at the point when technology threatened irrevocable marginalization of the Humanities in our culture, technology itself, in the form of the computer, provided a framework for showing that the Humanities offer a significant model for future technological development. A central role for the Humanities, after all, is to present models of the interaction between human beings and their environment, whether in the past or present, through the medium of archaeology, history, or literature. Yet until now there was no way of testing or verifying the interpretations of culture that the Humanities offered except, in the last resort (to borrow Keats's phrase) 'on the pulse.' So the work of the Humanities has long since ceased to provide the primary engine for shaping society or accounting for who we are. But if the computer is now, as J. David Bolter (1984) has argued, our defining technology, providing the metaphors by which we interpret both man and nature, the computer also now seems on the point of maturing sufficiently to embrace the thought worlds of the Humanities and, as a result, being humanized in its turn.

Central to this new role for computers in the Humanities is the development of knowledge based systems, powerful enough to take on the task of mapping the different logics of historical evidence or literary response. But there are other significant gains, of which the most promising is the new shape given to student learning that is assisted by the computer. In both cases the old conception of transmitting culture through the Humanities, and by extension, through teacher-dominated education methods, is being replaced: Humanities knowledge can be actively tested, explored and enacted through the computer, and an alternative conception of student-centred learning, which the computer tends to instill in us, sees students deploying the computer as a partner in individual and group learning activities. These are among the major themes to be examined in the pages that follow.

2   The Background to this Book

The use of computers in the Humanities has a long history, going back almost as far as the appearance of the computer itself. The first reported project, which began in 1949, was that of Father Roberto Busa to compile an index and concordance to the works of St Thomas Aquinas. Early work of this kind soon extended to computer-assisted authorshop studies, the compiling of computer archives of texts, and the development of databases for Humanities research. Until the 1970s, however, the computer was mainly confined to a role as a research tool, and computers were used by only a small minority of Humanities academics; there were very few courses in computing for the Humanities student (Hockey, 1987). With the advent of more user-friendly mainframe computers, then the rapid proliferation of inexpensive microcomputers in the 1980s, and now optical storage and other devices, the computer is beginning to play a significant role in the experience of students as well. Recent surveys of Humanities computing in British higher education in universities (Hirscheim, et al., 1987) and in polytechnics and colleges (Miall, 1989c) have revealed a steady growth in courses, particularly in the latter sector where it was estimated that over half of all Humanities students now take some course in Humanities computing.

Accompanying the growth in student involvement has come recognition of the need to think through issues for teaching and learning in higher education. The question of learning has been debated at conferences in the U.S.A. for some years, including a workshop devoted to the topic of teaching Humanities computing at Vassar College in 1986 (Ide, 1987). In Britain significant new innovations in computer-assisted learning were beginning to take place, but with no overall academic rationale. This realization led to the CATH conferences (Computers and Teaching in the Humanities), the first of which was held at Southampton University in April 1987 (Rahtz, 1987, brings together a collection of articles issued to accompany the conference). The second conference, CATH 88, also held at Southampton, took place in December 1988. This book is based on papers that were given on that occasion. A third conference, scheduled to take place in April 1990, will focus on the work of the new CTI (Computers in Teaching Initiative) Centres in Britain, a unique innovation begun in April 1989 with Government funding. Based on specific subjects, including several in the Humanities (such as history, literature and linguistics, and music) the Centres are designed to provide advice to all university teachers in their subject, and to act as a clearing house for information on computer applications and teaching methods. The Centres are the main follow-up to the CTI development grants, which provided funds to develop the use of computers in university teaching: many of the 139 projects funded since 1984 have been in the Humanities (see Katzen, 1988); several of the chapters in this book discuss CTI-funded projects.

The present book, therefore, emerges from a specific concern for the issues of learning and teaching in higher education (in which, as will become apparent, the emphasis has shifted onto learning). But surrounding this concern lie a number of other questions, including the wider issue of the place of the Humanities, as I have already suggested. Given that in Britain the main support for Humanities computing, in terms of funding, will go to supporting subject-specific developments, one major question that arises is whether Humanities computing is itself a discipline.

3 Humanities Computing: An Emerging Discipline?

In deciding on the title for this book, *Humanities and the Computer*, I have wanted to suggest that the question posed above remains open. Whether a discipline is emerging, with its own theoretical foundations and paradigmatic applications, called 'Humanities Computing,' has been disputed, most notably at the Vassar workshop. There is no doubt that a range of significant and often mature developments within the field have occurred, including both generic (i.e. cross-discipline) and subject specific applications (this claim can be verified by a glance at the magisterial survey provided by Lancashire and McCarty, 1988). But doubts must remain about the validity of a distinctive and coherent discipline while most of what is called 'Humanities computing' is carried out within specific Humanities subjects (as Ide, one of the convenors of the Vassar workshop, noted in an aside to her discussion: Ide, 1987, p. 214, n. 7).

What is 'Humanities computing' so far, then? Another of the Vassar participants, Robert Tannenbaum, provided a summary of the field as he saw it (bear
in mind that this was 1986). His list included a range of applications, each of
which has a role in all or most of the different Humanities disciplines: text editing, text formatting, and text analysis; statistical analysis, databases, spreadsheet
analysis, graphics for representing and analysing data, modelling and simulation,
data capture, and computer-assisted instruction (Tannenbaum, 1987: 222). These
various methods have undoubtedly increased the power of the humanist researcher,
in some cases dramatically. Yet it is also apparent that the rationale for employing
one of these methods in a given subject still comes primarily from the subject, not
from the computer. While the computer provides a means for undertaking work
that might have been much more laborious, or perhaps impossible, without the help
of a computer, the framework within which such work takes place—the research
method, the rules for interpreting the significance of findings—are still provided by
the home discipline. The computer provides a powerful and remarkably versatile
instrument for Humanities work, but it doesn't up to this point provide a way of
conceptualizing the Humanities subject itself or the Humanities in general.

The reason for this is not hard to see. For example, storing literary texts (such
as the complete works of Shakespeare) on the computer allows rapid access to
any word or combination of words that I choose anywhere in the text: but the
interpretation of the words that I have found remains with me, not the computer.
The computer cannot 'read' text, except in a purely mechanical sense. Similarly,
a well-designed relational database will enable a significant domain of historical
information to be stored and analysed: but the rationale for designing the database
requires the powers of analysis and imagination of the historian. Computer
methods of the type listed by Tannenbaum do not, in themselves, constitute a
new discipline. As Bantz puts it (later in this book), 'computer applications have
limited means for symbolically representing information.' The principle form of
representation, in other words, remains the mind of the Humanities researcher,
informed by the questions and concerns of his or her subject.

The proponents of Humanities computing as a discipline turn to computer
science to find a rationale, at least when thinking how to design and teach a course
in computing to Humanities students. The issues dealt with in such a course are
derived from computer methodologies developed within the Humanities, but refer
back to basic computational issues. Such courses, Ide (1987) argues, lead to an
emphasis on 'theoretical principles and conceptual foundations.' One important
method of enabling students to learn some computer science is to require them to
learn programming (in a number of courses Pascal, Snobol, or Basic is taught; a
few now teach Prolog): this gives students an insight into memory, file management, recursive operations, and the like. As a result students will be better able to
understand the standard programs they use, their rationale and limitations. Such
courses are obviously longer and more demanding than courses that aim only to
introduce the standard tools of Humanities computing, but Ide goes on to suggest

that, as a result, 'the next generation of humanists who use computers will actively contribute to the development of the field—both in methodology and software tools for its implementation.' It is also clear, however, that such courses will tend to centre on quantitative methods: Ide (among others) foresees, for instance, an increase in the scope of computational linguistics. In this view, Humanities work is being moved closer to what we conceive computers are best at doing, rather than computers being developed to make them more suited to the traditional ways of thought of the Humanities.

While a rapprochment between standard approaches to text and computational linguistics may be just over the horizon, the most impressive achievements of Humanities computing so far remain tied to data storage, retrieval, and analysis. At the forefront stand some notable examples: the Thesaurus Linguae Graecae, comprising over 8000 works of classical Greek literature (now available on CD-ROM), the research tool for text analysis, the Oxford Concordance Program, of which exemplary use has been made in a recent study of the novels of Jane Austen (Burrows, 1987), or the British Domesday Project, which brings together a wealth of textual and visual information on Britain in the 1980s. But it is debatable whether a collection of tools of this kind, remarkable though many of them are, yet constitutes a discipline.

The issue can be put another way. Bolter (1984) argues that, given the significance of the computer in our age, our thinking will in time come to be determined by the terms suggested by the machine. This is because 'the computer reflects, indeed imitates, the crucial human capacity of rational thinking . . . By making a machine think as a man, man recreates himself, defines himself as a machine' (p. 13). But, except in minor ways, the thought worlds of the Humanities seem particularly resistant to being defined in computational terms: the computer so far can suggest only impoverished and reduced definitions of thought. The data processing powers of the computer, as in the examples noted above, require supplementing at every point by the powers of human thought and imagination. The real difference between the thought worlds of the computer and the Humanities is suggested by another remark of Bolter, where he contrasts a tool with a machine. A tool 'extends human technical capabilities while remaining intimately under human control. A machine runs more or less under its own control, with its own sense of purpose and its own inanimate source of power' (p. 55). In this respect the computer in the hands of the humanist remains a tool rather than a machine. The 'sustained, autonomous action' which Bolter attributes to the machine (p. 233) resides in the mind of the humanist, in the form of his or her understanding of the field and the research questions which drive further inquiry (including the decision whether to use the computer).

Thus the question whether Humanities computing is a discipline is decided by the level at which we are able to conceptualize the thought processes involved. If our model of computer thought is derived from the processing of discrete, arbitrary, finite, and isolated elements of thought as in Bolter's account of the computer (p. 75–78), then this must exclude the mainstream processes of thought undertaken in the Humanities, however invaluable the computer has proved as a tool.

But there is reason to believe that this is about to change: the level at which computers are able to model thought will increasingly come closer to the Humanities. This book reports several projects deploying knowledge based systems in the Humanities, and these may be the first signs of major developments that lie ahead. Humanities knowledge typically involves degrees of uncertainty, whether in archaeological interpretation, reader response, or historical data. Reasoning in the Humanities is frequently based on incomplete data, thus alternative logics are required: modal, fuzzy, probabilistic. Attempts to model reasoning of this kind in artificial intelligence may have reached a point of maturity at which serious projects can be mounted to deploy them in the service of the Humanities. Compared with the standard techniques of text storage, relational databases, or videodisc libraries, such projects will provide more powerful means for representing knowledge in the Humanities, and will enable various interpretative processes of Humanities reasoning to be modelled and tested (see Gardin and Ennals, 1989).

The thrust of research in computing is already strongly influenced by the achievements of artificial intelligence. Commercial knowledge based applications (often called expert systems) are now being developed and implemented. It is to be expected that such advances will increasingly impact on the Humanities. A measure of the progress already made is provided by a comparison of the two CATH conferences and their associated books. Artificial intelligence techniques were mentioned in passing by two of the speakers whose papers appeared in the earlier book (see Ennals and Hall, in Rahtz, 1987), and was the focus of one speaker whose paper was not published (J-C. Gardin).[1] The present book, by contrast, contains two chapters focussing specifically on applications of knowledge based systems, including wider consideration of their role in reconceptualizing the Humanities (see Stutt and Young); several chapters mention other new developments in passing (Denley, Miall, Rahtz, et al.).

Perhaps the most significant implication of these alternative logics, argument structures, and models of interpretation is that they provide new ways of understanding the mind. The distinctive contribution of the Humanities is to provide a rich domain for developing and testing such models. Existing computational models of the mind, as I have suggested, are impoverished by comparison with the thinking of the humanist. The information processing paradigm which has dominated cognitive science for the last thirty years, and which has proved so fertile in suggesting productive lines of research, still remains unable to embrace typical Humanities processes—for example, understanding how we read a short story.[2] Now we may be within sight of a different approach, in which Humanities

---

[1] A shortened version of his paper was subsequently printed: see Gardin (1987b).

[2] A recent advocate of the information processing approach to literature, W. John Harker (1989), for example, is unable to quote a single example of research in this domain which successfully handles

methods of thought are modelled by the computer; these in turn will encourage computer scientists and cognitive scientists to reconceptualize their views of the nature of human thought. No doubt this is still a long step, but one result has already been signalled by Margaret Boden (1987) in her account of the implications of artificial intelligence. Contrary to the popular belief that work in computers is conspiring to dehumanize our world, she argues, such work actually 'confirms our insistence that we are essentially subjective creatures living through our own mental constructions of reality (among which science is one)' (p. 473).

If knowledge based systems do begin to model Humanities work effectively, as now seems imminent, this is more likely than any other development to bring to birth Humanities computing as a coherent discipline. The Humanities have many research procedures in common, and a common interest in processes of representation: these will be facilitated by the new methods emerging from artificial intelligence. Computer-based work in understanding natural phenomena, including the mind, will in turn be enhanced by the models that Humanities computing will make available. In this respect the Humanities will be working to rehumanize technology, allowing a more complex (and responsible) understanding of the powers and limitations of technological development.

As yet such achievements lie in the future, but much is being achieved already. The present chapters provide important evidence of the gains being made now from the use of computers in the Humanities.

4 The New Discourse of Computers

Besides the move towards knowledge based systems, another notable sign of progress since the first CATH conference is a better developed focus on learning. There is a consensus, apparent from a number of the chapters, that computers facilitate more independent and interesting work on the part of the student. Four chapters discuss the determinants of the learning process in detail (Martlew, Morgan and Trainor, Miall, and Denley); a number of others discuss learning in the context of a specific computer application.

What emerges from these different discussions is a new role for the computer as a medium for reflecting the discourse of the Humanities. The methods now available, including text analysis, music composition, or graphic design, engage students—often working in small groups—in debate about what questions to put, how to control and shape their investigations, and how to assess their findings in relation to theory and practice in their specific discipline. The computer, in other words, tends to foreground the act of inquiry, to require an active grasp of the implications and limitations of particular research procedures. A type of conversational learning is making its appearance around the computer: this was always available as a possibility without computing, but in reality it demanded

understanding of literary texts. For some analysis of the reasons why, with an alternative proposal, see Miall (1989a).

of the lecturer careful planning and the application of strategic knowledge about pedagogic practice which few were equipped or willing to provide (higher education in Britain still has much to learn from practice in primary and secondary education, as Martlew observes in his chapter).

The flexibility of the computer as a tool, together with the fact that attending to the screen shifts attention away from the teacher, encourages students to engage more actively in the debate that is central to the Humanities. Given also that the computer can now provide direct access to potentially massive stores of data (such as the primary source materials of the historian or the literary scholar), students are becoming involved in practices of research which were formerly open only to the postgraduate or lecturer. A number of the contributors to this book speak of the gains in student commitment and in students' awareness of their own learning that come from judicious use of the computer. The narrowing of the gap between research and teaching that comes from Humanities computing does, of course, have a political dimension: it comes at a time when official policy in Britain is to divide research from teaching through separate funding arrangements. This retrograde move ignores the changes in the Humanities that are described in this book, as well as disregarding the nature of the learning process that is carried on in higher education (Denley provides a more detailed discussion of the issues).

To see the computer as a reflexive and conversational medium for learning necessitates changes in course management and design in higher education. It will require changes in methods of assessment (a particularly interesting innovation here is discussed by Dyer and Milner); it will also require bringing computers into subject departments, with Humanities staff taking over some of the responsibilities formerly assigned to university computer centres (with implications for job descriptions and appraisal that have yet to be seriously addressed). But students seem increasingly aware of the vocational value of acquiring computer skills while taking a Humanities degree, and this will undoubtedly continue to be a major argument for funding computers in the Humanities. It would be a mistake to place too much emphasis on this vocational dimension of the Humanities, however: a discipline which is left to rely only on extrinsic justifications for its existence is surely destined for oblivion. The Humanities are worth more than a set of computer skills which can then be updated for use in commerce or industry.

The other principal implication of the new discourse of computers which emerges from the chapters in this book involves the concept of interdisciplinarity: the conversations which could (perhaps should) be taking place between disciplines. An eloquent defence of interdisciplinarity is mounted explicitly by Davis, who argues for seeing the computer as a catalyst for the creation of new cross-disciplinary subjects, giving music science as his primary example. But the issues emerge clearly from several other discussions: for example, Henry's proposal to focus on imagery in the interpretation of texts requires contributions from artificial intelligence, linguistics, and psychology. Computing, in its latest developments, is clearly more than one discipline already, drawing in particular on cognitive science. Now the Humanities seem set to extend the scope of computing to the models of human and natural processes available in the Humanities. However, one danger, as Young points out in the case of philosophy, is that inequitable funding arrangements will lead computing to develop faster than research in its sister Humanities disciplines, which have traditionally attracted little or no research funding—to the ultimate detriment of computing itself.

It has been argued (by Bolter among others) that the principal conversation that the computer will facilitate is that between the arts and sciences, overcoming the much-discussed and damaging 'two cultures' division. The computer will bring some understanding of the scientific domain to the humanist, while the technologist will gain access to the recorded knowledge of the Humanities through the computer (Bolter, 1984: 229–231). This seems an unduly heavy burden to place on the computer, but it is also a somewhat limited and instrumental view of the potential conversation. The convergence of the arts and sciences is already taking place in significant respects, through reconceptualizing the meaning of both domains: through the realization of the subjective nature of observation in science; through more explicit theoretical and empirical studies in the arts. The computer, aided by new knowledge based developments of the kind discussed above, will certainly help in this process. But the proper goal of such a convergence (if we can venture to propose one) is better understanding of the mind and of man's relation to nature. Here the Humanities will have a major contribution to make in enabling us to frame the issues and to propose research questions at an appropriate level. It is a contribution whose full extent can only be glimpsed, but it is being revealed in part by the work of those involved in Humanities computing.

5 The Scope of this Book

The arrangement of the chapters in the book enables a logical sequence of issues to be followed. The first two chapters, by Denley and Bantz, raise the most wide-ranging questions about the nature of Humanities computing: its promise and some of the dangers. In his chapter, Denley (a historian) points first to the precarious position of the Humanities in the late 20th Century, then indicates some of the opportunities for rethinking the Humanities that are provided by the advent of computing. He also examines the academic context of Humanities computing, and underlines the political difficulties that tend to hinder development in Britain. Bantz looks at some of the dangers for the Humanities of over-enthusiastic or technology-led developments in computing. He argues that the computing facilities we offer students should be directed by the fundamental concerns of Humanities education, and he describes examples of the work being done in this respect at Dartmouth College.

The next three chapters concentrate in particular on the implications of computers for reshaping student learning. Martlew analyses the relationship between teacher and student that is typical in higher education, where the teacher remains in control of both method and content. While computers can be (and have been) used to reinforce this, he advocates a shift to student-centred learning, in which students are given access to computer resources (such as videodisc technology) to pursue their own inquiries. In my own chapter (Miall), I make a similar case, using the example of English studies. I also try to demarcate the domains where computer use is appropriate in English (such as project work, taking place in small groups of students) from those where computers have, as yet, no role. Morgan and Trainor review the background to traditional teaching methods in history, particularly in Scotland. Their own practice provides an important contrast: based on workshop methods deploying the computer, students are given experience in framing and carrying out inquiries on historical databases.

Of the three chapters that follow, each points in different ways to the significance of knowledge based developments for the Humanities. Stutt describes a project for an argument support program, in which the underlying premises and reasoning typical of Humanities discourse are modelled by the computer. This would provide a tool for the student (or researcher) to reflect and test their interpretations, whether in archaeology or literature. Young looks at the promise of artificial intelligence for reshaping both the concerns and the teaching of philosophy. Knowledge based systems that model expert knowledge in various domains require research on alternative logics: these are best studied by philosophers interested not only in computational principles, but in the ethical issues involved in computer-based medical or military developments. Henry draws on artificial intelligence, cognitive science, and literary theory to examine the role of imagery in the way we read texts: he raises some fundamental questions about the nature of interpretation. To explore these adequately requires a new, intelligent computer-based model of reading.

The second half of the book moves into closer focus on the role of computers in several specific disciplines: they enable the implications of computer-assisted work to be evaluated in the study of texts, in art and design, typography, music, languages, and archaeology. The chapter by Friedman, McClellan, and Shapiro discusses a course on Galileo in which a full-text retrieval system is used by students to gain access to 2700 pages of primary and secondary sources. The results of this facility for student learning patterns are evaluated. In a comparable development at Oxford University, Hockey, Freedman, and Cooper describe a system for making text retrieval available across the university: the software gives access to a range of texts and two powerful programs for text analysis, and thus offers a highly flexible environment for students. Slatin's chapter examines the arguments for hypermedia (non-linear presentation of text and graphics), showing that recent literary theory provides a framework for validating hypertext as a medium for the study of literary texts. He illustrates his account with examples from a hypertext course on modern American poetry. Hypertext is also the primary focus of the next chapter, by Dyer and Milner. However, their approach, based on work in teaching Art and Design, points to the power of hypertext as a medium for student's assessed work: instead of presenting essays or a thesis, students produce their arguments, illustrated with graphics, in the form of hypertext. The authors show that hypertext is a type of 'painterly' medium particularly suited to bridging the practical and theoretical studies of their students.

The chapter by Black discusses students' use of the computer in typography: the design of document layout was carried out either on screen or on paper. A careful evaluation of students' responses to their work in the two media was carried out, which contains interesting implications for the ways in which computer environments are deployed in learning. Davis looks at the growth of computer-based and other electronic technologies in music. While his chapter argues the need for musicians to involve themselves in a range of disciplines beyond music (as traditionally defined), the issues he raises have wider implications: the new technologies will require a much greater respect and support for interdisciplinarity in all academic disciplines.

The next two chapters offer two different perspectives on the teaching of languages. Knowles and Kukulska-Hulme provide an invaluable survey of the impact of computing on the teaching of modern languages, from which it is apparent that the introduction of computational methods is bringing revolutionary changes to the concerns and methods of language teaching. Rash points to the problems involved in learning a medieval language, and describes a computer system for enabling students to make use of their knowledge of a 'cognate' modern language. Finally, in the last chapter, Rahtz and his colleagues examine a new role for computers in teaching archaeology: first a system for simulating the excavation of an archaeological site, then a program for providing comprehensive information to students about all three years of their degree course in archaeology.

As with several chapters earlier in the book, these last chapters also show how the use of computers effects changes in learning styles, shifting the emphasis from content to method. While it is clear that there are certain inherent dangers in applying the new technology in the Humanities, as Denley, Bantz and Black in particular suggest, the advent of the computer seems to be causing many Humanities academics involved in computing to rethink both the nature of their subject and the means by which students acquire their knowledge of it. The computer, in other words, offers to alter our perspective, shifting us from those angles of view where we or our students have perhaps grown too accustomed to standard responses and familiar modes of study. The longer term impact of computing on the Humanities is hard to estimate as yet, but it is clear from this book that the computer will have a major influence in redefining learning. Whether it will also serve to redefine our concept of the Humanities disciplines themselves remains to be seen.

The preparation of this book has been aided by the work of three assistant editors: Susan Hockey, May Katzen, and Sebastian Rahtz; they have provided invaluable help and advice throughout, and I would like to express my gratitude here. The first stages in planning the book occurred during 1988, when those of us who were preparing the CATH conference also acted as an editorial board to make the initial selection of contributors. Thus I would also like to thank the conference committee for their work on the book. Given that conference proceedings are now often ignored when research publications are being counted, it is worth saying here that the present chapters, while derived from papers given at CATH 88, are all specially commissioned; all have been subjected to a further review process by the editor and assistant editors, and most have been partly rewritten as a result. Thus the present book is not a conference proceedings! Then I would like to record my thanks to Sebastian Rahtz for taking on the arduous task of producing camera-ready copy from my word processor files. Needless to say, I alone am responsible for any errors that may remain in the following pages.

2

The Computer Revolution and 'Redefining the Humanities'

Peter Denley

1 Introduction

It is a commonplace that the advent of computers is epoch-making, and that it will
in due course be so in virtually every field of enquiry. All those at the CATH 88
conference shared, to varying degrees, a conviction that computing will come to
have a profound effect on humanities teaching just as it will on so many other
areas. These may still be early days, but already new techniques are sweeping our
disciplines.

It was particularly apt that the subtitle to the theme of the conference was
'Redefining the Humanities.' The humanities themselves were defined by educational revolution, in a process initiated by the humanists of late medieval
Italy. This chapter is based on a conviction that information technology may well
similarly bring about profound changes in the shape and role of the humanities.
The achievements of the CATH 88 conference itself— and there have been many
others—speak forcefully both for increased cross-disciplinary activity within the
humanities and for the benefits already gained from dialogue with computer
scientists and programmers. The computer revolution, coming as it does at a
time of fundamental reassessment of the role of arts subjects in education, offers
possibilities of reintegration with other subjects.

A clear statement of the impact that computing may come to have on the nature
and structure of the humanities is an urgent necessity. One of the contentions of
this chapter is that the realization of the full potential of humanities computing
is being hampered by the lack of clarity of purpose. But such a statement is no
simple matter; it will need to grow through consensus. The approach here will
be more indirect. The historian of education finds interest and relevance not just
in the nature of educational reforms but equally in the way in which they came
about. This topic speaks to us directly, for the politics of education have become
a dominant concern to all involved.

2 The Crisis of the Humanities

That the humanities are currently undergoing major crisis is much in the air. The cluster of disciplines we label in this way grew out of an ideal of education that had been intended as a common basis for education at school and early university level, preparatory to the higher university subjects. By the nineteenth century, pressure for the insertion of these subjects into the formal degree system and the 'professionalisation' of disciplines was leading away from the rounded educational basis of the humanistic programme and into specialisation. The humanities were becoming more 'scientific,' engaging in 'research.' Keith Thomas described this process very well in a paper recently published in *The Times Higher Education Supplement* (Thomas, 1988). By falling in with the German, Humboldtian, doctrine of the indivisibility of teaching and research (not new in practice but the more forceful for having been made explicit), the humanities acquired justification for their desire to pursue scholarship; not just 'for its own sake,' but because that scholarship was now recognised to be necessary for the continued training of the young. Yet this was a two-edged weapon. With the revival of utilitarianism the humanities are now in a position where this is the *only* justification for research. 'Scholarship for its own sake' no longer pays the rent; it is very difficult to persuade the outside world of the value of, say, historical or literary research, compared with the obvious practical benefits of scientific research; and the more esoteric and less populist that research is, the harder the task of persuasion (Thomas, 1988). It seems that at best humanities academics can be entertainers, writers of popular books, or advisers to television programmes, to show off or diffuse their learning; at worst, they remain stuck in their ivory towers.

These dangers were latent even before the twentieth century transformations, the widening of access to higher education and the end of higher education for narrow élites, undermined the original rationale for a broad humanistic education. The late twentieth century—and nowhere more than in Thatcherite Britain—has brought this fragility home with a vengeance. There is now a need to explain to almost every parent, every prospective student, every scientific colleague, every university administrator and every politician what the value of humanities subjects is. 'The training of the mind,' 'helping give perspective on life,' 'the value in itself of a broad education,' are phrases that may convince some humanities teachers; they cut no ice with utilitarians, especially as the humanities get upstaged not just by the sciences but also by more 'socially relevant' disciplines such as sociology and business or management studies.

So what is the way forward? The humanities are in a more exposed position than ever before. The possibility of a fundamental transformation, the disappearance of many single-subject departments and their regrouping into 'humanities' schools teaching for 'humanities' degrees, does not merely loom; the process has already begun.

All this is happening at a time of overall retrenchment, of the deliberate depression of the universities in order to bring about a shake-up. The profession is being put in a position similar to that of the courtiers of the Renaissance. There is no 'job security,' and very little funding, what there is being given on a 'one-off' basis; already the humanities, along with the rest of the university system, are having to justify every inch of ground, and having to apply for funding for every substantial piece of research, to be judged on its own merits and the merits of the supplicant, his/her department, faculty and university. There is no question of the general principle of the value of the humanities being accepted and their practitioners being allowed to get on with it. The transformation of humanities academics into skilled fillers-in of application forms, managers of funded projects, and producers of glossy public-relations literature is perhaps the most striking phenomenon observable in the humanities in the 1980s. Nor is it defensible to point to the new initiatives that have grown out of these transformations to the profession as justification for the new approach. University reforms of this kind, coming as they do at a time of contraction and upheaval, have done damage to quality, morale and the capacity for imaginative thinking and forward planning that far outweighs the potential benefits. The humanities are under siege.

3 The Advent of Computing

To introduce the computer at this point in the discussion risks an element of bathos, even ridicule, until we remember that the advent of the microcomputer and the dramatic advance of humanities computing coincide precisely with that period of retrenchment and crisis. It must be stressed, immediately, that the last thing that should be expected of information technology is any kind of panacea for the humanities. Only a minority of practitioners would argue that even in half-seriousness. Nonetheless, even in the short time that cheap computing has been available, there have been quite remarkable developments in research and teaching techniques in the humanities as a consequence; many departments now have a major investment of time, energy and money in humanities computing; and many of the most adventurous (if not the most mature or eminent) teachers are involved in pioneering work in this area.

With this development have come new working patterns and new kinds of interrelationship, some of which may well signal more profound changes to come. Those who have taken to computers have questioned and re-explored the fundamental methodologies of their own disciplines; they have worked closely with colleagues from other disciplines within and beyond the humanities; and they have found their students eagerly doing the same. There are intellectual and practical sides to this opening up of disciplines through the common language of computing, and one of the pleasant surprises is to find how well they go together. Teachers and researchers find that methods of organising information or preparing data, even when primarily undertaken for modest practical purposes, provide new tools for the subject and points of contact with colleagues working in other subjects.

A history student wishing to construct a database is both stimulated into rigorous historical definition by the task and given analytical and technical skills which will serve in later life; and there is no tension between the two.

The intellectual ramifications of the computer revolution for the humanities are, I repeat, not the concern of this paper. The subject is too vast, and the legitimacy of computing techniques within individual disciplines must in the last resort be a matter for those disciplines. What concerns us here is the practicalities of the computer revolution in the humanities. How is this revolution taking place? What have been the obstacles in its way, and how can they be surmounted? What are the practical implications of the new technology for the shape of the humanities?

4 Humanities Computing and the Scientists

Historically the first context in which humanities computing should be examined is that of academic computing generally, which was originally the exclusive province of the sciences and which is still overwhelmingly dominated by them.

The humanities were late arrivals to computing. This was not just a matter of lack of interest or will, but also lack of recognition of its validity, and lack of funding. One of the consequences of the peculiar status of the humanities, and the lack of a perceived 'utilitarian' dimension to humanities research, has been that the humanities were never seen as requiring funding beyond library and salary provision. There has been no provision for technical support because the subjects were not considered, in that sense, technical. Those in the humanities who have used computers for some time can all think back to the days when major projects were hampered, sometimes seriously undermined, by limitations of file space or budget over and above the limitations of computer capability at the time. Humanities computing began as a 'poor relation,' and is still in that position.

What has helped has been precisely the cheapness and popularity of arts subjects. University scientists may not feel that the humanities are 'useful,' but the fact remains that the humanities bring high-calibre, well-qualified students into the institution, and do so cheaply. Equally, though, university funding has been a matter of the slicing of a finite, limited cake. Scientists are understandably reluctant to contemplate actual cuts in their own budgets to help humanities computing.

The humanities have only got as far as they have in computing because the cost of computing has fallen so much. But they still have particular needs. If it is explained to the scientists that arts computing makes periodic but intensive use of CPU-time on a mainframe, and requires by and large more file storage, memory or magnetic tapes than the average scientific application, this is nowadays a surmountable problem. If the science-dominated computing committees are asked for microcomputers, laser printers, even optical character readers and phototypesetters for the humanities they are often happy; they can use this equipment too, and the request confirms the widely-held prejudice that arts computing is basically glorified word-processing. A request for an arts computing adviser is an altogether different matter. The opposition is not intellectual; many scientists understand that humanities students wishing or needing to be taught computing skills need to be taught in a different way from science students—that problem-solving approaches, with emphasis on detail, and the gradual emergence of the general picture, are not the most congenial to the arts-trained mind (Ide, 1987). The real reasons for opposition are the implications of such a post: for funding; for the computer centre's control over advisory services (few are geared to discipline-specific advice); for the computer science departments, many of which are still suspicious of special courses for arts students, and which consider themselves the natural arbiters of what computing courses should consist of. The shift here from scorn to polite apprehension indicates that humanities computing is now being taken seriously in these quarters, but not yet that it is considered respectable. The fact that it initially evolved outside scientifically-oriented computing compounds this problem.

This is a political battle more than an academic one. The humanities have had to learn all about grant applications—in which the sciences have long experience—but they have a long way to go. They have yet to convince bodies such as the British Academy of the need to fund computer-based projects on a systematic basis, and there is the larger hurdle of persuading the Computer Board to weight formula funding less to their disadvantage.

5 Humanities Computing and the Humanities

As well as having to defend its corner in the computing world, humanities computing has had to convince colleagues within the humanities of its value.

Again, there have been many recent conversions. The pioneers in the field were doing something which instinctively aroused hostility (and fear). The quantitative emphasis of what they were doing was hardly designed to endear their work to conservatives, and there was a certain amount of snobbery about 'getting machines to do one's thinking.' Now, by contrast, it is considered good for the academic profile, and good for recruitment, to have a computing dimension within arts departments or arts faculties. The more the humanities come to be measured—vis-a-vis other faculties, other departments within the faculty, or departments in other institutions—by the amount of funding they attract, the more computing is an attractive option. But there are dangers in this trend. The level of managerial understanding does not always bring with it an understanding of what computing is doing to the humanities, and that is a serious obstacle to real integration. Computing courses in arts departments are often left on the periphery, as an optional extra to the degree course. This may appear the safer path until what computing can offer is more fully appreciated, but it is self-defeating. The scope for introducing computing to humanities students, and the time teachers and students can afford to give to such courses, are severely limited if the course is not an integral part of the degree; and while such restrictions apply the full potential of computing will not be realised. At the other extreme, making computing courses a major compulsory element for students, and even forcing staff to acquire computing skills and teach such courses, may be counter-productive too.

Colleagues in the humanities still often harbour more profound reservations, some practical, many methodological. Amongst historians there are those who are wary of what the computer offers because they see computing techniques as 'emphasising the repetitive at the expense of the unique.' This is not just a new form of the old controversies about quantification or about the value of political history as against other branches of the discipline. There is a strong feeling that certain types of history are better taught in traditional ways, and that an overemphasis on computing might prejudice that approach. Advocates of humanities computing need to be sensitive to such fears, and to make clear that they are proposing ancillary skills, not wholesale revolution. Similar tact is necessary to deal with a more widespread but rarely admitted fear, the fear of many teachers that they will be left out and relegated to a subsidiary status by not becoming computer literate, let alone teaching with computers, if computer-based teaching comes to take too great a place in the curriculum.

More extreme—but no less widespread among those who think about such things—is mistrust of the importation of the new for the sake of the new. Notoriously the best spokesman for this attitude is Theodore Roszak:

> As for the general intellectual benefits of that skill [computer literacy], of these there is no evidence to be found beyond the claims of the computer industry's self-promotional literature, filled with vague futuristic allusions to life in the Information Age. Yet if the computer makers succeed in their hard sell, we may soon be teaching undergraduates who believe (with their lecturers' encouragement) that thinking is indeed a matter of information processing, and therefore without a computer no thinking can be done at all. (1988: 77)

To Roszak, networking and other 'artificial uses' are merely increasing technological dependence, 'a vice already ingrained in our culture.' Such apparatus does not assist the natural flow of ideas; it inhibits it. Free human dialogue, wandering wherever the agility of the mind allows, lies at the heart of education. If teachers do not have the time, incentive, or the wit to provide that, if students are too demoralized, bored, or distracted to muster the attention their teachers need of them, then *that* is the educational problem which has to be solved—and solved from inside the experience of the teachers and the students. Defaulting to the computer is not a solution; it is surrender (Roszak, 1988, 79–80).

Roszak's mistrust is at least partly justified, and most practitioners of humanities computing know, in their own work, about the dangers he refers to and aim to avoid them. Partly, though, such fears are possible because of a failure of communication. The fact is that humanities computing has not yet defined sufficiently clearly what it is trying to do. The task is in a sense much more formidable than that faced by previous educational reformers. Advocates and practitioners of humanities computing are looking forward in an age of dramatic and continuing technological advance in which the very task of keeping pace with change is exhausting. Humanities computing is still at an experimental stage, and it is in the nature of the undertaking that experimentation is its hallmark. There is a danger that the emphasis on experimentation—with which one could not for one moment take issue—is at the cost of cohesion in what is being done.

The problem is not so much that experimentation carries with it the risk of failure. Some of the experiments *are* failures, albeit sometimes spectacular ones, and they inevitably are the ones that give critics the most ammunition; but open-ended experimentation is nonetheless defensible, and within reason acceptable to colleagues who understand the nature of academic investigation. Rather, the grounds on which humanities computing is currently most open to attack are lack of clear direction and clear guiding principles. That so many different practitioners in different institutions are exploring different approaches is healthy; that they would probably give a range of different, and varyingly coherent, answers to the question what they were trying to do, is indicative of the complexity and profundity of the potential impact of computing on arts disciplines rather than because, as Roszak would have it, they were merely dazzled by new toys (though some of them rightly or wrongly give that impression). As well as experimenting in different ways, practitioners of humanities computing need corporately to elaborate a rationale, albeit an open-ended one which continues to allow, indeed to place high value on, experimentation. It is a matter of public relations, and public relations at a collective as well as an individual level.

In order to achieve that statement of what humanities computing is about, it is first necessary to be clear about the range of different activities encompassed in that phrase, and to discuss the implications of some of those activities. The remainder of this paper aims to provide an agenda for such a discussion.

6 Humanities Computing: A Typology

There are four basic kinds of teaching that in practice fall within the purview of those involved in humanities computing:

1. The teaching of word-processing skills

2. The teaching of basic computing skills

3. The teaching of discipline-specific computing skills

4. The teaching of discipline-specific skills with the help of a computer.

The first two categories are the most widely found and yet the least appropriate to the concept of 'humanities computing.' Such basic skills, of which humanities students see the value just as do others, could be taught by any qualified teacher. At the moment, given the historical development of computing within a science environment, experience is telling us that these basic skills are probably best taught to arts students by those who are attuned to the mentality and needs of those students. Since these skills are also the building-blocks necessary for progress in the third category, humanities computing teachers often find themselves having to impart these skills before going further. Yet there is no intrinsic reason why these two categories should be considered part of humanities computing, and indeed it would clarify the position considerably (as well as help to break down faculty barriers) if they were not.

The third category is the heart of the enterprise and intellectually the most exacting. But there has been fundamental disagreement about how it should be conducted. An international workshop held on this question recently at Vassar College identified two viewpoints. One, the 'holistic' approach, held that humanities computing should be taught as a subject in its own right, starting with general computing skills and building up to those most useful to the humanities (which are usually taken as a whole). At the other extreme was the 'expert users' approach, which regarded humanities computing as providing specific tools for the humanities, tools which were learnt to a high level (Ide, 1987).

Most practitioners in the UK probably operate somewhere in between these two poles. What we do varies greatly between them, while still being classified as 'humanities computing.' A standard policy is neither practicable nor desirable. The issue is not in any case 'soluble;' different approaches will suit different students. Also, institutions vary too greatly in their size, complexion and requirements for such standardisation, and few are yet in a position to offer the multiplicity of courses which would allow the full range of approaches to be offered under one roof. But we must recognise the fact that this variety of approaches, which in any case is dictated much more often by resourcing considerations than by academic ones, blurs the image of humanities computing amongst those not involved but in positions of influence. As long as the answer to the question 'what does humanities computing consist of' remains one to which no easy or consistent answer can be given, practitioners will have an uphill struggle persuading colleagues within the humanities, let alone colleagues in other disciplines, of its desirability.

The fourth category is fundamentally different from the other three, in that here the computer is simply being used as a learning tool without any attempt being made to evoke interest in computing *per se*. This is technically the most forward-looking area, and the most demanding for teachers developing the software. As the area in which most experimentation is taking place, it may also be the one with the highest failure rate. The fashion for simulation in history teaching at school level has not yielded all that was promised. Expert systems offer great potential, but they are still at a rudimentary stage, and the question of how their use is integrated with the rest of the teaching programme has not yet really been resolved. An outstanding example of this approach is the HIDES project in the History Department at Southampton University, where students use a variety of packages, authored by members of the department, as study aids for third-year history courses, and in the process obtain ready access to substantial data sets and text-bases which they can interrogate and handle with powerful software tools.

In the case of other learning software the potential gains are unquestioned. CALL, Computer-Assisted Language Learning, is rich territory, already widely accepted and used, and rapidly increasing in potential and sophistication. A recent and most exciting tool available for teaching purposes is hypermedia, of which much was seen at CATH 88. This promises new breakthroughs, and demonstrates beyond doubt that computers can open doors, giving access to methods of teaching and of information retrieval not seriously possible before the advent of the new technology. Perhaps the greatest scope for development is at a more modest level. At the recent Cologne Computer Conference, R. J. Morris, in an impassioned plea for the imparting of numeracy skills to historians, showed how computer-held information can be retrieved, displayed, re-run or re-drawn in the classroom, in the lecture, to help develop such skills. Here students need not touch a keyboard or even understand it (though one hopes that they will). It is the lecturer who has an invaluable new teaching aid.

A fifth category ought perhaps to be considered in connection with the last two; research. Historians in particular, in constructing databases for both teaching and research purposes, have been able to reassert, as R. H. Trainor did at the Cologne Computer Conference, the fundamental unity of teaching and research. The political value of this has already been alluded to; it is also a major asset for the discipline. In courses where students put together their own databases, in the form of project work, they are themselves undertaking research in a way unusual in history syllabuses in the past. This possibility links well with the new outlook on history teaching in schools; students are increasingly familiar with data sets and databases, and welcome the opportunity to interrogate them directly.

7 The Shape and Scope of Humanities Computing

Whatever the type or level of teaching within humanities computing, a number of practical questions remain. The first is the issue, discussed elsewhere at CATH 88, of whether such teaching ought to be addressed to the humanities as a whole or to individual disciplines. This is related to the question addressed by the Vassar Workshop but is not identical to it. In the UK, at any rate, the tendency until recently has been for humanities computing to be thought of *en bloc*. Although different institutions have adopted different strategies, for computing purposes the humanities have more often than not banded together politically, and have gained funding and advisory staff accordingly. But how much academic cohesion is there to support this? Are the needs of students of language and literature sufficiently similar to those of historians to warrant this association? At the research level it is true that historians are becoming more aware of the importance of preserving and analysing text, and literary and linguistic practitioners are increasingly interested in database approaches; but how far can this process go, and at what stage does it become relevant to undergraduates? A possible compromise lies in modular courses, as run for example by Project Pallas at Exeter, and at Royal Holloway and Bedford New College and Westfield College in London. Again, there are no answers to this question; different institutions have different needs. But a discussion of the relative merits of different approaches, and perhaps the formulation of some general principles that institutions might try to work towards without prejudice to their existing activities, might be helpful. Again, this is a political question about how humanities computing presents itself.

Another question on which consensus might be reached is the danger of merely recreating old patterns and structures with new technology. Some of the less good work done has been trying to mimic old teaching methods with new equipment. Should practitioners themselves not be more critical of this? Ultimately this is a matter of self-interest; the more effectively software mimics the teacher, the sooner teachers will be replaced by machines. Computers can at best complement teachers, and it does students, teachers and computing alike a great disservice to forget or blur that fact.

This raises a third, more fundamental question; how far should humanities computing go? To what extent is it right to build computing into arts teaching? Arts computing courses are invariably popular, but at the moment they are in the main optional. At what point would departments risk losing those students who elected an arts subject precisely to avoid the new technology? And how integrated should such courses be with the rest of the syllabus—is no corner of the subject to be immune? That this observation raised nervous laughter at CATH 88 was no surprise; it is all too easy to become immersed in humanities computing to the point where such natural questions are unwelcome. Yet the present phase of humanities computing must be transitional. The first generation of schoolchildren to whom computing is second nature has yet to reach higher education. It will be a great shock when it does.

Implicit in that question is the possibility that the whole subject is a transitional one, and that in a few years (or decades?) humanities computing courses will seem as implausible as humanities typing courses. This view seems fundamentally flawed, but practitioners must recognise that there are limits to what the computer can and should do for the humanities, and that it is in the interests of the subject not to overstep the mark either in practice or in the claims they make.

8 Humanities Computing: Infrastructures

In the absence of formal academic status for humanities computing, a number of less formal avenues for the diffusion of the subject have sprung up—centres, learned societies, newsletters and journals, advisory services. An assessment of the state of the subject would not be complete without an examination of some of these. It is right to pause and ask whether these are the best avenues, and whether some improvements could not be made.

Centres. A number of centres have been founded, in response to local initiative or to central funding opportunities. The key role of the Oxford National Facility for Computing in the Arts will be fully appreciated when the history of humanities computing is eventually written. The funding patterns of the 1980s have tended to put such centres on a competitive footing, in the positive sense of encouraging initiative and enterprise. Now that funds are leaner still, this has its dangers; but it says much for the collaborative spirit of humanities computing that these centres are all functioning in an open way. Mutual interest is, by and large, predominating in the subject.

Conferences. The most characteristic vehicle for the diffusion of information about humanities computing has been the conference. The conference is the most natural forum for such interchange. The subject is after all international, fast-moving, and multi-media; the amount that can be imparted solely by means of the written word about software, hardware or teaching methods in this field is severely limited. It would seem ungracious, therefore, to hold reservations about the medium. Yet it has to be asked whether the conference circuit is not getting out of hand. Conferences entail an immense amount of work, not only for the organisers (who may or may not reap rewards in terms of institutional profile), but also for those who attend them if they are to benefit to the full. Already it is possible for full-time humanities computing practitioners to spend a frightening proportion of their time taking in one conference after another, and the point where the same contributors reappear with barely modified products has been reached. The need for some self-denying ordinance within the community has surely come. It may be that the new bibliometric trend, with its suspicion of unrefereed papers and publications in conference proceedings, unwelcome as it may be on other grounds, will put a brake on excesses here.

Publications. The printed word, and now the electronic word, are substantially cheaper than the 'small world' of conferences, even if they do suffer from the disadvantages mentioned above. Furthermore, as practitioners of text-based computing, the interested parties are ideally placed to keep publication cheap and rapid, without sacrificing professionalism in matters of design, layout and accuracy. Yet there is a hidden danger here too, connected with the pace of change and the professional pressure to publish. The ephemerality of much writing on humanities computing has had a noticeable impact on the standard of writing. Pioneers of new computing methods who need to get their message across as quickly as possible simply do not have the time—or perhaps even the incentive— to write scholarly and polished reports of their work. What these writings gain in spontaneity they often lose in accuracy and clarity. The average standard of articles, and of edited books of articles, on humanities computing is frankly not always what it might be. This is not just regrettable; it is also dangerous, since the rest of the academic community is most likely to judge the subject initially by what appears in print. The worse the presentation looks, the feebler the message is likely to seem. To redress the imbalance, fewer breathless announcements of new projects or techniques and more reflective methodological papers would be helpful (just as small-scale workshops are at present more needed than jamboree-scale conferences).

Personnel. The biggest area of concern in anything but the short term must be the position of humanities computing advisers. They have been invaluable in promoting the subject, and their appearance has been a universally welcomed development, but it has not been accompanied by anything in the way of planning or career structure. A case could conceivably made for that situation to continue. It could be suggested that in this area, new ideas come in short bursts, not lifelong careers; that the most effective advisers are hybrids of the arts and the sciences, and that there are no clearly-defined career paths into the job, which is thus not definable with sufficient precision. It could even be argued that, if the need for arts advisers is temporary, if computers really do prove to be no more significant academically than the typewriter, considerable damage would have been done to careers and to the humanities by such a planning extravagance.

All these arguments are fundamentally flawed. They constitute a failure of nerve. There is by now surely evidence in superabundance of the value of humanities computing and of the advisers who have nurtured it. Far from treading so gingerly, arts faculties should be thinking of computing provision as a regular and substantial component of their activities if they are not to be left behind in a rapidly-changing scene. Should humanities computing advisers then be seen as the humanities' parallel to the scientists' technicians? That does not do them justice either. Much of what they do is not academically-related but academic. A handful of institutions now have academic posts in humanities computing. This is surely the way forward, and in political as well as academic terms will do more for the subject than any other of the developments that have been outlined here.

9 Conclusion

This paper has endeavoured to look at humanities computing in the context of the history and politics of education. It has concentrated on the ways in which computing has entered the humanities, and argued that greater clarity of purpose is needed to complement the sense of excitement and innovation that exists in abundance. To further this, I conclude by summarising some of the potential benefits of humanities computing and the reasons why it should be considered to have an impact on the state of the humanities disciplines themselves, an impact which might even eventually amount to 'redefinition.'

Computers can enhance the learning process. As practitioners of CAL in many fields agree, the computer can deepen the retention of information and understanding, and provide better opportunities for interactive corrective feedback. Its use places stress on the individuality of the learner and his/her learning pace, and, as Nicholas Morgan and Rick Trainor argue forcefully elsewhere in this volume, it can assist the democratisation of the teaching process, in that teachers become 'guides not dictators,' and students participate to a greater extent. Computers can 'liberate the imagination.'

The technical skills involved in computing can enhance the humanities disciplines. In the case of history, computing skills have widely been found to be an admirable accompaniment because they include skills in 'information handling' that complement those of the historian; history teaches about the complexity of data held in a database, while the database package demands rigor in the questions to be asked of the historical information to be entered. In other disciplines, too, computing can help the student to question and put in a different context the methodology of his/her subject.

Humanities computing has the potential to build bridges between disciplines and between faculties. In academic and in practical ways the advent of the computer has brought teachers and students in the humanities into close contact with those beyond the narrow confines of their subject. Arts students see the vocational attractions of acquiring computing skills alongside their main subject, but because these skills are imparted within the context of that subject (or at least sufficiently related to it) this need not bring with it the risk of fragmentation or the 'cafeteria degree.' The alliance of humanities to computing is welcomed eagerly by employers, who see practical skills being applied to subjects they already regard as training the mind; and this in turn is understood by students. The demands of humanities computing have contributed positively to the development of computer science itself, as practitioners have graduated from strictly quantitative applications to more complex techniques—record matching, fuzzy logic, rule-based expert systems and analysis of incomplete data sets.

It is these last developments that have prompted the reflection that computing may yet change the humanities, bringing them closer to each other but also to other disciplines. Computing offers the possibility of re-establishing a common language across faculties, or at least of providing a basis of commonality, which might help to resuscitate the pitiful level of dialogue between arts and sciences. It may seem an unlikely candidate for the role, but it is one that the humanities in their current state of isolation cannot afford to ignore.

3

The Values of the Humanities and the Values of Computing

David A. Bantz

1 The Values of the Humanities and the Values of Computing

Are the tacit values of humanities scholarship and humanistic learning at odds with the widespread intensive use of computing and computing techniques? The view I argue for here is that recent advances in computing have great promise of enhancing the humanities in ways completely consistent with and subservient to the values of the humanities, but that there is nothing automatic about the fulfilment of such promise. On the contrary, unreflective or passive adoption of computing applications—which are typically developed with scant attention to the needs of the humanities—can undermine or distort the aims of the humanities. I will suggest ways in which a self-consciously critical approach to computing may foster developments which enhance rather than distort the disciplines of the humanities.

2 Reductionism and Dogmatism

How might computing embody values at odds with those of the humanities? Given the ubiquity of, for example, text processing, retrieval of data, or electronic mail, it may appear tempting to regard the technology as inherently neutral or exclusively as enhancing productivity. This view is reflected in most computer advertising ('Develop your ideas in Digital Darkroom,' 'Let your creativity sail,' 'Increase Instructor Efficiency,' 'system will save you from a blizzard of time-consuming tasks.'). But any technology is capable of only some procedures; even to the extent that computing merely makes some tasks we care about easier, these may be thought of as having been advanced at the relative expense of others which are then comparatively more difficult, or even impossible within the confines of new technology. Computer applications have limited means for symbolically representing information—means through which texts and other objects of interest, problems and tasks must be (re)formulated. In thus transforming our concerns to a form in which symbolic computation is relevant, there is the possibility not only of failing to capture important aspects of our concerns but of transforming our understanding of what constitutes a significant, or even an intelligible, question.

If we focus first on the ubiquitous representation of information in standardized and formalized language or codes, then computation appears to confound the multiplicity and diversity of the literal record of human achievements—achievements which, humanists have often held, can only be well understood in their concrete and particular contexts. Does this apparent move towards a universal and standardized representation not urge us to pose our questions and forge our theories in similarly standardized and context-free terms? And what of material that resists being so comprehended? Is it not in danger of being relegated as peripheral or irrational—i.e., 'noise' in the 'data?' I will call such a threat to traditional conceptions of the humanities (following Booth's [1967] discussion of Crane's conception of the humanities) the threat of reductionism.

Suppose, to carry forward the implications of thoroughgoing computerization in the humanities, we focus on the implication of computational techniques providing answers—unambiguous, objective, and clearly delineated answers—to questions posed carefully in the constrained language of calculation. Then computation may appear inimical to the pluralistic and many-faceted appreciation of human achievements that constitute the humanities. In other words, when aspects of the human record, regardless of the forms in which they might have been originally presented, are translated into a more schematic and rigidly defined form suitable for storage, manipulation, and presentation on one or another computer system, we run the risk of viewing all of that record as though it could be comprehended by a single consistent and overarching framework. It would seem to be our task, then, or that of our students presented with such materials, to discover that single coherent framework. To parallel the threat of reductionism above, we can call this aspect of the conceivable threat to the humanities the threat of dogmatism.

Against such seemingly abstract concerns we expect sober and practical rejoinders pointing out the various ways in which computing can—indeed now routinely does—serve the ends of the humanities. Writing has been supplanted by word processing; the labours of producing concordances, indices and variorum editions have been greatly relieved by the straightforward use of computing on 'machine-readable' versions of texts. Without doubting the utility of such techniques, it is still possible to question whether their net effect on the humanities is beneficial, for the very ease with which such computational techniques can perform some of the traditional work of the humanist suggests a reorientation, and conceivably a distortion, of research and learning within the humanities. The utility of some computational techniques in the work of humanities thus does not of itself settle the issue raised in the previous paragraph. However, it does, I think, show that there is no necessary opposition between computing and the humanities, and it focuses our attention properly on *practice*.

When we turn to practice, there are some disturbing features of the ways in which computing is currently conceived and used within the disciplines of the humanities. I consider those features under three headings: (1) writing, (2) the presentation of texts, and (3) thoughtless educational software. Under each of

these heads I will illustrate some of the as yet unmet needs of computing for the
humanities, and consequently some of the directions in which humanists should
be forcing the evolution of computing. Concrete illustrations will be based on
actions and decisions we have taken at Dartmouth aimed generally at providing
enhancement of learning and scholarship based on the needs of disciplines, and,
more specifically, on discussions of the capabilities needed in a 'language workstation:' a computer workstation which could usefully support many aspects of the
work of language students, teachers, and scholars in humanities. Some portions
of these capabilities (though not their needed integration into a total environment)
have been illustrated through prototypes and specialized programs running on the
Macintosh. These provide the basis for further work aimed at a refinement and
enhancement of tools for the humanities.

3 Processing Words versus Writing?

Writing has, of course, been the principal entry of computing into the work of
both humanists and students. All of us, surely, are aware of colleagues who saw
no point whatever in computing, even ridiculed the interest of those humanists who
struggled with recalcitrant hardware and software, who have been not only won
over but virtually transformed by their adoption of 'word processing.' The enthusiasm of some of these converts—in some cases bearing disturbing similarities
to the enthusiasm of religious fanatics—and the apparent match of the possibilities for revising written work with recent research suggesting the importance of
revision as fundamental to the practice of good writing, have generated (at least
in the U.S.) computer writing laboratories and writing courses reworked to make
revision with a word processor a central feature.

There is little doubt that, once mastered, a word processing program can be a
valuable tool for writing. Yet there is virtually no evidence that using a word
processor improves one's writing. And what should we make of the fact that
in discussions of new writing programs and computer writing laboratories, so
much attention is placed on the underlying technology? Despite the fact that word
processing is billed as a technology which will enable and enhance writing, a large
portion of the effort seems to be directed toward issues of the selection of 'the most
appropriate' software, in training—that is the correct word—students and faculty
alike in its use, and toward maintaining and enhancing the hardware on which
word processing is done.

Dartmouth has a rich microcomputing environment: since 1984 entering students have been strongly urged to purchase a Macintosh computer for their own
use. Currently 85% or more of our students own a Macintosh. We have supported
these with a campus-wide network reaching virtually every office, classroom, and
dormitory room on the campus. The network supports ready access to the college
library catalogue, terminal sessions on several mainframe computers, electronic
mail to all individuals on campus, and remote printing on laser printers. Despite
this computer-saturated environment (or perhaps because of it, as I am about

to describe), we have neither built a computer-writing laboratory nor structured courses in which writing is central around the use of word processors.

Instead, we have viewed writing with computer support in all its aspects as an essential activity throughout the academic community, and a primary component of work in all disciplines. Rather than using a particular course and laboratory environment to teach or train students in the use of word processing, we have tried to establish an environment where students—and faculty and staff too—can make use not only of word processing but of other writing tools (outlining aids, formatting, equation processing, and desktop publishing) as and when appropriate. To make such *ad hoc* use feasible, we have endeavoured to provide a computing environment in which users of all levels of interest and ability can make use of basic tools with little or no training and support—that is, we have tried to provide tools to make users self-sufficient and able to utilize tools as and when they need them. Before microcomputers were deployed, we relied on intelligent terminals and on-line help for software running on central mainframe computers: a partially successful strategy in that many humanists with no other interest or skills in computing used this system for serious scholarly writing.

Supporting writing requires a much broader range of applications than word processing: note-taking, 'brainstorming,' outlining, re-organizing, commenting, constructing bibliographies, and applying style conventions are all part of the overall writing process. Facilitating each of these processes without refocusing our attention on the technology *per se* requires a sophisticated computing environment. Unfortunately, because writing is often considered fundamental in the sense of rudimentary, the notion is abroad that writing requires only minimal computing support, far less than in, say, the sciences, where people may more routinely write computer programs or use graphics for design. But the variety of tasks in writing places its own severe demands on the computing environment.

To maintain broadly based use of writing tools by largely self-reliant users in a rapidly evolving microcomputer environment, we have come to place great value on an easy to master graphical interface, such as that available on our Macintoshes (and gradually becoming available with advanced versions of IBM's OS/2 and Windows). The advantages are only partially captured, and perhaps distorted, by the oft-repeated 'easy to use' label; beyond this, the aptness of the metaphors employed in the interface, and above all the consistency of the interface across a range of applications, allow users to focus on their ideas rather than the computer interface: the computer interface itself becomes in an important sense 'transparent.' It really isn't that difficult to learn the commands of even the more intimidating of microcomputer word processors, such as Nota Bene; and the techniques used in graphical interfaces are of course not self-evident but conventions with which users have to acquire familiarity. But surveys bear out what anecdotal evidence suggests: that such 'transparent' interfaces enable users to routinely use a broader spectrum of software, and hence provide greater support for their work (Diagnostic Research, 1988; Peat Marwick, 1987).

Beyond the needs arising from the use and integration of a variety of traditional writing tools, flexible graphically-based writing tools may provide an alternative visual basis for the organization of writing. 'Storyspace,' for example, allows elements of writing to be represented as individual windows or 'frames' which can be dragged and rearranged, or nested one within the other to any depth, as Chinese boxes can be nested. Additionally, 'paths' through this potentially complex 'space' can be constructed and indicated visually (Bolter & Joyce, 1989; Joyce, 1988).

4 Texts versus Text Databases?

Computer applications for manipulating texts antedate microcomputers and are apparently more directly related to humanistic scholarship and research. The creation and use of concordances are now almost routine with the use of a variety of concordance programs. We can look forward to electronic versions of a variety of reference materials, including the full text of important works, with consequent abilities to locate rapidly passages of interest, or even, as suggested in the advertising for the electronic version of the OED, obtain numbers—such as the number of words of Arabic origin illustrated with quotations from Shakespeare—without bothering to see the texts in question.

But humanists have endured very low standards for the presentation of texts in electronic media. Despite longstanding availability of high resolution graphics displays used in computer-aided design and other applications, texts have been displayed on small low-resolution screens, in often poorly designed and inadequate fonts, with the result that only a small portion of what could be displayed on a printed page can be viewed at once, and that small portion devoid of the stylistic variety and formatting available in printed materials. Font and style variations and the layout of printed pages convey information—at the least providing important visual coding of the structure of a text—and the loss of this information constitutes a degradation of the text.

Recently, somewhat more powerful software combined with 'bit-mapped' (rather than character-based) screens has allowed a more literal copying of the appearance of printed text, but of course reproducing the appearance of a small portion of a printed page is not a fully adequate representation of that text! Chapter and other divisions, running heads, and traditional scholarly apparatus, for example, not only display material in a variety of styles and sizes and physical locations, but allow a reader to 'navigate' through the material on the basis of interests or needs, using a variety of visual distinctions as navigational guides through a volume. Unless this structure is itself reflected in the electronic version of a text, allowing analogous navigational skills, the text does not have the same utility as a printed document and may encourage a more passive (or perhaps more frustrating) reading. Once recognized as an important need, the provision of a rich structure to a text is even more suited to electronic media than print. Much current writing about structured electronic text focuses on the concept of 'hypertext' which contemplates the association of any portion of text as having (possibly several) 'links' to other texts (or, indeed, to non-textual information) which can easily be followed or ignored depending on the interests of the reader.

While hypertext holds promise, many existing computer applications in the humanities still suffer from fragmented and unstructured presentation in electronic form. Even the modest requirements for displaying text in multiple natural languages (diacritical marks for European languages, alternative character sets and typing modes for many others) strain the resources of most commonly available microcomputers.

At Dartmouth, we have been working on strategies to make electronic text data bases an integral component of the computing environment on the desk of every scholar, teacher, and student. Of course, this is largely a motivating vision rather than a fully implemented environment. We currently have two large text databases 'on line' at Dartmouth, the Thesaurus Linguae Graecae, the product of a long-term project based at the University of California, Irvine to provide essentially all classical Greek texts in electronic form; and the Dartmouth Dante Project ('DDP') database, which will eventually include the text of sixty commentaries on the *Divine Comedy* in several languages; currently, the *Divine Comedy* itself and twenty-three edited and indexed commentaries are incorporated (Dartmouth Dante Project, 1989).

Currently, these two databases reside on one of our central VAX computers; non-English characters and formatting of texts are encoded. Our interface to the DDP database illustrates the extent to which such computing artifacts can be hidden from users. Using the standard personal computers employed for writing, and software conventions familiar from that environment, users can easily read commentaries in a variety of languages and time periods on any portion of the *Divine Comedy*; they can also search for the occurrence of any text string in the *Divine Comedy* and/or the commentaries, and restrict those searches or combine them with previous criteria to reduce or enlarge the number of passages found. Brief references to texts meeting the criteria are displayed, and clicking on any reference displays that text. The text is properly displayed in the appropriate language; any portion of it may be copied into a word processor document for quotation or further editing. All the details of connecting to and 'logging onto' the VAX over the campus network, the construction of syntactically valid queries to the database manager on the VAX, transferring text files from the VAX to the workstation, and conversion of encoded diacritics and formatting is transparent to users.

We want to expand the utility of such databases by increasing the number and variety of texts available and by including non-text materials, such as still images, sounds, and full-motion video. While we have developed interfaces to the TLG and DDP databases which properly display those languages, each has been written as a special case. Our target is to have a quite general scheme for displaying any number of languages on the same screen, respecting not only the character sets and diacritical marks needed in that language, but also such features as alternative keyboard layouts, left-to-right versus right-to-left input, and alternative string-comparison routines (for finding and sorting). Each of these aspects of the language should be available without any explicit action by users—i.e., other than retrieving text in that language. There is nothing in principle difficult about this task, other than the fact that commercial vendors have generally taken inadequate account of this elementary need in working with multiple natural languages.

We are able to demonstrate some portions of this capability through Dartmouth-created extensions to Apple's product HyperCard. These extensions allow the display of large, fully formatted texts; using conventions analogous to those in print, notes and other materials are indicated unobtrusively in the text (Calhoun, 1989). When a reader points with the mouse to any portion of text to which material has been linked and clicks the mouse button, an appropriate window opens displaying text notes, illustrations, or, with the addition of appropriate hardware which is now becoming commercially available, a video sequence (see Figure 3.1.) Another Dartmouth application using HyperCard provides a combination index and controller for video images stored on videodisc (Humanities Computing, 1988). Not only can one search for images through text descriptions and display those images virtually instantly, but entire sequences can be constructed in advance and displayed in any order. These tools are being used by instructors as classroom presentation aids. But they also give students ready access to materials they would otherwise see only once briefly (in a lecture) or not at all (because the image was not part of the instructor's message) by making the images with their indices and video display from videodisc available to students as a resource.

While the underlying enabling technology is thus largely in place for delivery of multimedia hypertext or 'hypermedia,' we continue to be confounded by copyright restrictions which prevent us from making many materials available in such an interactive electronic environment. The resistance of traditional publishers to such innovations is probably the single most important factor impeding the development of widespread hypermedia.

5 Learning versus Computer-Aided Instruction?

How might computing enhance the teaching of humanities? The market now contains a lot of computer 'courseware:' software that is supposed to teach students ancient history, or geography, or a foreign language. Alas, a good deal of what is available, and particularly what is available from commercial publishers, is all too aptly described by the perjorative 'drill and kill.' It is relatively easy to translate information from a printed page to the computer screen, then follow it with multiple choice questions to test 'mastery' of the material; this is indeed the most common form of computer 'courseware.' It is very difficult on the other hand to anticipate students' requests for help and provide appropriate responses in advance, or to recognize incomplete answers in idiomatic English. It is even more difficult, apparently, to imagine and create a learning environment on a computer

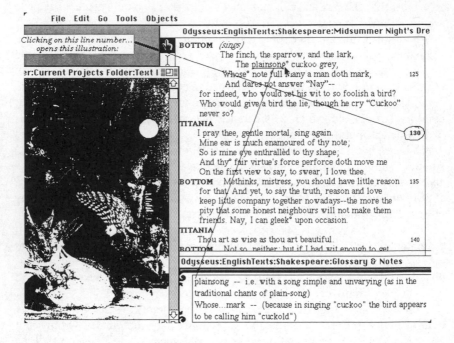

Fig. 3.1: Hypertext with linked apparatus and illustrations

which goes beyond these classroom techniques to provide something we could not provide in a classroom.

The most imaginative—and intriguing—uses of computing to encourage learning in the humanities either provide students with a simulated environment to explore, or, even more straightforwardly, make available to students a body of tools and information to be explored or queried at will. Examples of such innovative uses include the examination of the rights of patients to refuse extraordinary treatment illustrated by the Dax case (a severe burn victim who repeatedly demanded that his treatment not continue, allowing him to die) in an interactive video environment by Carnegie Mellon University's Center for the Development of Educational Computing (Covey & Roberts, 1988); 'Tarski's World' which allows one to construct three dimensional 'worlds' which can model sentences in first-order logic (Barwise & Etchemendy, 1987); and the historically-based role-playing in 'The Would-Be Gentleman' based on bourgeois economic and social life in 17th Century France (Lougee, 1987). Analogous efforts have been described in the CATH 88 conference, notably by Morgan and Trainor and by Susan Hockey, et al. (see chapters in this volume).

These beautiful examples represent quite substantial commitments of resources, most especially the time of faculty authors. Most faculty continue to believe, however, that such activity is inadequately supported or rewarded by their institutions; so long as this perception continues, the number of elaborate innovative software packages will remain small. If, then, the direction of instructional computing in the humanities is to be determined by academic humanists rather than a business-oriented market (as I have been arguing it needs to be), we need ways of encouraging innovative developments on a more modest scale. It is for this particular niche that Dartmouth is actively pursuing the use of Apple's HyperCard: that is, as an extremely flexible tool allowing faculty—or faculty-student teams— to produce software targeted precisely on a need or opportunity identified by the faculty member with a modest investment of the faculty author's time. HyperCard is sufficiently flexible, particularly in screen design and in providing 'navigational aids,' to allow the software to be designed to an author's specifications, rather than imposing either the standardized environment of a commercial 'authoring environment' which imposes its own preconception of the learning process, or a vastly simplified environment in which only a few choices are available to users at any point in the program. At the same time, HyperCard does not require much programming expertise or training in its use as a development environment; consequently, faculty can undertake projects with the expectation of usable results with modest investment of their time.

Several examples in the humanities lend credence to this contention, two of which are briefly described here. Both were direct responses to needs of teaching faculty without computer programming backgrounds, developed and refined to meet precisely specified instructional needs; each was developed within a few weeks.

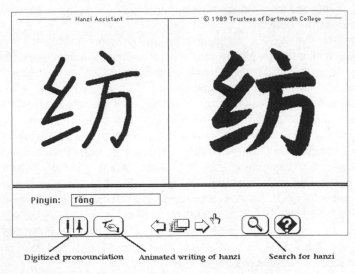

Fig. 3.2: Hanzi Assistant screen and labelled buttons

'Heavenly Mac,' a project in the history of astronomy (Kremer & Chadowitz, 1988), is an example of using HyperCard as a presentation medium: text and graphics describing episodes in the development of models of the motions of planets are organized chronologically, but students can easily search for particular topics of interest. Several kinematic models of planetary motion, based on the theories of Ptolemy and Copernicus, have been incorporated as animations, which greatly adds to the understanding of fundamental issues. These animations were written by a collaborating undergraduate student in a traditional programming language, but all aspects of the interface and overall design are the work of the history faculty member; there is seamless and instant transfer between the animations and the rest of the presentation package.

A second example, 'Hanzi Assistant,' incorporates animation, text and sound into a reference tool for students of Chinese. *Hanzi* are displayed in a large size; a standardized phonetic representation (pinyin) and an English translation for each *hanzi* are available at the student's option (see Figure 3.2). Learning to write Chinese entails learning the proper stroke order, so each *hanzi* may be 'drawn' on the screen in the proper stroke order. Finally, because spoken Chinese is a tonal language, we have included pronunciation by a native speaker for each *hanzi* (Humanities Computing, 1989).

The software described here is typical of a wide range of applications developed at Dartmouth. Our applications empower students with tools and resources not otherwise available to them; they are not tutorials or programs for teaching per se. We typically do not record student responses, score or grade performance, or even provide a guided path through material. The use of these materials at all is often left to the discretion of students themselves. Those of us—instructors and developers—who provide these applications do so in the belief that we are providing the means for students to explore material, formulate questions or hypotheses, or receive immediate feedback which they could not effectively do in lectures, with printed materials, or in tutorials. Our applications originate with instructors who see opportunities to enhance and supplement traditional instruction, rather than replacing or making such instruction more 'efficient.' This strategy has seemed to most faculty developers to render moot many standard evaluation tools. Most are content to see a perceived need addressed, and to see that students in fact make use of the software developed even when it is optional. Student and peer evaluations are routinely used to refine applications. In some cases, such as software in the areas of music, statistics and molecular genetics, and the Hanzi Assistant described earlier, strong demand for the software from Dartmouth students and from other institutions reinforces our beliefs.[1]

6 Humanists Need to Ensure that Computing Enhances the Humanities

Finally, and most importantly, I want to turn very briefly to the implications of computing as a nascent technology. Born of electrical engineering, mathematics and signal processing, computing has appeared to many humanists as simply a new feature of the environment, perhaps usefully turned to work in some aspects of the humanities, but without any potential for guiding its further development. If, as I suggested above, much of current computing practice is at odds with the core values of the humanities, what computing can be is still very much to be determined. There is no good reason that the humanities themselves should not have an important, if not preeminent, role in this shaping of the future of computing so as to enhance learning in the humanities and our appreciation of the record of human achievements.

To merit widespread use in teaching in the humanities, computing should reinforce learning by exploring and doing rather than tutoring in the sense of presenting material to be 'gotten' by passive recipients. This point was made forcefully during the CATH 88 conference, e.g., by Martlew (see his chapter in this volume). Computing has the capacity to empower students and give them general tools and skills, and we have examples to illustrate not only the possibility, but the great fun of doing so. Whether the infusion of computing into our institutions achieves this promise depends on a reflective, critical and activist stance on the part of humanists; only thus can we have confidence that the technology will enhance the values of the humanities.

---

[1] Instructional software developed at Dartmouth is generally available at nominal cost for non-commercial purposes; for information on the Dartmouth software described in this paper, write to the author. Electronic mail may be sent via Bitnet or Internet to dbantz@Dartmouth.edu.

4

Videodiscs and the Politics of Knowledge

Roger Martlew

1 Introduction

A university or college lecturer in the UK is employed to teach students and carry out research—whatever the balance may be between these two activities. Much has been said and written about the use of new technology in Humanities research, while applications in teaching are relegated to second place if they are considered at all. Computers have the image of Pandora's box, with a small band of enthusiasts emphasising the good that can come out of them, and a large group of detractors ranging from the cautious to the 'technophobic.' This paper examines the changes which computers can bring to Humanities teaching, and highlights those which may make lecturers feel uncomfortable with new technology. The paper also describes an educational philosophy which supports the positive aspects of educational computing, and which is particularly relevant to applications in Humanities teaching. Finally, the paper considers the mechanisms by which these positive aspects may be developed and disseminated beyond the small group which has already accepted them.

Traditional styles of Humanities teaching in universities impose specific roles on both lecturer and student. Similar relationships between teacher and pupil in the secondary sector are changing under the influence of the latest pedagogical developments. Computers have contributed to the changes, and valuable experience has been gained in this sector in the educational and management issues which arise from their use in the classroom. At all levels of education, however, computers have the potential either to fossilise the traditional roles of teacher and pupil, or to encourage new approaches which will improve the quality both of our teaching and also of our research.

In this paper I shall examine the traditional roles of lecturer and student, and indicate the potential impact which new technology can have. These generalities will be illustrated with reference to the interactive videodisc project in the Archaeology Department at Leicester University, funded by the Computers in Teaching Initiative (CTI).

2 Traditional Roles in Humanities Teaching

In crude terms, university lecturers control the educational process by controlling knowledge. If a topic is central to their own research, they will be steeped in the latest facts and opinions—published and unpublished. If the topic is not closely related to their own work, as is often the case in these days of highly specialised research, their power is based on familiarity with the subject through having taught the course before, or through having access to source material in advance. This position of power is confirmed by examinations, set and marked by those who have taught the courses, which emphasise the recall of factual knowledge.

The cherished academic freedom given to lecturers means that individuals usually have complete control over the styles of teaching which they use. There could hardly be a greater contrast in the traditional teaching styles employed at university level: the mass lecture at one extreme, with a single lecturer addressing maybe a hundred or more students, and the small group tutorial at the other, with three or four students closeted in a lecturer's room for intensive discussion. There is little interest in the pedagogical justification for using these widely different teaching styles, and there are few rewards for investigating alternatives. Individuals are mainly required to show competence in research and publication, in order to be regarded as successful in the post of lecturer.

3 New Technology and Traditional Teaching Styles

Information Technology often appears threatening to those who have not yet come to terms with it. There are incentives to encourage the use of new technology in research, where it is seen as being progressive and keeping up with the latest developments in the subject. This involves changes in methods and areas of emphasis which have created a revolution in Humanities research. The introduction of computers into teaching also involves changes, but those who are established in the traditional ways of teaching are often resistant to the idea of such changes. A strategy for keeping change to a minimum would be to fix computer-assisted teaching into existing teaching styles and management structures.

Laboratories of twenty or more machines come closest to the numbers involved in a traditional lecture, causing a minimum amount of disruption to timetables. Students have access to machines on a one-to-one basis, and the lecturer retains close control of their progress through structured sequences of CAI (computer-aided instruction) programs, or by leading students through demonstrations. The idea of a teaching laboratory is often also politically attractive within an institution, in that it allows a centralised computing service to retain contact with the undergraduate computing carried out for or by individual departments.

Outside any centralized facilities, computers are most easily introduced at the individual or tutorial group levels. This is particularly true if departmental funds can only stretch to the purchase of one or two machines. If a few machines are available on an 'open access' basis, students can be directed to use CAI software for remedial or revision work just as they would be given reading to do in the library. Computer programs could also be used to prepare students for tutorials, seminars or practical work by taking them step-by-step through basic information or techniques. Single workstations can be used in tutorials as a demonstration tool by the lecturer.

4 New Technology and New Teaching Styles

The introduction of computers into schools in the early 1980s focused attention on educational and management issues (Thorne, 1987). Teachers with a professional commitment to education were anxious to exploit the power of the technology, but there was a long learning period when many mistakes were made. There is good and bad educational software, just as there are good and bad teachers, but almost a decade of experience on a nationwide scale has revealed the major possibilities and pitfalls.

The most positive response to computers from both staff and students often comes when new technology is allied to student-centred learning styles. These styles require new techniques of classroom management which are much more flexible than the strict 'chalk and talk' approach. The increased emphasis on group work can make the use of one or two computers a practical possibility in a class of thirty or more pupils, providing the management issues have been taken into account in the initial development of the courses. In the secondary sector this new approach to the organisation of learning has led to a change of emphasis from the memorising of facts to the skills required in using them. The examination system has been changed to accommodate the increasing attention which is being paid to skills, in addition to the subject matter.

Negative responses to the use of computers arise from merely trying to fit them into existing methods. Experience has shown that the 'electronic blackboard' may have value in some restricted applications, but in general terms it under-utilises and may even trivialise the technology. Computer laboratories limit interaction between students, and between students and lecturers. Rather than widening the range of learning styles available, they tend to concentrate on narrow and often mechanical approaches. Computers can provide useful opportunities for revision or remedial work to supplement traditional teaching. This, however, is a specific application which does not make full use of the technology to encourage and support new learning opportunities.

5 'Technophobia'

The implications for introducing computers into university teaching are clear, and unsettling. New technology may already be familiar to many lecturers in a research context, but its effective use in teaching obviously requires changes to some long-established traditions. These changes appear to erode the power base of the traditional teacher or lecturer. She or he need no longer be in total control of the knowledge which the student is trying to assimilate, and may therefore feel that control of the educational process is being undermined. Didactic software may be used in an attempt to avoid this, perpetuating the subordinate role which the student is expected to take in the learning process. This tends to shift the burden of responsibility from the lecturer to the computer, and the quality of the software becomes the main influence on the quality of learning. This may not present any problems if those involved in designing the software are familiar not only with the subject matter, but also with the theories of learning on which current teaching practices are based. On the other hand, experience has shown that a good teacher can create a valuable learning exercise from a poor piece of software. Although it is a common fear, there is no way in which a lecturer's role can successfully be transferred to a machine, nor should the computer be seen as the one and only way forward for university teaching.

6 New Technology in Humanities Teaching

New technology has tremendous power to liberate the student from over-controlled learning styles. In order to facilitate this, the lecturer must cease to be a controller of knowledge, and must become a manager of learning. The traditional power base is eroded, so lecturers must come to terms with a new role in which they have less of the absolute power to which they have become accustomed. This is particularly important in the Humanities, where a university degree is seen by employers as an indication of a general level of education and intellectual competence, rather than as something which has direct relevance to specific vocations. Many of the aims which supported this in the past have become buried under the increasing amount of specialized knowledge which students have to assimilate. New technology provides opportunities for students to take responsibility for their own learning, to work in groups on the solutions to problems, and to manage information for themselves. These are skills which will improve the quality of the graduate workforce: the short-term recall of factual information in examinations does not have the same value.

Many current Humanities courses recognize this, and continuous assessment is giving higher prominence to skills related to 'process' in addition to 'content.' New technology provides powerful tools for supporting this, in more rewarding ways than by training students in the use of word-processing and database packages. Computers supplement the roles of lecturers and textbooks, without replacing them. Their main impact is in facilitating access to information, which students can use in an active way to gain knowledge and understanding of their subject.

The following illustration of these general comments shows not so much how the Humanities might be redefined by new technology, as how the ownership of knowledge in the Humanities might be reallocated in order to improve the quality of undergraduate education.

7 Images in Archaeology

Archaeology is a very visual subject. The traditional lecture is illustrated by a series of slides, and lecturers often use the images as an *aide memoire*, rather than consulting notes. A lecturer will build up an often extensive slide collection while teaching a range of courses, and they will be kept in personal or departmental archives. Some of the slides (copyright laws notwithstanding) will be taken from published sources: they will be illustrations which the students can expect to see when doing their reading. The most valuable slides, however, will be those which an individual has been able to collect personally, by visiting museums, excavations and field monuments. Visiting lecturers will bring their own slides, which have an enhanced rarity value. These images are not just background illustrations: they represent the most efficient way of recording many of the basic facts of archaeology. A verbal description of Stonehenge, of a flint arrowhead, or of a skeleton with associated grave goods, would not be very elucidating. One picture is worth many thousand words.

To have a unique image in one's personal slide collection is to possess an important piece of information. The power which ownership of that information brings is similar to the status conferred by being responsible for a particularly exciting archaeological excavation. The parallel in the study of history would be if a lecturer owned the only copy of a manuscript which lay in a distant museum archive, or which had been completely lost. Naturally, ethics dictate that the information should be made public, and disseminated widely in the relevant academic community. This would not be a problem with a single piece of evidence such as a manuscript. However, the process of publication is a costly one, and it is particularly restrictive in the case of corpora of visual information. The prohibitive cost of publishing photographs means that it is usually only the best objects or sites which are selected, and even they are often only reproduced in black-and-white.

Access to Images

The control of access to visual information in archaeology confirms the lecturer's power over the educational process. Access is restricted by practicalities, and by the necessity in most cases to provide contextual information such as site name or artefact type to clarify what the picture actually represents. The practical problems of locating a slide, displaying it and protecting it from loss or damage prevent lecturers in most cases from allowing students free access to their personal or departmental collections. In order to convey the required knowledge, the lecturer needs to arrange and re-arrange the images, and supply accompanying information and comments. The students' role is passively to receive the knowledge which has been processed from basic information by the lecturer. The power structure which supports this is clearly represented by the way in which slides are used in teaching archaeology. The formal lecture is highly illustrated, with sometimes fifty or more slides being used per hour. The tutorial, in which students are made responsible for preparing information for discussion, commonly uses little or no visual material at all.

The Videodisc—Usage and Abusage

The technological background to videodiscs has been described elsewhere (Martlew, 1988). Videodisc players linked to computers (known as IV work-stations) provide rapid and flexible access to a vast number of images. Control of this information can be preserved in the hands of the lecturer, reproducing the traditional teaching style described above, or it can be handed over to the students. The decision is the lecturer's, and should be based on pedagogical rather than political criteria.

Despite their tremendous potential, videodiscs can be used to perpetuate tra-ditional authoritarian styles of teaching. The teacher can retain control of the learning process by using 'programmed learning' software, in which the videodisc workstation presents stimuli and checks responses. If the response is correct, the next stage of the program is presented; if incorrect, the software diverts to a remedial section before moving on. This approach, which is by no means confined to videodisc-related software, is based on the work of behavioural psychologists. It is heavily machine-oriented, putting a computer in the place of the teacher. Programmed learning is favoured by commercial training packages, but while it can be useful in some circumstances, it requires a tremendous amount of planning and software development if it is to rise above a narrow, mechanical learning experience. The user may interact with the system, but the interaction is totally controlled, and must be totally anticipated, by the program developers.

8 Flexible Approaches to Learning

There are occasions when programmed learning using a videodisc will be perfectly adequate. There are also many applications which will not be best served by this approach, or where programmed learning may only be the first in a hierarchical series of learning tasks. As in any educational planning, the first consideration of the lecturer who wants to use educational technology should be the identification of goals. What do you want the students to know or to be able to do when they have completed the assignment or course? The next questions follow logically: what is the most appropriate method which will enable students to achieve these goals, and what is the most appropriate way of assessing how successful students have been in achieving them? This may sound obvious, but the logical sequence and the emphasis on student learning, rather than teacher control, should be noted. It may well be decided at this stage that the videodiscs available offer no significant improvement on traditional methods, or it may be realised that goals may be defined which would be impossible to achieve without using interactive video.

No single method is likely to achieve all the goals effectively, and it should also be recognised that different students will prefer different ways of working on similar tasks. In archaeology, a hierarchy of goals shows the videodisc's flexibility in supporting different learning styles. The example applications which follow also reveal the changing roles of lecturer and student.

Any archaeology graduate should be able to identify major sites, recognise important types of pottery and interpret different types of evidence such as pollen, animal bones and charcoal. This is basic knowledge which could be taught by programmed learning in a mechanical way. Students would be shown a picture of a group of bones from a sheep skeleton, to take an example from *The Archaeology Disc*. At the lowest level they would be expected to identify them as bones, naming the individual bones next and finally identifying the species. This exercise might constitute preparation for a practical tutorial or seminar, in which bones could be closely examined for butchery marks, and the implications for reconstructing the economy of a past society discussed. If actual examples of the bones are not available, of course, the pictures on the videodisc might be the only access which students have to this information.

This approach corresponds closely to traditional teaching, except that students have access to the information via the videodisc, rather than via an anatomical textbook. The pictures will inevitably be better than those in the book—they will be in colour, and may show the bones from several different angles. Students may run through this exercise at any time, in preparation for the tutorial or as a revision exercise before an examination. The software may test the students' knowledge and provide remedial action where necessary, and could provide the lecturer with a final score to record the progress of each student.

An alternative approach to the same learning task could use exactly the same pictures on the videodisc. Students are given access to a text database which contains brief descriptions of each image on the disc, such as the names of bones and the species to which they belong. They are set a problem: a collection of bones (shown on the videodisc, or available as actual specimens) has been found on an archaeological excavation, and the students have to describe, identify and interpret them in the sort of specialist report which is a normal part of published excavation reports.

In order to complete this task, the students will need to look at published bone reports to ascertain the type of information which is required, and to see how it is set out. They will be able to use the videodisc to identify the bones, and then determine from which part of the skeleton they derive. By looking at similar collections of bones in published reports, they will be able to interpret the significance of the examples with which they are dealing, drawing their own conclusions about the economy and lifestyle of a past social group. When they have completed their reports, the students can compare and discuss the results in a tutorial setting. The lecturer has specific content to assess—the understanding and knowledge shown in the reports—but she or he is also able to assess the students' skill in processing archaeological evidence to produce the reports.

Both of these approaches can be described as interactive, although some people steeped in behavioural conditioning might not acknowledge the second approach as 'Interactive Video' *sensu stricto*. The role of the lecturer in the first approach is diminished by the computer, which is in control of the learning process. In the second example the lecturer has a major role in guiding students through the resources and in assessing their achievements. Qualitative assessment of performance is possible in the second example, whereas the computer provides mainly quantitative assessment in the programmed learning context. Students actively engage in problem solving in the second approach, but work their way along prescribed routes in the first.

Problem solving in groups is closer to working practices in the 'real world' of business and commerce than the one-to-one interaction with the computer in a programmed learning context. Opportunities are created for the acquisition and practice of additional skills such as teamwork, leadership and decision making when students are working together on an assignment. If a university education is to be a preparation for life in the modern world, attention has to be paid to these important areas in addition to the traditional skills of essay-writing and memorising facts for examinations. Involving students actively in their own learning is more likely to improve motivation and raise standards than the pedestrian exercises of programmed tutorials, or the mass-production of lectures.

It is clear from the example videodisc applications that merely introducing new technology is no guarantee of improvement in learning opportunities. The most significant development lies in the adoption of new strategies of learning. These strategies rely on students having easy and flexible access to information, and well-prepared guidance on how to use it. Videodiscs put the control of visual information into the hands of students. Lecturers need no longer 'talk through' sequences of pictures, but instead they must provide guidance for students as they use the images in a variety of activities. This development has the effect of placing equal emphasis on the lecturer's role as teacher as well as subject expert, a change which has serious implications for management in universities.

9 Implementing New Technology in University Teaching

The primary and secondary sectors of education have well-established support mechanisms for developing curricula and providing in-service training. Although often severely stretched, these mechanisms provide a valuable medium for the discussion of new ideas, the generation and funding of research projects, and the dissemination of good practice. In universities, however, a lecturer is lucky if a journal in his or her discipline contains a section devoted to the uses of computers in teaching the subject. In the UK the humanities are fortunate in having the CATH conferences on issues related to computers and teaching, but it is questionable whether this mechanism ever could—or should—do more than preach to the converted.

When computers are introduced into university teaching, pressure is exerted on the subject specialist to become expert in educational methods. Few lecturers already have appropriate skills or training in this area, and there is little incentive for them to spend time and effort on developing such skills. However, it is no longer sufficient to be an expert in one's own field of research in order to teach a subject at undergraduate level. Being a lecturer involves teaching, but expertise or even interest in teaching has never been a general prerequisite to appointment, or a high priority in promotion. One only has to compare the institutional support given to developing pedagogy in universities with that available in schools, to see where education is regarded as worthy of a professional approach.

The Computers in Teaching Initiative is an attempt by the University Grants Committee and the Computer Board to encourage the use of new technology in university teaching. As with the Microelectronics Education Programme in the primary and secondary sectors (Fothergill, 1987), it is a 'pump-priming' initiative, which means that money has been made available to address a problem, without any commitment to supporting or implementing the work which has been funded. In recognition of this, follow-on money has recently been provided to enable a few individuals to work in an advisory capacity on computer-assisted learning (CAL) in specific subject areas.

The presence of CTI-funded projects in departments has undoubtedly raised the profile of CAL in the short term. Once the projects have finished, however, the fundamental problem of resourcing developments in this area is felt more strongly than ever due to this increased interest. Most of the traditional sources of funding in universities are concerned with research rather than teaching, and some specifically exclude teaching-related projects. The resource which is perhaps more important than money is time, not only for the development of software but also for its implementation. The pedagogical changes described in this paper create a serious need for staff development. This is currently met by a very wide range of provision in different institutions, and usually involves staff on a voluntary basis. Many are glad to remain in fearful ignorance of new technology, and even those who might be converted often do not want to become involved because of their existing burden of work.

If the CTI is to have any long-term influence, and if CAL in universities is not to stagnate after the initial burst of enthusiasm, management at the highest levels will have to recognise the implications of paying more attention to pedagogy. Interactive videodiscs in particular and computers in general can make undergraduate learning a more exciting and rewarding experience, or they can perpetuate the worst aspects of traditional teaching styles. With universities competing for decreasing numbers of school-leavers, and facing financial cuts and restructuring, there is likely to be a move towards increased accountability in the major revenue-earning service which universities provide—the education of the highly skilled and professional workforce which is demanded by industry and commerce. This is likely to be the public face of the politics of knowledge in the coming years.

5

Rethinking English Studies: The Role of the Computer

David S. Miall

1 Introduction

The theme of the conference for which this chapter was first written was 'Redefining the Humanities?' We wanted to ask what effect computer methods may be having on our understanding of the Humanities disciplines we study. Are the disciplines themselves changing? I will argue that one central implication of this shift in understanding, if it is happening, is that learning methods in the classroom must also change. Partly under the impact of the computer, the teaching of the Humanities can no longer be seen only as the transmission of authorized bodies of knowledge. A part of the redefinition lies in seeing the Humanities as a debate that we have with the past, but more importantly, with ourselves: the Humanities offer us alternative perspectives on the world. The classroom itself can become a forum within which we rehearse that debate with students.

In his paper in this volume, Peter Denley refers to the shift in consciousness of the Humanities that took place during the Renaissance. I will refer to another key Renaissance figure, Doctor Faustus, as he is shown at the beginning of Marlowe's play. Faustus has the whole of pre-Renaissance learning at his command. He can cite Aristotle, quote the Bible, cure whole cities of the plague. But he is bored with this knowledge: he wants something else. What he really wants is to transform himself, to transcend the limitations of his knowledge—and of course he turns to magic to achieve this. But such transformation, in the end, is what the Humanities are for: they are for altering the self. Through acts of imagination we change our consciousness and our feelings—whether it is through learning a second language, through an act of archaeological reconstruction, or by reading a poem.

The question I wish to put is this: How do we create a learning environment within which such changes in consciousness are possible? And what role does the computer play in this process? In short, what are the issues for learning, and what does one actually do in the classroom? In discussing this my main examples will be drawn from the teaching of English literature, which is the area I know most about; but I suspect that there are implications here for other Humanities subjects.

2 The Computer and Literature: Four Issues

The advent of the computer in the literature classroom provides an opportunity to rethink English studies, and to centre it explicitly in a more rational and systematic approach to texts on the one hand, and learning methods on the other. If one aim of the way we educate students in English literature is to increase the power of the student, to give her more control over her learning, then a central aim of our computer facilities must be to give the student more immediate access to methods for pursuing the issues that arise from responding to texts and questioning their origins and contexts. In what ways does the computer either integrate with, or require changes in, current teaching methods and assumptions about the subject?

Students arrive at our institutions with certain expectations and subject-specific skills. We expect that the curriculum that we offer them may change, or at least widen, their view of the subject; it will also require the development or acquisition of skills relevant to their studies. In English, as in other Humanities subjects, there may be students who will not be expecting to find computers in the seminar room. A few students may even have embarked on a Humanities degree in order to escape from a world being reshaped by technological determinism. But the computer confronts all students with the prospect of learning new skills, integrating new methods into their approach to texts, and, above all, developing a perspective in which their conception of English studies embraces the computer as a medium for formulating, testing, and sometimes resolving questions about texts.

In this respect computer methods oblige us, if we would be effective, to develop cognitive frameworks or maps on which to locate the information and processes of a given procedure, including our own role in initiating, or interacting with, the computer. The model that we have of our role, the self concept that we have as students of English, may be called into question by this demand. Thus the computer also interacts intimately with our affective understanding, our underlying and often subconsciously held commitment to the subject. The use of the computer does not merely supplement what is already being done: it is likely to change our assumptions about our role as readers, about the nature of our subject, to impel new theoretical accounts of literary texts, and to lead to different teaching and learning methods. As computer-based studies gain a place in the English Department, it will be essential to think through these issues in order to avoid confusion about the aims and methods of our discipline.

Perhaps the first issue is that of student motivation. Our curriculum, revised to include an element of computing, will provide students with a set of guidelines to direct their learning. But the computer-based tasks we can design do not necessarily address questions that the students themselves would have posed or the difficulties that they experience in understanding the chosen texts. If the computer is to cast genuine light on the texts being studied, the students themselves must be enabled to formulate their own questions, and to see in what ways the computer provides a tool to assist their inquiries. This points to a shift to workshop or project-based methods, where students work for major periods either singly or in small groups.

In any case, the very nature of the computer, where the user faces a keyboard and screen rather than a room of other students and a lecturer, suggests that computer work must frequently be autonomous, except for limited and predefined exercises that can be carried out by a whole class. At other times a network of computers will provide a medium for a different type of dialogue between students, as they write responses and read and comment on what others have written. In either case the emphasis falls on the responsibility of the individual to manage their own interaction with text and computer.

But effective computer work assumes some existing competence. Thus prior to the workshop stage students must receive systematic training in the rudiments of the hardware and software they are to use. Both the skills training and the workshop methods may be unfamiliar to many students within the context of English studies: the former follows a more inflexible pathway, the latter provides for considerable autonomy—the student may have encountered neither of these in the English seminar. Thus the rationale for both types of learning must be explained and discussed.

Motivation and method are thus closely intertwined: if students are given training in a range of methods, including those based on the computer, they are better placed to choose a method for pursuing the questions that interest them, and will be better motivated to direct their own studies. But the use of skills training and workshops then raises the issue of students' accountability for their learning.

In more traditional seminar and lecture based teaching accountability is well understood: in seminars students debate ideas with each other and the lecturer, they are assessed on seminar papers or essays, and they sit examinations. Where skills training is assessed, however, it has been found that Humanities students may be uneasy at being given marks for the exercises involved, which seem not to tap the competencies normally expected of them (Wardley, 1988:56). At the other end of the spectrum, assessing the self- or group-defined work undertaken for projects is more problematic than the conventional essay. Do students report such work, and if so how? Does a group share a mark between them? Should project work be assessed at all? Where the computer plays a significant role, the lecturer may also need to consider how far the software program being used is self-evaluating, providing students with feedback not only about the issues being investigated but about the effectiveness of the inquiry itself.

Finally, the question of accountability raises an additional question: whose criteria are to determine the basis and methods of assessment? In a traditional system, once again, it is clear that the authority of the lecturers as subject specialists makes them the primary source. If the student is to gain greater autonomy in choosing the focus and methods of their study, however, as computer methods suggest, the student must also acquire greater authority in evaluating, perhaps even assessing, their own work.

These four main issues—motivation, method, accountability, and authority—provide a framework within which to consider the shifts in learning that come from the introduction of computers to English studies. I will now outline some of the key concerns of learning in English, and suggest how project or workshop techniques are already leading to more flexible patterns of learning and more explicit reflection on the nature of the subject. In the section that follows I suggest how computer methods can be used either in a focal or in a supporting role within the context of project work.

3   Reading and Re-reading

My first central point is a negative one. The central experience of literary studies cannot in itself be facilitated by the computer. Reading a poem or a novel is to commit not only cognitive and intellectual skills, but resources of imagery and emotion to that engagement with the text. The text may require that I shift my perspective on myself, on my position in the world, or on the world itself. An act of reading is a complex process of imagination, in which ideas, memories, images, feelings are reconfigured, enabling a new whole to exist within our being. In accounting for the experience of reading, such metaphors of existence (growth, wholeness), seem inescapable, although recent critical theory has insisted that we distrust them. It is an experience signalled by some alteration at the level of being, the sense of a process taking place in cooperation with the text, for which the term *imagination* still seems the most appropriate (accepting that the term marks out problematic territory, both historically and theoretically).

To this central experience of reading the computer in itself probably has nothing to offer—at least, not yet. The sequential algorithms of the Von Neumann machine do not provide a congenial medium for reflecting or enhancing the processes involved. The transformations that are initiated by reading—revaluations of ideas, shifts in feeling, anticipations denied or fulfilled unexpectedly—cannot be effectively modelled by the information processing capabilities of the computer. Information processing requires organization within a frame, a semantic network or schema: literary texts function within us in part by invalidating our schemata, by requiring that we create new ones. Reading at this level is still rather poorly understood; but it seems likely that the creative process within it is directed primarily by our affective rather than our cognitive resources (as I have tried to show elsewhere: Miall, 1989a).

At a practical level, extended reading of texts on screen is simply less efficient (as Slatin points out in his chapter in this volume). A computer screen is not an appropriate interface for the primary act of reading. Enhancements to the medium of presentation (alternative typefaces, graphics, etc.), of the kind recently celebrated by Lanham (1989), are unlikely to have a significant impact on the reading process—they may indeed work the other way, trivialising the process by distracting the reader. Although major developments are taking place in how text is presented on screen, such developments are not informed by an understanding of the process of reading literary texts: too little is known about the process in any case. In this respect technical know-how is (as usual) in advance of our grasp of psychological realities.

Although the act of reading cannot be directly served by the computer, however, the case is different when we consider re-reading. Under the term *re-reading* I want to include the various modes of inquiry that can facilitate analysis of the literary text: to re-read is to consider, by detaching some fragment or aspect of the text, information that may inform or illuminate our reading. Such information can range from the meaning of a word that must be checked, to the situation of a text within its historical period. We re-read in order to work the new information back into our understanding of the text as a whole, a procedure that may require several re-readings of one passage, or an analysis of the relationships between several aspects of the text. Such work is analogous to the pianist acquiring a new fingering for a difficult turn in a piece of music: he may need to practice the same few bars several times; but eventually the new fingering is subsumed within an unbroken performance of the whole piece. In the same way, re-reading serves the return to reading.

The distinction between the two modes of reading should be made clear in the classroom, since it touches an issue which is encountered more starkly when the computer is introduced. Some students initially find it troubling if they are asked to examine a text closely: they prefer to discuss the issues they perceive in the text as a whole, such as its relation to general moral questions, or the character of the author. Their sense is that the integrity of the text is violated by the use of detailed analytic methods; they will say that the text has been destroyed for them. Such students must be helped to see that the two modes of understanding are necessary and complimentary: re-reading rests on a prior act of reading, and leads forward to a renewed and reinvigorated act of reading—a cycle that may be repeated several times. In the classroom, however, as well as in the computer room, the primary focus will be on various components of re-reading. The inquiries of re-reading are shareable, in a way that the affective transformations of reading are not; re-reading is based on processes of analysis and discussion that can be practised in the classroom and, to some extent, instantiated on a computer. Given that the classroom can be made the site for such shared inquiries, the computer will more readily find its place as one significant resource, alongside the library, other students, and the lecturer.

Perhaps the best way of summarizing the themes I have discussed so far, from motivation to re-reading, is this: that English studies call for the project approach. Such an approach assumes that students require training in relevant skills (including some systematic study of computer methods), but that as skills are acquired students take increasing responsibility for designing and implementing programmes of study, both as individuals and in groups, that deploy those skills. The students will be formulating problems that they wish to pursue out of the issues arising from their own reading. This will enable them to see more purpose in using the skills they have, but also help them to see what additional skills they need to acquire.

This process can be illustrated by considering the pathway of students studying poetry within the degree I help to teach. Among their first year classes, students have a weekly two-hour seminar on poetry. The first few weeks of the seminar are given mainly to detailed analysis of poetic diction, to ways of examining the structure of short poems, to the question of poetic voice, and some standard poetic forms, such as the sonnet and pastoral. A handbook (which I helped to write) containing notes on some of these matters is given to each student. Either through the handbook, or verbally, I suggest a particular procedure for analysing a given poem. My practice is to require the students to work through the poem individually, then compare their findings with others in a group of four or five. Out of their agreements and disagreements (the latter can be just as interesting), they produce a report on a sheet of paper, which is eventually placed on a noticeboard in the seminar room (it remains there for two or three weeks for others to consult). At the same time, one student from the group will tell the class about their more salient findings. Such reports, taken from four or five groups, usually lead to a general discussion, in which we debate the meaning of the poem and any further problems and issues that have arisen.

By the second term students have acquired a range of techniques for analysis, avenues to different aspects of poetry together with a vocabulary for describing them; they have gained some confidence in methods of analysis, and they have learned to profit from the perspectives of other students in their group. They can track some of the issues they have tackled through the communal reports on the noticeboard. By this point students are beginning to take more initiative in proposing their own topics for seminar work, and in choosing their own methods and the poems they will work on. Some groups will now pursue a topic for two or three weeks, and agree on work that will be done individually in between class sessions, such as finding source materials for a poem, or relevant letters by the poet, or an illustration for the noticeboard.

A more conventional lecture and seminar system would largely be determined by the lecturer, whose own interests need not coincide with those of the students, and whose preferred readings of poems may depend on contexts for analysis that remain out of reach of the students. The advantages of the project approach have already been outlined: students become better motivated, they acquire methods which can be generalized to other poems and different contexts, and their reports provide a more systematic and productive way of accounting for their own learning.

The first year work provides students with ways of working and a sense of the issues and problems raised by poetry: these inform the broader concerns of Year II, in which (alongside other classes) the students take a course in Romantic writing, consisting mainly of poetry. Here the primary concern is to understand the historical moment at which the Romantic writers emerged, to see how contemporary concerns shaped their poetry—concerns about politics and social reform, the country and the city, about poetic diction (a revolutionary issue, as Hazlitt noticed), the status of the poet. A secondary concern later during the year is to test how far the shift in consciousness of the Romantic poets determined the concerns of literature and literary theory beyond their immediate period, through to the twentieth century.

Here, then, are a new range of concerns, and a corresponding need to develop additional skills of re-reading. Once again, it is the project approach, now supplemented by a few short lectures, that forms the working method of the seminars. But in comparison with Year I, the library now provides a wealth of essential resources, and students are given practical training in the research tools required for effective library work.

Finally, in Year III students move to twentieth century poetry and begin to assay the emergence of modern literary theory and its dependence in part on influential poet-critics. In describing the curriculum in poetry I have left out of account other major strands in the student's work: prose, drama, popular culture, other historical periods (according to the options chosen by the student). But I have limited the account to poetry to provide a more specific illustration of how the project approach begins with training in analytic skills and leads to self- or group-chosen work of a demanding kind. It is a learning method (or rather, range of methods) which may end by giving the student less extensive knowledge, in terms of curriculum coverage, but which provides them instead with a much wider range of competencies, including greater confidence in their own powers of study.

It is within this context that the computer in English studies will most readily find its place. While the computer has been in use as a research tool among literary scholars for over thirty years, its use as an aid to undergraduate work is only just beginning. In the next section, still confining the account to work in poetry, I point to ways in which computer skills and methods can be integrated into project work.

4 The Computer in Undergraduate English Studies

A significant minority of students of English are now arriving on our degree courses with some computer skills. These generally need retraining to use the equipment available within the institution: in Britain, at least, there has been a tendency for schools to provide specifically educational computers (so called), whereas higher education institutions have more commonly provided professional equipment. The latter is more powerful, but often difficult to learn how to use. Until more friendly systems are available, the difficulties students can have in logging on and negotiating the operating system may be a serious barrier to productive work and eventual acceptance of the computer.

Thus, ideally, all students early in their first year would be given a basic course in computer familiarization. Such a course should be taught by lecturers in the Humanities, or computer staff familiar with the needs of Humanities students, able to discuss with students the role of computers in Humanities work. In the case of English, it is important to dispel the myth held by some students that a computer is of use only for mathematics and science, requiring of the student a high level of numeracy before it is possible even to switch one on. Since computers will be unfamiliar to some students, prior discussion of their role, if only as tools for thinking and writing, is highly desirable. In our College we provide a basic introduction to word processing, single file databases, and text analysis, with some additional help available on an ad hoc basis either for students who are experiencing difficulties or for those who want to explore more widely. Such a course is most helpful as a background, since other lecturers responsible for English are not obliged to start from the beginning if they wish to introduce some computer work into their own seminars.

In the Year I poetry seminar the main concerns are poetic diction, structure, standard forms, and voice. There are programs for studying diction: some provide students with definitions of technical terms, such as ellipsis or metaphor, and allow example poems to be analysed or searched for significant features. At least one program is now commercially available, *Litterms* (Rust, 1988). Other programs, still at the prototype stage, enable a student to explore the implications of arguments about poetic structure and meaning, tracking response statements in ways that involve the reader in a dialogue, using expert system principles (Miall, 1989b; Stutt, this volume).

Such programs require a certain skill of the user: gaining some familiarity with the scope and limitations of the programs calls for an initial phase of whole class instruction, using one or more standard, example analyses of poems. Later, the students, working individually or in a group, can be encouraged to choose the poems for analysis, and the computer facility that best suits their project. Where the students are already working with some degree of autonomy, using the range of resources available to them—such as the noticeboard, the lecturer, or the library—the computer (provided it is accessible, available in the same or an adjacent room) will more readily be adopted as an additional resource. The technical demands of the computer, moreover, will be more acceptable if students are aware that the acquisition of skills forms one essential component of their work.

Moving to the second year, the students in the Romanticism course will have a more extensive range of computer methods to deploy. The methods I will mention are either already available or in the course of development. Firstly, where students have defined a particular topic for a project, and now wish to pursue it with relevant reading in the library, efficient and rapid access to the location of journal articles and chapters in books can be provided through an annotated bibliographical database. Items are chosen by searching on the titles of poems or by key words relating to the themes of the project. Students can also be asked to improve the usefulness of the database: when they have read a given article, they can propose additional key words that would assist future users.

Another important computer facility is text analysis. Here students have available a computer-readable copy of the texts in which they are interested (such as *The Lyrical Ballads* or the poetry of Keats), and can examine the uses of particular words or co-occurrences of words via a concordance. For example, through *WordCruncher*, a student becoming interested (say) in the concepts of time or love in Keats's poetry can quickly find all examples of poems that use these and related words. Recent projects in the Romanticism class that made use of the computer facilities included a study of memory and landscape, and a survey of significant repetitions in Coleridge's imagery. A second text analysis program which we are considering introducing, *Personal Librarian*, enables the user to find words that occur in significant co-occurrence with one or more search words (see Friedman, et al, this volume, for a fuller account of the software). In this way the computer enables the student to move beyond the level of word locations in literary texts, to a grasp on concepts and themes – whether in a body of poems, such as the complete poetry of Keats, or in a novel or play.

In examining the relation between texts, or a text and its background, hypertext systems are now also being developed to allow significant words, themes or ideas to be pursued from one text to another (see Slatin, this volume). Thus a student interested in, for example, the section of Wordsworth's *Prelude* dealing with his experience of the French Revolution could trace key ideas out to Wordsworth's letters, back to previous writers on the issues, from Burke and Mary Wollstonecraft, forward to such later writers as Hazlitt or Shelley, and then on to modern critical discussions of Wordsworth's poems. Such links must be specified by the author of the hypertext system: this predetermines the routes through a body of texts that a student can take; but used with caution, such a facility provides a way of conveying essential background information easily and quickly. It can be used to alert the student to links which they would not become aware of while engaged in ordinary reading.

These and similar techniques are available to facilitate students' pursuit of questions they have formulated within a project. The computer can also be used as an exploratory tool, simply to see what can be discovered. One technique, offered by *MTAS* (Presutti and Lancashire, 1986), is to list word frequencies. To take a long poem or a group of poems and find which words are used most frequently can sometimes provide a first insight into a poet's vocabulary. For example, a listing for Coleridge's 'The Rime of the Ancient Mariner' will reveal a number of the words 'like' and 'as.' If the incidence of these words is significantly higher than other Coleridge poems it would indicate that the poem features an unusual number of similies. Another program called *Litstats* (Reimer, 1988) quickly provides summary data on a text, such as word lengths. 'The Mariner,' it may be noted, has a greater proportion of short words than Coleridge's conversation poems written in the same period. Both these findings may suggest to the student stylistic features worth pursuing in greater depth.[1]

More usually, however, the computer will be used when students are already involved in a particular project, and then turn to the computer with a specific problem where available software provides a method of analysis. To be able to formulate a question that is amenable to further inquiry, whether by computer or other means, is itself an important step in learning, one which students accustomed only to conventional classroom methods often find difficult to take. The next step again is to recognize that although there are many possible and important questions, some of the most interesting have a range of potential answers or have no answer.

The computer methods I have described support such open-ended inquiries. In disciplines other than English inquiries may be based more closely on numeric models (such as history, economics) or on logical systems (philosophy, archaeology), so that software can be designed to provide some evaluative, self-correcting feedback to the user (Laurillard, 1988:8–9). But in English studies involving the computer the quality of the outcome is more likely to depend on the rigour with which the inquiry was initially formulated and then pursued. A computer method will support, but cannot be a substitute for, the discipline of analysis, discussion, and systematic reporting.

5   Conclusion: Redefining English Studies?

In many departments of English the computer has had little or no impact so far, except perhaps as a word processor for staff. In considering how the subject is changing, it is clear that currently there are much stronger forces effecting change than the computer, not least the general decline of this and other 'soft' Humanities subjects in North America in favour of the 'hard' technologically-based disciplines, with their lines into profitable scientific research and the commercial world.

Where the computer will make an impact, if I turn to speculation, will be in underpinning certain developments within the subject and discouraging others. The formulation of debates about texts through argument support programs will tend to reinforce an existing, and growing, tendency to focus on the role of the reader in producing the texts that he or she reads. All texts are 'writerly' rather than 'readerly,' in Barthes's (1975:4) terms, including the canonical texts which were the focus of Barthes's argument. Interactive programs to support

---

[1] Comparing 'The Mariner' (including the Gloss) with a group of Conversation Poems ('The Eolian Harp, 'To the Rev. George Coleridge,' 'This Lime-tree Bower,' 'Frost at Midnight,' 'Fears in Solitude,' and 'The Nightingale'), the data are as follows:

		Mariner	Conversation Poems
No words in sample	:	4811	4864
similies:	'like'	25	16
	'as'	18	8
mean word length		4.04	4.39

interpretation and debate about texts will tend to foreground the constructive and often experiential functions of the reader in understanding literary texts. Thus the reader will return, not just as the putative or ideal reader of Culler or Riffaterre (Freund, 1987), but as an actual reader empowered by the computer to investigate her own response processes, and better situated as a result to debate the determinants and outcomes of her reading with other readers.

English studies, as everyone knows, is the site of alternative and often incompatible theoretical positions. There can be no return to some previous, a-theoretical condition of Leavisite innocence. But the computer offers English studies in the classroom a powerful tool to help assess and discriminate between alternative views. Its command over a potentially massive bank of references, textual data, response statements, and the like, facilitated by the developing resources of artificial intelligence, will enable alternative conceptions of literature to be explored and tested against the experience of real, historically situated readers. Such computer-based methods of re-reading should lead to a more finely tuned and better grounded understanding of the act of reading itself. This is perhaps the most important contribution that the new technology has to offer English. If the computer is deployed to support a more rational and productive approach to reading, it will come to play an important and critical role in the classroom.

6

Liberator or Libertine? The Computer in the History Classroom

Nicholas J. Morgan and Richard H. Trainor

1 Introduction

What are we trying to achieve when we teach history? As Sir Geoffrey Elton (1969a: 186) has written:

> the purpose of teaching history to undergraduates is to equip them
> with the special intellectual training embodied in the study of history
> at any level. This intellectual training consists of two elements: a
> sharpening of the critical analytical faculty, and a deepening of the
> imaginative and constructive faculty.

This chapter, based on the experiences of the DISH project at the University of Glasgow (see Trainor, 1987; Morgan, 1987), will argue that in many institutions of higher education these objectives have become clouded by a tendency to impart facts rather than by undertaking 'intellectual training' or the development of critical and analytical skills. The integration of source-based computerised teaching with the more creative aspects of 'conventional' instructional methods offers a remedy for this situation, and at the same time redefines the traditional relationship between teacher and student.

2 Learning in the Classroom

Facts about the past, and generalisations based upon them, have become more important in our teaching than those sources of information from the past from which facts are culled. As a result the process by which sources yield generalisations is largely hidden from students. Yet this process is the essence of historical analysis: the key to independent judgement (surely the desiderium of the history teacher) resides in the first-hand study and understanding of the nature of these sources. In the absence of this independence it is the authority of the lecturer or the course textbook, in other words the providers of facts, which counts.

Facts are especially easy to examine, and are particularly easily taught in conventional lectures, traditionally the staple diet of the history undergraduate. Within the Scottish educational system they have long been the stuff of both secondary and higher education, and this tendency is nearly as marked in England. When John Buchan arrived as an undergraduate at Glasgow University early this century his first impressions were that he had travelled back in time: 'in my day,' he wrote in his autobiography, 'a Scottish university still smacked of the middle ages' (Buchan, 1940: 32). Buchan, ('a diligent student, almost medieval in my austerity') could have been forgiven for this mistaken view. To be sure, the main Gilmorehill buildings of the University date back only as far as 1866 rather than 1451, when the University was founded (on 6th January of that year), but they had been designed by Gilbert Scott to invoke a Victorian's view of what a medieval institution of learning might (or should) have looked like. However, the heavy stonework and crow-stepped gables of Gilmorehill alone could not have persuaded Buchan that he had stepped back five or six centuries. No doubt one of the aspects of the University that might have seemed most medieval was the style of teaching, with its heavy emphasis on lectures and the primacy of place given to the lecturer— frequently, of course, a professor.

Buchan had no reason to know then that this, far from being a medieval style of teaching, was rather the result of great innovations in University teaching in Scotland in the eighteenth century. With the reforming spirit well kindled by the much vaunted Scottish Enlightenment, universities had begun to expand the range of courses they offered, at the same time abolishing the 'regent' system, where a single teacher carried a class of undergraduates through their entire university careers, in favour of the specialised lecture course. Academic life was further 'electrified' in 1729 when Francis Hutcheson began lecturing philosophy to his students at Glasgow in English rather than in Latin (Smout, 1969: 448–9). It was here that the tradition of the 'great professor' lecturing to awe-struck students was established. By the early twentieth century it was unchallenged. The memoirs of an undergraduate at Kings College Aberdeen, John Adam Lillie, paint a striking picture of both teacher and taught in Scottish universities at the start of the century. 'The great adventure of the Arts course,' he wrote,

> was that in a new setting, the setting of the untrammelled mind, whole continents of thought were opened up and their riches displayed to the wonder of thrill and discovery. This was a new and exciting world of the mind and our guides were men themselves thrilled by the fathomless significance of their worlds, and their almost prophetic task of telling it. The dullness of a textbook did not suffice in those days and fortunately such were little available or relied upon. The expositor in class was unhampered . . . The expositor was a man uniquely designed for the task, with the personal beauty and the poetic imagination which gave to his expositions a dimension and vivid vitality which permeated the eager receptivity of those who sat at his feet.

'The lecture system,' he wrote, was 'an irreplaceable instrument of education in breadth.' Nowhere was this more so than in the classes in Scottish History taught by Professor Sanford Terry (Lillie, 1970: 27–28).

The system described by Lillie was one where learning was defined by the dominance of the lecturer. The content of the class was all important, and the content was literally owned by the lecturer or professor—at Glasgow, as else-where in Scotland, professors had continued to sell their knowledge through the collection of class fees until the late nineteenth century or even beyond. So the teacher was dominant, the learner subservient, their relationship mediated through the transmission of knowledge in the lecture theatre. This relationship between teacher and taught remained even in systems where the lecture was less dominant, for example at Oxford and Cambridge. Buchan, although later a convert to the city and its University, recalled of his early Oxford days that 'the lectures which I attended seemed jejune and platitudinous, and the regime slack, after the strenuous life of Glasgow' (Buchan, 1940: 48).

At Oxford the tutorial system broke down the formality of the lecture room (to replace it with the even subtler formal atmosphere and architecture of the tutor's study), performing a function analogous to the tutorials, classes and seminars which have proliferated since 1945 in 'provincial' English and Scottish univer-sities. Yet, however relaxed such teaching formats might be, they usually retain great advantages for the tutor over the student. For the raw material of such teaching has consisted mainly of secondary works written by the 'authorities,' among whom students are invited to take sides on the basis of common sense, background information derived from lectures and the guidance of the tutor, rather than on the basis of independent judgement rooted in original historical evidence. Moreover, although the seminar has been extolled for providing students with 'better training in group cohesion and in verbal self expression' (Harrison, 1968: 383), history teachers will know that 'the seminar is an unpredictable vehicle, often difficult to get out of the garage and on to the road, treacherous in inclement weather and beset by uncooperative passengers' (Bourne, 1986: 59).

The increasing professionalism of history, the mushroom growth of historical writing, and rising esteem for cognate disciplines have tended to augment the number of courses and the weight of facts and received opinions on students, rather than altering the basic methods of instruction. Insofar as the style of historical teaching has altered, change has tended to increase the dominance of content rather than reduce it. In 1944 F. M. Powicke bemoaned the increasing professionalism of history: 'we have,' he observed, 'turned history into a "subject" ' (Powicke, 1955: 230). The rise of the new universities in the post-war era, and the general expansion of history teaching changed Powicke's single discipline into an almost bewildering variety of subjects, reflected in the growth of departments, 'schools' and interdisciplinary courses. But as a number of scholarly surveys of the profes-sion clearly show, changes have been most widely effected in the range of courses available (and therefore in the content they offer) rather than in the methods of teaching. Brian Harrison's survey of 1968 (which provoked stern rebukes from G. R. Elton, who likened those offering new courses to 'hucksters competing for the custom of purchasers who can have no idea what goods they really want' [Elton, 1969b: 63]) showed that of forty universities only nine demanded a research-based dissertation (Harrison, 1968). Although J. M. Bourne's study of 1986 was more optimistic ('what resistance there was to dissertations seems to have evaporated' [Bourne, 1986: 59]), many historians will know that one colleague's research-based dissertation is another's survey of secondary literature.

To be sure, there is a long tradition of source-based 'special subjects,' deriving from Manchester, where Tout had introduced the research based undergraduate thesis into the History School before the first World War. Yet, in most universities, then as now, this liberation came only in the final year of teaching, after an apprenticeship dominated by lectures: even so great an admirer of this system as F. M. Powicke found this a 'bewildering' though also a 'wonderful' experience (Powicke, 1955: 21). Moreover, the special subject has restricted itself very largely to 'documents,' individual pieces of text found in such sources as charters, parliamentary debates, official reports and memoirs. The bulky and complex materials so central to much recent historical research on all periods—Domesday Book, pollbooks, censuses, and national income statistics, to name but a few— have found little place here. It is therefore ironic that these materials have for a number of years held an increasingly central role in the teaching of history in schools (see *inter alia*: Blow and Dickinson, 1986; Blow, 1986; Randell, 1984; Wild, 1986, 1989; Wilkes, 1985).

3 The Computer and Learning

In the university classroom, as in the schools, computers offer a means of returning to a form of teaching—complementary to special subjects, but permeating the history curriculum—that places intellectual training at the forefront. It does this through detailed source-based assignments modelled on a workshop format, in which 'facts' are relegated to context. The computer enables students to approach and interrogate types and amounts of information about the past that would, without new technology, be unavailable to them. In the process their work becomes less passive, more participatory and, potentially, more imaginative. Likewise instructors can free themselves from the necessity to rely overwhelmingly in their teaching on lectures and tutorials based on secondary works.

Yet how do these apparently liberated teachers and students avoid enslavement to the computer as libertine, a promiscuous mistress of information? In particular, can the creative processes of the computerised classroom avoid being overshadowed by the complexities of computerised datasets and accompanying software?

This tension, though presented flippantly here, is real. The complexity of computers and enthusiasm for their educational utility produce a strong temptation for academics to immerse their students and themselves in a plethora of technical specifications, complex data, background information and mundane tasks. Degree programs and individual courses can easily become over-computerised, driven by technological targets rather than historical issues. Even when this imbalance is avoided many pitfalls remain. Quite apart from the intricacies of the hardware employed, the nuances of network software and applications packages provide a snare for the overzealous instructor and his or her student audience. Likewise, study of the provenance and structure of the relevant database or computerised text can easily absorb much of the time available for preparation and classes. Similarly, historians convinced of the academic utility of the computer may be tempted to bombard their students with an unwieldy accumulation of questions to be answered on 'the machine.' Finally, such instructors may trap themselves and their classes into dealing with a huge quantity of paper in the form of manuals, background handouts, data samples, and exercises. Such a profligate approach is wasteful of the strictly limited time that students can devote to particular courses. It also risks transforming the inevitably labour-intensive process of developing computer-based teaching, which entails constant revision as well as careful initial preparation, into an insupportable burden on academics themselves. Not only is undisciplined computer-based teaching impractical: it becomes far less rewarding as the 'means' overwhelm the supposed educational 'end.'

At the most general level, the self-discipline required to avoid this sorry state of affairs entails using the computer for teaching only when it is suitable to the academic task in hand; it also necessitates the careful integration of such teaching into the rest of the students' instruction. The problem of suitability is easily circumvented when entire courses are devoted to historical computing, but 'methods' courses often contain non-computerised elements, and in any case the integration of computing methods into a student's overall programme is often a difficult task. Teachers must deal with issues such as how the methods course will be examined, and whether students will have the opportunity to use the computer in other courses.

Even more problematical, though in many ways more academically rewarding, is the role of the computer in courses where the subject is not the computer itself, and where the computerised class session is used in conjunction with more conventional teaching formats. In such situations, historians must deal realistically with the examination problem, ensuring that students are not in effect penalized for absorption in computerised work. Also, computer-enthused historians must avoid the temptation to overload such courses with computer exercises: these should be restricted to occasions when the computerised material advances the overall aims of the course. Experience at Glasgow suggests that this is not an unduly negative prescription, if the computerised class follows lectures which provide necessary background and precedes collective discussion of the results of a machine-based tutorial. For example, the analysis of electoral trends and the study of changing occupational patterns are more easily approached by students with the computer than with either lectures or discussions in isolation, or even through a combination of the two 'conventional' formats.

Within individual workshops the teacher must structure computer-based teaching carefully if congestion and chaos are to be avoided. Fortunately, the nature of educational computing makes such structuring pedagogically appropriate as well as logistically essential. Computerised classes require careful planning: the improvisation which can sustain an awkwardly timed lecture or tutorial courts total disaster in a computer workshop. Query systems based around simple boolean logic demand the precise manipulation of regularly structured hierarchical or relational data: a well-structured session allows students to make the most of such software even when their original questions are vague or imprecise. Thus computers discipline as well as liberate: they force instructors and students to think logically about the structure of the information about the past that they are using. In the absence of such discipline, students and instructors find themselves either in electronic cul de sacs or in states of abject confusion.

4 Computer Workshops: the DISH Example

Thus the avoidance of computerised libertinism also demands that the historian provide his or her students with a structured exercise which isolates the most important questions and the minimum of data necessary to explore them properly. One method of accomplishing these goals is the 'workshop' format adopted by Glasgow's DISH Project (a discussion of the approaches of some other history projects is available in Trainor, 1989).

At least a week before the computerised tutorial, students are given a hard-copy exercise which provides them with necessary background information, structures the lab work they undertake in search of 'results,' and provides more general questions to be answered on the basis of this 'output.' The exercise has several parts:

1. A discussion of the historical issues in the course to which the workshop relates;

2. Information about the source (including a photocopied facsimile) on which the computerised dataset is based;

3. An example of the data, illustrating the way in which it has been constructed from the source, and indicating its structure with explanations of any coding;

4. Instruction in any additional software (or features of software) not previously used in the course;

5. A series of problems to be explored on the computer;

6. An indication of the more general historical problems for which the student's results may have implications;

7. An opportunity for 'feedback' on the structure and content of the exercise.

Sometimes the paper exercise is handed in at or soon after the conclusion of the workshop; ideally the workshop forms the basis of collective discussion at the next class session.

This method can be illustrated from exercises used in two Glasgow University history courses: Approaches to the Study of the History of Scotland (in the Scottish History Department), and Elites in Nineteenth Century British Society (in the Economic History Department). The courses are based on the same source, the Scottish Calendar of Confirmations, and they are concerned with the same general historical issue, the geographical and occupational distribution of wealth in Victorian and Edwardian Britain.

Preliminary lectures and the opening sections of the exercises introduce students to a debate in the historical literature concerning the extent to which southeastern Britain—and the landed, commercial, financial, and professional classes disproportionately found there—continued to dominate structures of income and wealth despite the Industrial Revolution (see Rubinstein, 1981; Britton, 1985; Morgan and Moss, 1986, 1989; Morgan and Trainor, 1990). Students are then acquainted with a sizeable, but manageable, teaching dataset (1155 records), based on the Calendar of Confirmations, the Scottish counterpart of English probate calendars: this contains estimates of the personal wealth (plus details of age, occupation and address) left at death by the best-off fifth of the population who died in Glasgow in 1901 (see Figure 6.1.).[1] Having provided the students with a facsimile of the Calendar, the exercise then instructs them about its history, function and structure, which serves to illustrate both its difficulties and its value in comparison with related types of evidence used by historians interested in the subject. In the exercise in the Elites course, which occurs earlier than in the Approaches course, some further software instruction is also provided.

The exercises then move on to a series of general questions. In the Elites course, where the students have only one week to spend on the subject, students use a series of subfiles of people whose Confirmation values fall in various ranges of wealth: they attempt to discover the extent to which the various major occupational groups (industrial, professional, commercial, etc.) are represented in each range. In the Approaches course, where two weeks are allocated to the subject, students are confronted by more general questions relating to distribution of wealth by size of estate, wealthholding by sex, wealthholding by occupation, the occupational background of top wealthholders, and the spatial distribution of wealth within the city (in the Elites course these additional topics form an optional supplementary part of the exercise). An example of the results they obtain—in this particular case, concerning the clustering of confirmed estates within the city—is presented

---

[1] They represent all those who died in that year and whose estates, by 1906, had gone through the legal process of confirmation in the Glasgow Sheriff Court. These estates consist mostly of those valued at £5 or more, thereby including nearly all those large enough to be relevant to the debate about patterns of wealthholding, which has concentrated on large fortunes. The dataset was compiled by Nicholas Morgan.

```
┌──────────────────────░░░QWEST - CCG1901░░░──────────────────[↓][↕]─┐
│RECORD  :0394                                                     ▲  │
│NAME    :LAIRD,SIR WILLIAM                                           │
│ADDRESS :7 KEW TERRACE KELVINSIDE GLASGO                             │
│DISTRICT:PARTICK                                                     │
│SEX     :M                                                           │
│DDEATH  :14/08/1901                                                  │
│AGE     :71                                                          │
│OCCO    :IRONMASTER                                                  │
│CODE    :2108                                                        │
│TESTATE :Y                                                           │
│DCONF   :07/09/1901                                                  │
│EST     :313648.85                                                   │
│EIK     :                         ┌──────░Search Summary░──────┐     │
│TTL     :313648.85                │                            │     │
│RANGE   :7                        │ Total records:     1155    │     │
│──────────────────────           │                            │     │
│                                  │ Records searched:  516     │     │
│RECORD  :0397                     │                            │     │
│NAME    :LANGLANDS,WILLIAM        │ Matches found:     15      │     │
│ADDRESS :41 LANDSDOWNE CRESCENT GLASGOW │                      │     │
│DISTRICT:KELVIN                   │ Size of gap(s):    0       │     │
│SEX     :M                        └────────────────────────────┘     │
│DDEATH  :06/11/1901                                              ▼  │
└───────────────────────────────────────────────────────────────────┘
```

Fig. 6.1: The Calendar of Confirmations 1901 dataset. ADDRESS gives residence at date of death; DISTRICT refers to the registration district of Glasgow of that residence; CODE is a four-digit occupational coding based on the Registrar General's scheme of classification for 1881; DCONF is the date that the estate was confirmed; EST is the value of the estate at confirmation; EIK the date of any additional inventory; TTL is total value of the estate (i.e. EST plus the value of any EIK); RANGE is a coded field indicating how high in the range of wealthholding TTL falls (in the case of Sir William Laird the highest, £100,000–£500,000).

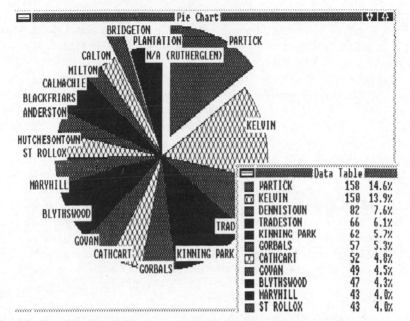

Fig. 6.2: The Calendar of Confirmations 1901 dataset: a distribution of wealthleavers in Glasgow. As students of the social geography of Glasgow will know, at the turn of the century Kelvin and Partick contained prosperous middle-class areas.

in Figure 6.2. Finally, in both courses, students are invited to speculate about the implications of their results for the historical debate about wealthholding, paying particular attention to the extent to which the case study in question—a 'provincial' city, but one of considerable wealth and occupational complexity— confirms or qualifies the prevailing historical orthodoxies.[2] In this way students proceed step by step from issues to dataset to questions to implications and back to issues again, acquiring the minimum of necessary technical knowledge and handling the minimum of necessary data.

Yet, as this outline of the Confirmation exercises suggests, while the workshop method avoids libertinism, it promotes liberation, for exploration is as integral to the method as its structure. The exercise is framed to permit learners to pursue a variety of routes (either individually or, as often occurs in DISH workshops, in impromptu student groups) to an outcome which, like the conclusion of an adventurous student essay, is a plausible resolution of a complex problem, rather than a single answer to a simple question. For example, Figure 6.2 from the Confirmations exercise provides information on the geographical distribution of

[2] The results (revealing a great many non-industrial wealthholders, especially at lower and middle levels of wealth, but a substantial proportion of industrialists among the very wealthy) have complex, ambiguous implications for the debate.

wealth, but there are several reasons why this chart is not in itself an 'answer' to the question of wealth distribution: first, it requires interpretation (which to be well informed must draw on information not available on the computer, such as the social characteristics of particular districts); second, it suggests further computer-based queries, notably the extent to which the wealthiest individuals, as well as the highest number of wealthy individuals, were found in the same areas; and third, it points to more fundamental queries, such as speculation about the four-fifths of the dying population whose estates were not confirmed. Such flexibility becomes increasingly practical in the later stages of courses, when students have become comfortable with the hardware, software and computerised material in use, or when a substantial part of the course can be devoted to a particular set of material. Yet even single exercises presented relatively early can be shaped so that students, although guided toward particular questions, are forced to realise that the 'answers' obtained are only the building blocks for personal interpretation of the major issues involved. In either situation, students are encouraged to play an active role in the exploration of the topic, and instructors find themselves exploring the subject alongside them, not always with superior results!

5 Conclusion

The change in the teacher's role that we have been describing, from unhampered expositor to computer-assisted fellow investigator, fundamentally challenges current assumptions about the function of the university teacher of history and, no doubt, of other humanities disciplines as well (the pedagogical opportunities in this respect in the various humanities disciplines are discussed by Trainor, 1987). Indeed, at one extreme it could be argued that for historians this approach liberates academics from having to teach history at all: instead they can become guides accompanying their students in an exploration of the past. Their role becomes more participatory and more challenging, without any abdication of responsibility for the basic structure of courses. The lecturer is liberated from the tyranny of content, although at the clear expense of the time and effort that is implicit in the preparation and presentation of computer workshops. As a consequence the traditional relationships between teacher and taught are modified (as indeed are relationships between students). But the instructor's relationship with his subject is revolutionised.

7

Argument Support Programs: Machines for Generating Interpretations

Arthur Stutt

1 Introduction

In this chapter I will explore the possible use of the computing machine as arguer: that is, as generator and critic of interpretations. I will suggest that there should be limitations on the autonomy of the machine and that, therefore, it is best viewed as a means of producing a range of possible arguments with selection left up to the user. Nonetheless this will provide a useful contribution in an area where formal teaching is often neglected. At the same time the theoretical underpinning of the disciplines which make use of such a machine will not be affected since only the model of argumentation is imposed on the user. The main uses of such a machine will be: in learning (rather than teaching since the student is not directed by a teacher); in the storage and retrieval of viewpoints as well as facts; and, as a tool for researchers who want to clarify and test their arguments.

In the following sections I will discuss some design principles, suggest how they overcome objections to the use of knowledge based systems in the humanities and present a program design based on them.

2 Design Principles

As an introductory preamble to the idea of the machine as arguer, I want to introduce two notions in order to set the scene for the project I will be describing later. The first notion is that a novel is a machine. This comes from Umberto Eco's discussion of his novel *The Name of The Rose*. Eco says, 'A narrator should not supply interpretations of his work; otherwise he would not have written a novel, which is a machine for generating interpretations' (1985: 1–2). The second notion is of the machine as author. In an essay entitled *Cybernetics and Ghosts* Italo Calvino makes the following observations:

> The literature machine can perform all the permutations possible on a given material, but the poetic result will be the particular effect of one of these permutations on a man endowed with a consciousness and an unconscious, that is, an empirical and historical man. It will

be the shock that occurs only if the writing machine is surrounded by
the hidden ghosts of the individual and of his society. (1986: 22)

What strikes me about the first of these quotes is the use of the word 'machine.'
Eco uses the word as a metaphor. He is suggesting that a novel can be considered
in some respect like a machine. He doesn't say what respect, but it is easy enough
to suggest possibilities. Both have parts, structure, power, effect. Perhaps the
metaphor doesn't work for us because we have a certain view of the machine as
something composed of metal parts and used in some industrial process. However
this view of the machine is no longer tenable. Consider the computer science
notion of the 'virtual machine.' This is the machine as experienced by the user as
opposed to the machine which really exists for the designer of an operating system
(or at a lower level the machine which the chip maker knows about). Computer
science has expanded the notion of what a machine is. Thus it becomes possible for
Eco to suggest that the novel is a machine and for us to accept the metaphor. But
the use of metaphor is a two way process (at least according to Black's influential
interaction view: Black, 1962). Thus to say that a novel is a machine is also
to some extent to say that a machine is a novel. Other contributors to this book
(see the chapter by Bantz) have suggested that the interaction between computer
science and the humanities should be a two way process. For me the metaphorical
use of the word 'machine' suggests that any great divide between technology and
the humanities is much exaggerated.

The Calvino essay discusses a notion which has been widely canvassed ever
since the birth of the computer: The computer as author. There have been
countless attempts to produce poetry writing programs using various stochastic
techniques. There have also been attempts to get the computer to produce stories.
For instance, James Meehan produced a program in the seventies for the generation
of fable-like narratives (Meehan, 1977). The Calvino quote expresses both why
this has been felt to be a possibility and why it must ultimately fail. Since the
machine is capable of tirelessly producing all the permutations of some set of
basic data, if we could find a way of representing characters and situations we
could, for instance, encourage the machine to act as a scriptwriter for a TV soap.
Of course there is more to the soap than the permutation of words or characters.
Calvino suggests what this might be. The machine-author is not a human being
with a human being's sympathies, needs, desires, emotions, sense of humour or
interests. These characteristics are necessary even for the creation of an episode of
a soap. Calvino suggests further that they are not something that can be codified
since they are part of our lived experience. In this he is surely right.

We can accept, then, that there are analogies between the products of writers
and programmers and that artists, critics and other interpreters will go on using
this technology both as a tool and as a source of metaphors. But as Calvino
points out the machine has its limitations as creator. These limitations are not
confined to the writing machine. All software machines are limited in what they

can do. This is especially true of those which attempt to emulate or model aspects of human cognitive skills and is something that critics of artificial intelligence have always seized upon. Hubert Dreyfus (Dreyfus and Dreyfus, 1986) and John Searle (1980) are prominent among the philosophical critics. More recently Winograd and Flores (1986) have cast some doubt from within the discipline about the viability of the AI enterprise. They argue that since it is impossible to capture all the background knowledge utilized by humans in solving problems it is better to use the computer not as an autonomous problem solver but as a kind of assistant which models only a subset of human skills. There are of course visionaries in AI who claim that the encoding of background knowledge is possible and therefore, by implication, that at least some of Calvino's ghosts can be confined within the machine. For instance, work has recently begun on the Knoesphere project (Lenat, Borning, McDonald, Taylor and Weyer, 1983) to represent all the basic concepts necessary for the understanding of a standard encyclopaedia. Before moving on, I propose to encapsulate the above discussion in terms of the following principle which I have honoured with Calvino's name.

> *Calvino's Principle*: Since computers are good at the combination, permutation and matching of symbols but not at judging the results of these operations, designers of computer systems should attempt to produce systems that assist in the task of forming judgements rather than systems which make final judgments.

The work I shall introduce below is an attempt to design a machine which can produce interpretations, criticize user interpretations and allow the user to criticize the system interpretations. In accord with the above principle, the system should make no authoritative pronouncements but should always be prepared to argue for its interpretations and criticism. Therefore, the project I describe should best be situated not in the domain of automatic inferencing (or expert systems) but in the domain of cooperative approaches to work (such as Winograd's 'coordinator').

Whatever the outcome of the debate within AI exemplified by Winograd and Lenat, I suggest that expert systems as oracles are largely inappropriate in the humanities. While in a domain such as oil exploration the user may require the system to produce a single result (the most likely place to drill for oil) with perhaps some rationale for this result, in the humanities we need to explore the many possible interpretations of our data. The difference in the needs of the two domains (oil exploration and the humanities) results from differences in their overall aims. The principle aim of oil explorers is to find oil and to exploit their findings. The principle aim of, say, the archaeologist is to add to the sum total of human knowledge. The role of the archaeological writer is not to hand down oracular judgments but to produce evidence or interpretations of evidence as part of the ongoing debate which constitutes the discipline of archaeology. Thus traditional expert systems, viewed as quasi-autonomous problem solvers, have only a minor role in the humanities and, if knowledge based systems are to fulfill a significant role, an attempt must be made to produce a design in accord with the following two principles (due, not to Calvino, but to common sense and my own experience):

P1 Any system which is to be used in the humanities must take account of the nature of the humanities.

P2 Any system which is to be used in the humanities must provide something by computational means which could not easily be provided in any other way.

3   The Use of Knowledge Based Systems in the Humanities

Before presenting a brief overview of a system which complies with the above design principles we must deal with the following questions which are naturally raised by the above: Do the humanities need knowledge based systems at all? And, if so, what sort of knowledge based systems do they need?

My answer to the first question is that while the humanities do not need such systems, they may have a useful role to play. Standard expert systems (while failing to have a significant role) may yet be of use in the more technical areas of the humanities where rules can be stated formally. For instance in archaeological dating, prosodic studies or the interpretation of statistical results. On the other hand we have no way of telling whether other more powerful knowledge based systems will destroy the disciplines they are used in because alien theories and models are imported or whether, by avoiding their use, we may miss out on some fruitful flowering of the discipline as the result of technological changes. There are obvious analogies between the humanities today and the position of monastic scribes confronted by the presses of Gutenberg and Caxton. We may be more aware that technological change brings with it other changes but can we predict the outcome of any innovation? While my principles can help to avoid some of the grosser dead-ends, ultimately we'll just have to try and see.

What sort of systems are needed? These will be systems which satisfy all three principles given above. As I have already hinted, I view the humanities as an arena (or set of arenas) where debate at conferences and through the medium of published papers is at least one means of advancing the body of knowledge which constitutes a domain.

If this view of the humanities is correct, then it seems obvious that the sort of system we need to satisfy P1 is one which can participate in one or more phases of that process. The *ideal system* would be one which can store, display and allow single or multiple users to interact with vast bodies of data and opinion, which can provide and accept new interpretations of that data and argue in support or against these interpretations. This is not something that can be done easily either by a human lecturer or by the use of, say, libraries and paper documents. The ideal system thus satisfies principle P2. At the same time, in accordance with Calvino's Principle, such a system should not impose its interpretations and evaluations, leaving the decision between competing interpretations to the user. In other words the system does not act as a decision-maker but as an aid to acquiring a considered view. The provision of multiple justified interpretations minimizes the risk of importing inappropriate interpretations, while imposing only a model of argumentation.

There seem to be three main uses for this kind of system:

(a) *Learning*. Non-directive arguing systems of the kind envisaged will avoid the tedium of computer based training or the inadequacies of intelligent tutoring systems. Because the user can try out arguments such a system would provide a means of honing argumentation skills. In general this central aspect of the humanist's discipline is not taught explicitly. This can certainly be rectified by our ideal system as well as, to a certain extent, by systems capable only of storing and displaying arguments. As Stephen Shennan (1989) has recently pointed out, in discussing interpretation in archaeology, the use of AI enforces the explicit formulation of all the steps necessary in producing or changing an argument. In this, the approach I am advocating is similar to that suggested by Gardin (1987b).

(b) *The storage and retrieval of facts, opinions and argued positions*. For example, the system could be used as an interface to the results of an archaeological excavation coupled with the opinions of researchers about the significance of these facts.

(c) *A tool for research*. It is not only students who could benefit from such a system. Researchers could make use of it as a means of testing and developing chains of argument about particular topics.

4 A Design for an Argument Machine

In the remainder of this chapter I will briefly present a design for knowledge based systems for use in the humanities which model user/system interaction as *stylized argument exchange* (see Stutt, 1988 for more details). To emphasise the non-directive nature of these systems I have called them Argument *Support* Programs (ASPs). The user interacts not with the real machine represented by the hardware (or the operating system) but with the virtual machine produced by the ASP.

The design is consistent with the above ideal system. However the programs which are being constructed within this approach are limited in various ways. For instance without a natural language component the interaction will be conducted in a form of constrained English using windows, menus and a mouse. Again the arguments which can be produced and understood will not be very ambitious. This is because of the difficulty of acquiring and representing the complex bodies of knowledge required for realistic arguments. These systems must therefore be understood as prototypes for a real arguing system which would take on the characteristics of the ideal system mentioned above. At the time of writing the only system which has been implemented using this design is a small demonstration program for debate in archaeology. Nonetheless, even without a full implementation, we can see that the ASP satisfies principle P1 since it will provide a means for storing, retrieving and interacting with arguments and P2 since its capacity for storage, inference and display far outstrips that of any human arguer. Calvino's Principle is satisfied since no decision will be made which is not, in theory, arguable.

In brief outline, a knowledge based system exemplifying the stylized argument approach can be seen as one which allows either the system or user to put forward propositions and their supporting grounds and expects the other to criticise these by finding weaknesses or alternative arguments as part of an on-going argument exchange. The significant aspect of the approach is that the system is capable not only of analysing user arguments in terms of the canons of informal logic (Toulmin, 1979) but also of entering into an argument exchange.

ASPs rely on a model of argumentation which is loosely based on that of the conduct of legal proceedings (derived ultimately from Toulmin, 1958) and on the work on the computational modelling of argumentation pursued by Alvarado, Dyer and Flowers (1986), Cohen (1987), Flowers, McGuire and Birnbaum (1982), and Reichman-Adar (1984); a model of interpretation which is based on the work of J-C Gardin (1980, 1987a, 1987b); and a threefold model of argument fields in terms of domain, model and theory levels. This last allows a classification of arguments as either inter or intra level while the varying transformations possible within the model of interpretation provide a framework for a discussion of the differing modes of reasoning which underlie argument types. This capacity to analyse arguments in terms of their different types is one of the main contributions of the ASP design. The display of interpretive and critical arguments in terms of the different types of inferences used at each step (combined with the making explicit of backing theories and models) informs the user's argument with a high degree of perspicuity. In their capacity to display different links between propositions, these systems have much in common with hypertext systems (see Slatin, this volume). Given the ease with which the chunks of text can be linked in a hypertext system, researchers such as Trigg and Weiser (1986) and others have made use of hypertext systems as tools for argumentation. However, unlike ASPs, these systems only provide a means of storing and accessing rather than assessing or responding to arguments.

An ASP is made up of: (a) an argument module which contains a system knowledge base with knowledge about how to argue, and (b) an underlying domain knowledge base. The domain knowledge base is similar to that for a standard expert system. The argument module is composed of a series of knowledge bases which encode strategic and assessment knowledge as well as procedural elements which enable the program to act as a participant in an argument, as a storer of the argument and as an assessor. In order to identify weaknesses in user arguments, it has been necessary to provide rules for assessing these interpretations and criticisms. In the light of Calvino's Principle these rules are used by the system to justify as well as determine its decisions.

The basic function of these systems is to provide interpretations about some domain and to enter into a debate about these. An interpretation is a claim with full supporting grounds (each of which may have supporting grounds and so on). This is produced by processing the domain knowledge base which is stored as facts and rules. In simple terms, the system deals with a user argument by checking that the user interpretation is in fact possible and then selecting an appropriate response. In order to keep track of the debate, the argument module maintains an argument network which stores details of the argument as it proceeds. This network functions both as the system's primary knowledge source about the course of the argument and as the basis for various graphical displays of the argument which the user can request.

This rather abstract account can be made more concrete by the hypothetical example in Table 7.1. In a real example, the exchange would be contained in a number of graphical displays with which the user interacts rather than as straightforward text. The argument it contains is loosely based on Stephen Booth's reading of Shakespeare's Sonnets (Booth, 1969). The text in the rightmost column represents an analysis of the argument.

The argument here is conducted at the level of the domain facts and makes no appeal to external theory. The dominant reasoning mode is deductive or rule-based. The response is an *alternative argument* (not due to Booth) in which the original claim is attacked indirectly by supporting a relevant alternative claim. This latter argument might be produced directly from the knowledge base provided for the domain. Alternatively it might represent the contents of a previous user's argument.

The HyperCard mock-up illustrates how the argument (input using a dialogue like the above or some menu-driven interface) can subsequently be browsed. Figure 7.1 illustrates the top level claim given above. Each of the grounds for this claim is associated with a 'button.' When this is selected (as in Figure 7.2) the sub-argument for the ground is presented. Further selection of grounds will lead (as in Figure 7.3) to the evidence available in the text itself. Figure 7.4 illustrates the result of selecting the different argumentational pathway provided by the system's alternative argument.

The enormity of the representational task can be illustrated by the fact that even in this brief argument, the system would need at least rules for relating: (a) the concepts of oxymoron and paradox; (b) certain words, their instances and the lines and sonnets they occur in; (c) certain words and the concept of oxymoron; and, (d) certain words and the concept of spirituality.

5 Conclusion

To conclude, ASPs are machines for producing justified interpretations. Unlike a novel they are machines for entering into a discussion of these interpretations. An

Table 7.1: A hypothetical example

User:	The purpose of Shakespeare's sonnet is to express the paradoxes of experience.	Claim 1
System:	Why?	
User:	There are paradoxes of substance and paradoxes of syntax.	Ground 1 Ground 2
System:	What is the evidence for the Claim: There are paradoxes of substance	SubClaim 2 = Ground 1
User:	Sonnet 20 contains the line 'Hast thou, the master-mistress of my passion.'	SubGround 3
	and	
	this line contains the compound word 'master-mistress',	SubGround 4
	and	
	this is a paradoxical use of language.	SubGround 5 = SubSubClaim 3
	because	
	it is an oxymoron	SubSubGround 6
	and	
	oxymoron is a kind of paradox	SubSubGround 7
	. . .	
System:	Is there other evidence for your Claim	
User:	No	
System:	There is an alternative argument: The purpose of Shakespeare's sonnets is to express the role of forgiveness in experience	System Claim 1
	since	
	there is a line in sonnet 145 'Straight in her heart did mercy come'	System ground 1

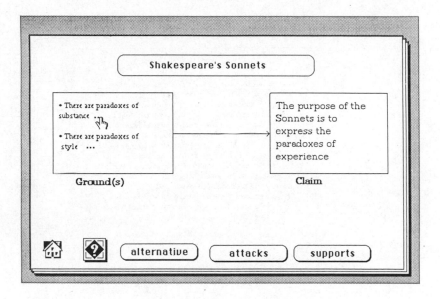

Fig. 7.1: The top level claim

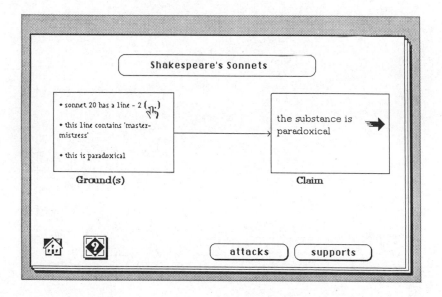

Fig. 7.2: Displaying a sub-argument for the top level claim

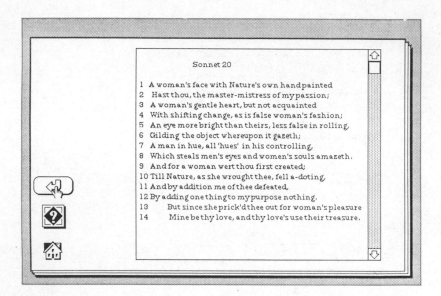

Fig. 7.3: Displaying the text associated with the argument

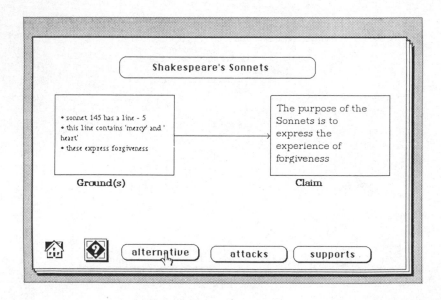

Fig. 7.4: Displaying an alternative argument

ASP aspires to be a *Reflections on the Name of the Rose*. Perhaps one day there will be a generic ASP capable of arguing in any domain and of presenting and defending its own theoretical assumptions. There may even be machines capable, like Eco, of producing the object for interpretation and the interpretation. Who knows. I, for one, think it is extremely unlikely. In the meantime we will have to do with flesh and bone authors and, for the foreseeable future, machines which can aid in the interpretation of their texts and therefore provide a valuable educational and research tool. These machines will, nevertheless, be limited in that they will be unable to produce valuable interpretations on their own. The ghosts will have to stay where they belong: as part of our lived world not as encoded and dead forms within the machine.

8

Philosophy and Knowledge Engineering

R. A. Young

1 Introduction

Computers may be used in philosophy in order to provide support for traditional philosophy teaching, but they may also be used because philosophers and their students are developing new interests, which are cognate with computer science, artificial intelligence, cognitive science, or knowledge engineering. If we consider support for traditional teaching then it must be confessed that many philosophy departments have not yet found a use for computers in the presentation of their standard courses, or in concordancing, or other computational study of texts. The most widespread use of computers in the philosophy classroom is the use of tutorial systems as an aid to logic teaching. Prolog (the most widely known logic programming language) may itself be used as a vehicle for logic teaching. From the point of view of a traditional logic teacher tailor-made tutorial systems may be helpful, but the use of Prolog in logic teaching is considered questionable, because programming in it distracts students from pure logic: they may become interested in the question of the efficiency of their programs, which is a question that is not central to logic.

From the point of view of other philosophers, such as myself, programming in Prolog is of interest precisely because it does introduce philosophy students to problems of efficiency and complexity in the application of logical reasoning. These are questions that are relevant in many fields of philosophical inquiry. Therefore at the University of Dundee we have a course on Logic and Computing at Honours level. This is not the primary introductory course in logic. Taught in the third or fourth year, it is a course on the application of logic to artificial intelligence, knowledge engineering and cognitive science. The course is intended to demonstrate the relevance of formal logic to these disciplines, to explain to philosophy students problems of complexity and efficiency and other computational problems that arise in such applications of logic, and to provide support for discussion of computational issues in other philosophy courses, and indeed in other cognate degree subjects.

As well as being available to Honours Philosophy students the course is available to Honours Psychology students. An advanced version of the course is given to students taking our Diploma in Logic, Text and Information Technology (run in conjunction with the English Department), and to M.Phil students, and in future it will be a component of our University's planned integrated B.Sc in 'Computer Science and Cognitive Science.' We are also introducing a course for our Honours students entitled 'Knowledge Systems.' This course, a version of which is already taught at postgraduate level, complements our Logic and Computing Course by considering departures from classical deductive and inductive logics, which have been developed in the application of expert systems to uncertainty and in learning systems such as those based upon genetic algorithms and neural networks. The need to use heuristic methods in order to cope with computationally intractable issues is also discussed.

These courses are not run in isolation from the rest of our degree program. In our first year course on 'Understanding People through the Human Sciences' we introduce students to the possibility of studying people through cognitive science and explore this as one component of the human sciences. Issues concerned with cognitive science and artificial intelligence also arise in our Honours philosophy of mind course, and are being introduced in our philosophy of language course and philosophy of science course.

If philosophy is being radically redefined because of the use of computers in teaching and research, then this is because philosophers and their students are becoming convinced that computational issues are integral to philosophy itself. Even here we need to distinguish the traditional interest philosophers have had in the comparison between mind and machine from the change in the subject that arises when the formal aspects of problems can be modelled on computers. At one time it was usual to say that 'Modern Philosophy' originated with Descartes—and he did of course present arguments for distinguishing between thinking things and automata (Descartes, 1637/1911). Thus there has been interest in the prospects for 'artificial intelligence' for centuries and philosophers have been divided about its potential. In this century Turing (1950) published his proposal for the Turing test in *Mind*, a philosophical journal, and philosophers responded with a debate that has lasted up to the present time. A feature of this debate about the Turing test is that many philosophers have felt able to follow it, or even contribute to it, without doing more than perhaps learn a little about the theory of Turing machines. In contrast we can consider various philosophers who pay serious attention to computational studies, such as Churchland (1986), or, as in the case of Thagard (1988) or Young (1990), who even report on their own computational studies. What are the reasons for this philosophical interest in computational studies? Is this engagement likely to deepen and become more widespread? If so to what extent can this interest on the part of philosophy staff be reflected in the undergraduate curriculum?

It is perhaps to be expected that analytic (formally-minded) philosophers will have interests that are cognate with computer science. It is not so obvious that philosophers who hold that human thought cannot be captured by formal analysis can also use computational models to express some of their own ideas. I shall first of all consider the position of analytic philosophers and then consider those who are opposed to them.

Philosophy is a discipline that has traditionally dealt with fundamental problems that we have with our systems of thought. At the core of its approach there has often been an attempt rationally to reconstruct these systems using formal techniques. In the hands of some philosophers, such as Leibniz and Russell, rational reconstruction has involved the formalization of knowledge through the creation of artificial, formally specified languages. Neither of them would have been happy to agree with the view that the human mind can be analysed as being identical with an artificial intelligence program. But the design of artificial formal languages for the analysis of human thought is similar to some of the work that is done in artificial intelligence and knowledge engineering. In the next section of this chapter I shall discuss these similarities and their impact on philosophy teaching. Later I shall argue that even philosophers who claim that it is misguided to analyze much of human thought in formal terms may find that they have allies in cognitive science and knowledge engineering.

2 Rational Reconstruction and Formalization of Knowledge

Many contemporary 'knowledge engineers' are also involved in the formalization of knowledge. At the moment this formalization generally takes place in very specific subject domains. On one definition the job of a knowledge engineer consists in articulating the knowledge of a human expert and in translating this knowledge into a specialized 'Knowledge Representation Language' (KRL). KRLs are meant to be intelligible to human experts as a means of formalizing their knowledge. They are meant to be intelligible independently of an understanding of how a machine processes them, whilst at the same time having the formality required to provide a basis for mechanized inference. Furthermore they are meant to allow representation of rules and of relationships between concepts. Thus knowledge engineers have concerns in common with philosophers who attempt formally to analyze knowledge. Indeed many KRLs are based upon systems of formal logic ranging from the first-order predicate calculus (first developed by Frege, Russell and Whitehead) to more recently developed systems of modal, temporal, epistemic, fuzzy, and other logics. Philosophers have played a key part in the development of these formal systems. They have also, until recently, been the major appliers of these systems to the analysis of human knowledge.

Moreover knowledge engineers are often led to engage in rational reconstruction of the human expertise from which they start. This may occur because of the constraints of machine inference. It may occur because human experts contradict each other or even contradict themselves. But it can also occur because some of the human 'knowledge' does not consist of premises and rules of inference. Consider the case of medical diagnosis: a human diagnostician may rely on habitual responses to patterns of symptoms rather than on any internally-represented rules. A knowledge engineer using a KRL that is designed to express statements and rules will attempt to identify a system of statements and rules for diagnosis which are at least as reliable as, and hopefully more intelligible than, the diagnostician's informal know-how.

Are the concerns of the knowledge engineer precisely the same as those of the formally-minded philosopher? One contrast that we may draw here is between the very specific domains in which knowledge engineers work and the interest which philosophers have in attempting to identify general principles of formalization and of interpretation. But this does not give us a clear-cut distinction between the two: to the extent that knowledge engineers are interested in building systems which have the capacity to integrate knowledge from different domains, they will be interested in general principles. Even if this kind of integration is not successful, because of difficulty in building systems of such complexity, knowledge engineers will still have an interest in identifying general principles that can be applied across several, or even all, specialist domains. Indeed expert system shells are designed to provide a general inference engine and interface that can cover a range of specialist domains.

Thus knowledge engineering and formally-minded philosophy are concerned with the formalization of knowledge, where this involves rational reconstruction and the attempt to generalize. Work on the computational philosophy of science, for example, is quite close to Knowledge Engineering, and some works (e.g. Holland, et al., 1986) happily combine the work of knowledge engineers, philosophers of science, and cognitive scientists. It is possible for philosophy students to develop their skills in epistemology, logic, and philosophy of science by working on knowledge engineering projects. In this way they are able to explore philosophical issues whilst simultaneously gaining vocationally relevant skills. At the University of Dundee we are implementing this approach in our teaching. In our Honours program we use examples taken from knowledge engineering and natural language processing. Instead of using examples such as 'All men are mortal, Socrates is a man, therefore Socrates is mortal,' we can leave Socrates to his mortality and consider practical examples from medical diagnosis. We can look at certainty theory, which was developed in the classic MYCIN system, and ask how it relates to logic and probability theory. We can ask whether it provides a sound way of reasoning to diagnostic conclusions and explore alternatives to it. A problem that arises in applying probability theory to diagnosis is that calculation of probabilities can become horrendously complex unless simplifying assumptions are made, but different sets of simplifying assumptions can be made and choice between these sets is controversial. There is a tradeoff between purity in handling probabilities and practical efficiency in calculation (Charniak and McDermott, 1985: 453–482; see also Adams, 1984).

We have seen how the concerns of philosophy overlap with those of knowledge engineering. A worry here for philosophers is that serious research in this area of overlap will come to be the preserve of knowledge engineers and computer scientists, rather than of philosophers. A crucial factor here is that it is easier for knowledge engineers and computer scientists to get funding for equipment and support staff than it is for philosophers to do so. This is true of funding for both teaching and research. There is a danger here, from the philosophical standpoint, of philosophical work on logic and formalized epistemology, or philosophy of science being marginalized. Just as physics and other sciences were once closely integrated with philosophy, but are now quite separate disciplines, applied logic might completely depart from philosophy.

A possible response to this worry is to say that analytic philosophy still has a role to play in cognitive science. Cognitive science is distinct from the activity of knowledge engineering, because its role is to develop models of natural human and animal mental processes. It is carried on with the presumption that human and animal mental processes are inherently computational. Thus it has affinities with knowledge engineering and theoretical artificial intelligence, but it is distinct from them because they may develop knowledge systems which work on principles that are quite unnatural to human beings. Whereas other disciplines may be involved in rational reconstruction, or even in the construction of radically new forms of knowledge processing, the role of cognitive science is to model natural human or animal processes, however inadequate or deficient they may be. Therefore the central discipline in cognitive science is empirical psychology, even though it is true that cognitive science does draw, and should draw, on other disciplines such as linguistics, artificial intelligence, and philosophy. A possible role for formal philosophy within cognitive science is to develop those systems of logical inference which human beings, given their nature, find most intelligible.

Some philosophical logicians have indeed seen it as their role to develop 'natural' systems of deduction. But it is very questionable whether philosophical logic should restrict itself to this role. Surely philosophical logicians should be concerned to identify those systems of logic that are best from the point of view of the expression and further development of knowledge. It is very questionable whether just those systems that humans find easy to understand will be best from this point of view. Perhaps we can differentiate the role of philosophical logicians by saying that whereas cognitive scientists are interested in logic insofar as natural processes of reasoning are logical, and computational logicians (e.g. the logic programming fraternity) are interested in logics that are suited to implementation on machines, philosophical logicians are interested in logics that are best for articulating knowledge itself.

This is a possible view. If it is adopted on the grandest scale then it approximates to the position that Russell (1918/1960) and other philosophers took in the 1910s, 1920s and 1930s: an ideal logical language was to be developed. It was to be ideal from the point of view of the exact expression of knowledge rather than from the point of view of utility in everyday discourse, even everyday scientific discourse. It was to be a language, i.e. possess a real-world semantics; it was not to be just a formal system. Unfortunately, when one attempts to develop a language which is supposed to express the totality of knowledge one runs into paradoxes of self-reference. There are various ways of coping with these paradoxes and this, together with other considerations, has led to a proliferation of different perspectives on philosophical logic. Philosophers are not in a position to give a definitive answer to the grand question of which logic should be used for the expression of knowledge.

Therefore I do not want to propose precisely Russell's view of the task for philosophy. But there is a role for people who will consider knowledge domains, and who will identify formalizations of knowledge that are designed both to improve upon natural human expressions and to improve upon the deficiencies of current knowledge systems. We need to be able to identify the limitations of ourselves as subjects of knowledge and of our computational knowledge systems. We need to discover the best way of integrating our human capacities with those of machines. This all needs to be thought out not just on the basis of what is narrowly advantageous from the point of view of a knowledge engineering project; nor should it be thought out in terms of what is most natural for human beings: what is most natural is not always what is best. We need to consider what our purposes are in designing systems. This again needs to be thought out on the basis of more general considerations, including ethical and other broad cultural considerations (Council for Science and Society, 1989; see also Young, 1988). It may seem strange to move from discussion of applied logic to ethical considerations, but it must be remembered that there are, for example, projects to advise on the law and on social security benefits, and, at the other end of the spectrum, projects for military systems. In the first example the content of what we need to formalize is normative, and may have ethical aspects. Here it should be noted that a great deal of work has been done in philosophy on special extensions to logic or, in some cases, special logics for the analysis of ethical and normative reasoning. The second example suggests there may be profound considerations of human responsibility that should be taken into account.

If philosophers are to concern themselves with such issues then they will need to verse themselves in the developments of applied logic that are being made in knowledge engineering and in cognitive science. It will not be adequate for them to surrender their interest in applied logic to some combination of knowledge engineering, computer science, mathematics, and cognitive science. Moreover I do not believe that keeping up with these developments should be seen as the task of a few specialists in philosophy. Developments in computer science and in cognitive science must be attended to by a significant proportion of philosophers.

3 Anti-Formalism in Philosophy and Neural Nets in Artificial Intelligence

I developed the argument of the previous section of this chapter by reference to formalism in philosophy. At the end of the section I raised considerations of ethics that take us beyond issues of philosophical logic. But I could be accused of ignoring, both in my discussion of philosophical logic and in my discussion of ethics, a certain important tendency in philosophy. I mentioned this tendency in the introduction, when I referred to the rebellion of philosophers such as Hume, Kierkegaard and Wittgenstein against formalism in philosophy. It may seem as if the thinking of this tendency must be opposed to Knowledge Engineering. This is indeed so, if by Knowledge Engineering we mean the activity of representing knowledge in a KRL. But the activity of Knowledge Engineering may be more broadly characterized than that. Instead of attempting to provide a Knowledge System with its knowledge by feeding it in as data, which is then processed by an inference engine, one can attempt to build systems which learn their knowledge 'by experience.' If these systems are based upon a formal procedure for inductive inference then they may be regarded as still embodying the formalist approach in philosophy.

But there is great interest at present in the construction of systems that are designed by analogy with the human brain. It is argued that if only we can understand how neural circuitry is designed then we will be able to build a learning system by mimicking the circuitry that does the learning. Progress has been made in the design of these neural nets: systems have been produced which do some learning. Most of these systems recognize patterns, and typically they show a response to degraded versions of a pattern. Thus their response is not a simple yes/no response: it is a matter of degree. This response arises as a function of the design of neural circuitry; the systems are not designed to correspond to any system of fuzzy logic. There is an argument that certain of these systems respond in a 'holistic' way. They recognize large-scale patterns from the large-scale firing pattern of neurones. If one recognizes a neighbourhood that one has been in before, say the New Town in Edinburgh, then this recognition will not consist in the firing of a special 'New Town' neurone, but in a complex pattern of excitation of neurones. If a few of those neurones are destroyed, this will not make much difference to one's recognition or to one's response to one's recognition, because both these things will be a matter of degree.

There are interesting analogies between the behaviour manifested by neural nets and some of the human behaviour upon which the later Wittgenstein focused (Wittgenstein, 1953). He stressed the fact that human language, action and thought cannot be thoroughly analysed in terms of any comprehensive system of rules. The rules that we can identify are imprecise and open-textured. Our responses in applying these rules are a matter of degree. Of course, we can say that a rule is to apply in two situations if they share common properties, but it is up to us to determine what counts as a relevant property. The correctness of any one person's decision about the application of a rule is determined by whether other people find it natural to make the same decision or not. We can see in Wittgenstein's philosophy an account that is appropriate to pattern-recognizers: these learn to make discriminations and to express them in language and action without having any clear-cut rules that are represented in their internal processing. The 'rules' for them arise as a necessity of language and social organization: they have to correct each other's 'mistakes' in order for there to be sufficient in common in their behaviour for them to be intelligible to each other.

In current neural nets we have pattern recognition systems, which are not programmed to follow high-level symbolic rules, but which nevertheless learn to recognize patterns. For example, it is claimed that some systems can discriminate human faces. We do not have any nets that have the integrated capacities of human beings. Nor do we have any account of how a society of networks might be expected to interact with each other. But I would propose that research into neural networks suggests that they might provide a physiological underpinning for many of Wittgenstein's arguments. Thus, as I see it, philosophers who are opposed to a highly formal account of human thought and action have potential collaborators in the world of cognitive science and knowledge engineering. At Dundee we raise issues connected with this anti-formalism both in Philosophy of Mind and in our course on Knowledge Systems, which is available to our postgraduate students.

Personally, I am not a whole-hearted supporter of this anti-formalist approach. One of my concerns is that I believe its explanatory value to be very limited. If it were successfully followed through then what would be its results in cognitive science? I think that what we could expect would be a vast variety of models of subsystems of human neural processing. This would be underpinned by an advanced theory of neuro-anatomy, but it would not give us a general theory of human mental processing. Now suppose that someone asked to what extent the set of models and the advanced theory of neuro-anatomy explained the human capacity to do arithmetic. Let us say that a neural net system had been produced which it was said could learn to perform basic arithmetical operations. This claim would be supported by empirical testing of the system. The claim that the system was explanatory of human behaviour would be supported by pointing out that the system modelled aspects of the relevant neuro-anatomy in humans. Could this count as a sufficient basis for saying that the system explained how humans do arithmetic? It seems to me that it could not.

It is a well known feature of software systems that extensive empirical testing of them may fail to reveal bugs, so we cannot simply rely on empirical testing of neural net systems. Also neuro-anatomy is itself highly complex and, if neural net systems model neuro-anatomy at all, it is usually only a very abstract aspect of this anatomy. We can only be sure that a neural net system is modelling all that is relevant to arithmetical capacity in human anatomy if we can prove that the neural net system does itself have the capacity for arithmetical processing. The best way to do this is not by empirical testing alone. Our aim should be to produce a formal analysis of the required arithmetical capacity, a formal specification of the network, and a proof that a network of that kind has the required capacity. There are serious problems with doing this. For one thing there are formal limits to provability that apply to logics that are designed to analyze arithmetic; and for another, there is great complexity in formal proofs for non-trivial systems.

		Prisoner B	
		Keeps Silent	*Gives Evidence*
Prisoner A	*Keeps Silent*	A:2 yrs. B:2 yrs	A:10 yrs. B:0 yrs.
	Gives Evidence	A:0 yrs. B:10 yrs	A:6 yrs. B:6 yrs.

Fig. 8.1: The Prisoners' Dilemma

Nevertheless I believe that we should attempt to make formal analyses of these systems.

4 Computation in Ethics and Political Philosophy

But I do not want to say that the only relevance of computing to philosophy lies in the issues already discussed. I would like to illustrate the pervasiveness of computational issues in philosophy by referring to Axelrod's (1984, 1987) computational studies of the Iterated Prisoners' Dilemma. The Prisoners' Dilemma has been widely discussed in many disciplines, including moral philosophy (Cooper, 1981: 258–282). It shows how rational self-interested choice may fail to gain the benefits of cooperation. The Simple (non-iterated) Prisoners' Dilemma is shown in Figure 8.1. Two prisoners are implicated in the same offence, and, because of the way in which the authorities have offered to vary sentences, both A and B have reason to give evidence, whatever the other prisoner does. For example, if B keeps silent, then A will get 0 years for giving evidence as against 2 years for keeping silent. If B gives evidence, then A gets 6 years for giving evidence instead of 10 years for keeping silent. Thus rationally self-interested prisoners, in a one-off situation, will both choose to give evidence and therefore they will get 6 years each instead of the 2 years they would have got if only they had stayed silent. They would each be better off if they maximized joint welfare by remaining silent. But rational self-interest dictates the opposite policy.

The Prisoners' Dilemma has been used as an analogy for many situations. For example it may be compared with the situation in which two countries, following a policy of national interest, maintain equally strong armed forces. If only they could adopt a policy of maximizing joint welfare they would be able to devote more of their resources to civil production, and thus both countries would be better off. However the decision to maintain strong armed forces is not a once-for-all decision. It is a decision that can be reviewed constantly by each country taking into account intelligence about the military activities and political intentions of the other country. Thus we have what is called the Iterated Prisoners' Dilemma. Axelrod describes a computer tournament that he held for programs designed to maximize individual benefits in this Iterated Dilemma. The winner was a program called 'Tit for Tat,' which was willing to take temporary risks in order to seek the benefits of cooperation, but which was also committed to competitive behaviour in cases where the other player was non-cooperative.

More recently Axelrod has tried a learning algorithm in the Iterated Dilemma. This algorithm was trained on an environment of the eight best algorithms from Axelrod's computer tournament and, on different runs, it discovered a variety of strategies that performed as well as 'Tit for Tat.' Indeed, in 11 out of 40 runs strategies were discovered that did substantially better than 'Tit for Tat.' As Axelrod points out, even if we consider strategies which respond to just the history of the last three moves in the Iterated Dilemma, we find that there are 10 to the power 21 different strategies of this simple kind. This provides a huge search space that cannot be searched exhaustively for the best solution. The learning algorithm that Axelrod used was a genetic algorithm: an algorithm based upon the principles of natural selection as they apply to sexual beings in biological evolution. The idea of a genetic algorithm is to keep a population (database) of candidate solutions to a problem (different strategies in this case). This population is constantly regenerated using a process of recombination that is akin to mating. Selection for 'mating' is weighted according to fitness, but nevertheless there is a strong component of random selection in the mating process. Fitness is determined in this case by the history of benefit obtained in the Iterated Dilemma.

Philosophy students are introduced to the Prisoners' Dilemma in their first year at Dundee. We have not yet included discussion of Axelrod's computational studies in our ethics courses, although their inclusion seems probable. Genetic algorithms are discussed in our Knowledge Systems course, since they are a particular research interest of mine.

5 Postgraduate Courses and Research Interests

Indeed, at the postgraduate level, it is not desirable thoroughly to separate teaching from research, even if this is appropriate at the undergraduate level (which I doubt). A major recent area of my own research[1] consists of an attempt to integrate genetic algorithms with neural networks and some work derived from logic in order to design parallel algorithms or systems for handling complex problems of cognitive modelling (Young, 1990). I have implemented various systems including one on the Meiko Transputer Surface at the University of East Anglia and one on an Alliant VFX4 multiprocessor at Dundee. While this area of research can be mentioned in undergraduate courses and discussed in greater depth in my postgraduate courses, it is difficult enough for a philosopher to get facilities to pursue this research, let alone obtain adequate facilities for undergraduates to learn about such systems by hands on experience. This is a problem which philosophers will face increasingly as their involvement with computers develops.

---

[1] Some of the research mentioned here was done when I held a visiting Fellowship at British Telecom Research Laboratories in 1988 and some was done during my year as a Senior Visiting Fellow in Computer Science (Declarative Systems Project) at the University of East Anglia in 1987–88.

9

The Image of a Word: Computer Generated Programs for the Transformation of Descriptive Language into Pictorial Representations for an Analysis of Axiomatic Thought Processes

Charles Henry

1 Introduction: The Status of Imagery

In 1820 a rather impassioned, somewhat eccentric book appeared by Johann Pestalozzi (1946) entitled *Wie Gertrud ihre Kinder lernt* (*How Gertrude Teaches Her Children*). Building upon some of the psychological approaches to education in his day, and on a wealth of personal experience, Pestalozzi described not only a successful teaching method, but a theory of how the human mind accumulates information, processes it, and synthesizes a myriad of sense perceptions into articulated thoughts. In one of his more passionate entries, Pestalozzi describes the world as a sea of chaotic sense impressions. The business of teaching, and thereby learning, is first to separate the impressions one from the other, then to reassemble them according to their properties in the imagination, where they are thus clarified by association; finally it is to give them the correct sounds (words), which, in a sense, helps to categorize and reinforce this association, as well as allowing the mind to integrate the new with the images of past experience. Proper teaching would lead to clearer images, clarified thoughts, and a more precise articulation of them. But image recognition comes first.

It is an interesting turn that Pestalozzi's intriguing ideas should be recalled in a recent and groundbreaking book, *Imagery in Scientific Thought* (Miller, 1987), which investigates the role of mental images, mostly pictorial or visual ones, in the creation of 20th century physics. Einstein, Poincaré, Heisenberg, and a distinguished list of other modern physicists, have left record of their musings and imaginative ruminations involved in rethinking some of the basic laws of nature. While Miller does not attempt to define precisely how a new scientific revelation comes to life, he evocatively underscores the cognitive role of mental pictures in assisting or perhaps creating a fresh scientific hypothesis. Images of a serpent swallowing its tail, twins travelling through space at different speeds, rising and falling elevators, so simple in themselves, belie an immensely complex and little understood process of the mind to abstract images from a mathematical or verbally stated formula or problem and to reshape this into a newly articulated form.

The relationship between knowledge acquisition and visual imagery has been discussed for millennia. Plato's and Aristotle's writings address it; philosophers as diverse as Kant and Sartre spent considerable thought upon the issue. Visual narratives have long been the concern of art historians (Gombrich, 1961), as has the correspondence between the pictured image and the written word, generally termed *ekphrasis*. In the field of literary analysis, one of the most articulate proponents of the importance of mental images in the understanding of a text is Wolfgang Iser (1982). Iser describes this process pointedly:

> the reader is situated in such a position that he can assemble the meaning toward which the perspectives of the text have guided him. But since this meaning is neither a given external reality nor a copy of an intended reader's own world, it is something that has to be ideated by the mind of the reader. A reality that has no existence of its own can only come into being by way of ideation, and so the structure of the text sets off a sequence of mental images which lead to the text translating itself into the reader's consciousness. The actual content of these mental images will be coloured by the reader's existing stock of experience, which acts as a referential background against which the unfamiliar can be conceived and processed. The concept of the implied reader offers a means of describing the process whereby textual structures are transmuted through ideational activities into personal experiences (Iser, 1982: 38).

It should not be surprising that newer fields, especially the cognitive sciences, share with the humanities an increasing interest in the mind's processes that generate pictures or images in the acquisition or understanding of knowledge. Indeed, in disciplines such as computational psychology, to which this paper owes some debt, heated debate exists as to the nature of mental images, and to the concept of imagery itself. As Boden points out (1988: 27–44), the concept of mental imagery or 'having an image' of something, is 'fuzzy,' and will most likely remain so for some time to come.

Whether a unified computational model of the mind might eventually be drawn from the work of Boden, Pylyshyn, Kosslyn, and others, cannot be directly considered here. However, in order to understand how computers might contribute to more effective teaching methods, some recognition of the processes by which the mind accumulates and interprets meaning will be essential. The above references to Plato, to 20th Century physics, and to reader response theory, all share an intriguing concern for one aspect of the acquisition of meaning that computers have not begun to address in the humanities: ideation, to user Iser's term, holds significant implications for the teaching of literature. In this chapter I examine the possibility of the computer emulating the ideational process. Concordance generators, word searches, syntactical field analysis, and other word-based computer programs are already substantially changing humanities teaching and research; but something deeper may be worth an exploration.

Some justification for embarking on a project of this nature is rooted in language itself. Here, one fundamental purpose of descriptive language appears to be to create an image or picture of reality in the mind. As mentioned above, investigations of the relationship between particular literary stories, such as myths, poems, and novels, and works of plastic art, such as a painting or a sculpture, have been debated for centuries. Yet until now the capability has not existed to create pictures *directly* from a descriptive passage, other than in the confines of the individual mind.

The ideational function is, of course, only one aspect of language. This is underlined by I. A. Richards' quarrel with T. E. Hulme: Hulme had pronounced that poetic language is exclusively a means to make the reader or listener 'see' physical objects, while Richards correctly contended that the language of poetry is often too abstract—intentionally so—to enable any visualisation of concrete, physical reality to take place (1936: 128–134). For many passages of poetry (Richards cites Shakespeare for his examples) visualising specific objects would interfere with the poetic intent. Language, however, does at times create pictures in the mind, and it is the premise of this paper that those pictures or images are of fundamental importance in deciphering and understanding a literary work's meaning.

If the capability of imitating the ideational process with computers could be developed, it would allow, firstly, a closer study of the relationship between the spoken/written word and the human faculties of vision (how visual is language, and by extension how visual is the memory which underlies the use of language); secondly it would facilitate an understanding of the meanings of verbal relationships that may not be readily apparent. The latter could be accomplished by analysing the series of images a text produces for patterns and variations on established imagistic configurations within a work, perhaps building upon the kinds of narrative maps described by Galloway (1979).

2 A Project Outline

Is such a project feasible in the present computer environment? Kosslyn (1981) developed IMAGE over a decade ago, and his work could serve as a prototype to the model presented here. A computer, so programmed, could (1) generate images from a body of text, using a predesigned database of word/image correlations; and (2) analyze those images once generated. Critics of Kosslyn's project, particularly Pylyshyn (1984), have argued against the more theoretical aspects of his models, though often enough accepting the basic mechanics of his experimental method. Using some of the paradigms Kosslyn describes, we can expect the results of such an undertaking to have important implications for the teaching of humanities and to help to suggest new models for the way we understand the act of reading.

The advent of HyperCard and the non-sequential correspondences it allows between images, words, and even speech, provides a particularly suitable model for this project, although only a nascent model, given the complexity of an ideation-emulation program and the speed with which it would be required to perform. Whereas in the past construction of this kind of database and its analysis would have cost a good deal of money and involved thousands of hours of programming and debugging—IBM's InfoWindow system and Digital's IVIS do not approach the speed and flexibility required of this project—newer technologies would facilitate a much easier and more elegant execution of the first stages described below. There is also an array of further technological advances relevant to the project, including fibre optics, vastly increased memory storage, and the prospect of parallel computing (seemingly apt for a project like this one).

Other research in cognition, especially studies that investigate the relationship of pictured images in the mind with thought processes (Pinker, 1985), suggest theoretical underpinnings for the project, as well as offering guidelines for the construction of the various databases that will be utilized. Herbert Simon (1977), who has been a leading advocate of understanding the mind as a symbol processing machine, analogous in many ways to a computer, suggests that a primary feature of this processing activity is the formation and interpretation of images; our ability to visualize the abstract appears to be generally more powerful than our logical thought processes. In fact such studies argue for a primary ability of the mind in creating 'pictures' of disparate concepts which provide an intermediate step between conception and understanding of a new idea. The process is considered an elusive but basic link in the architecture of human thought.

The recent work of Johnson-Laird (1983) on mental models points to the universality of the mental models people use to interpret the meaning of sentences. While the actual formation of mental pictures is not required by Johnson-Laird's theory, it is probably of frequent occurrence. In Johnson-Laird's account, mental models are themselves a type of framing device: such framing is of critical importance both in providing a tool for interpretation and as a determinant of semantic meaning. In this respect models or images appear to be more significant than their verbal equivalents. Campbell (1982), for example, who cites Bransford's (1979) experimental work on sentence structure, meaning, and memory, notes that people do not easily remember sentences word for word, whether written or spoken, but significantly resort to paraphrase. Those tested in Bransford's studies 'were able to store the meaning of the material rather than making a verbatim copy.' Thus, Campbell concludes, 'we forget the surface structure, but retain the abstract relationships contained in the deep structure' (Campbell, p. 219). It seems likely that in representing such relationships, the deep structure will include a set of 'core' images or pictures. It is from these that the verbal paraphrases of Bransford's subjects are generated.

Any project of this kind must of necessity deal with aspects of artificial intelligence. Minsky's work (1975) on the causal/symbolic nature of linguistic structures at the sentence level provides a guideline for engineering this project: nouns serve as object-symbols and verbs as difference-symbols; cause-symbols are contextually arrived at through syntactical arrangements, including clause structures and phrases within a sentence.

Nouns will be the first and easiest linguistic group to tag with pictures. Prepositions, which are inherently the most idiomatic part of speech from language to language, could more easily be addressed, perhaps using HyperCard, as spatial designators relating to other nouns or object-symbols in the sentence. Adjectives could be colour coded, although more abstract adjectives, such as 'beautiful,' should perhaps be left on one side in the first phase. The images generated in this way in the first phase of the project would be predominantly noun/preposition based, to exploit the spatial/pictorial component of language.

The concept of time involved in sentence-level images will be of less importance, at least at first. As a point of contrast, music must be considered a 'timed art:' a performer can play the e-flat that Beethoven wrote, but if played at the wrong time the note is incorrect. The written and spoken word, by contrast, is more of a spatial art. In the ideation process temporal 'properties' such as past and present have little meaning. An interactive imaging analysis program, because of its fluidity, would work against or not be constrained by a linear time line. The accumulation of images and thus of new meaning is time independent. In the initial phase the program will simply generate its pictures sentence by sentence, using punctuation as picture delimiter.

For the first phase, it would seem prudent to start with shorter pieces of literature that are realistic in nature: texts which consciously attempt to visualize the world in which the characters appear. Drawing upon a lexicon of pictorial equivalents in the database, images will appear, then small scenes. Each scene, before erasure to allow formation of another scene, will be stored in memory. Thereafter, several scenes will be analyzed for their image content and parallels and contrasts drawn. While it is true that the images loaded in the initial database may be somewhat idiosyncratic to the humanist user, the program will not attempt at this stage to determine the truth or falsity of object- or causal-symbol relationships; only the generation of analyzable patterns is sought, using an accessible 'dictionary' of pictorial signs.

Various permutations of image generation and analysis will undoubtedly occur. Substantial changes in the direction of the project may also be necessary. Possible future applications seem reasonably predictable. As the programming becomes more sophisticated and the semantic nets more fluid, it will be possible to generate images from more complex texts, such as a Dickens' short story. A highly visual but immensely abstract work such as Milton's *Paradise Lost* could be 'pictured,' perhaps revealing visual patterns not readily discernible from a non-computer assisted reading of the twelve books of blank verse.

3   Toward a Deepened Understanding of Verbal Symbols

The analysis of ideation in literature seems only possible with the advent of the computer, which gives an intermediary, more objective tool for analyzing conceptual relationships. Many of the objects referred to in a given text are repeated and nuanced throughout the novel or poem, or over a series of poems by an author, building upon simple analogies to create in essence a new meaning for a word. For example, 'chat,' in Flaubert's *Madame Bovary* accrues meaning by virtue of the context in which it appears, eventually becoming a symbol.

Perhaps this transformation from syntactic to contextual to symbolic expression itself promises new applications for the software and hardware currently available. While a concordance can produce each appearance of a word and the other words around it, an image generating system will create with fluidity a more primal context for those occurrences, allowing access to the visual component of symbolic thought. Literature is, in certain respects, the rearrangement of reality in order to redefine reality; it often invests a simple object with relationships quite different from those the object traditionally represents. The invisible becomes visible. The computer could be an unrivalled tool for tracing this process.

4   Beowulf and Footprints on the Fen

So far a rather rough amalgam of linguistic theory, image recognition, and literary theory has been presented in support of a project that does not yet exist. To make this discussion more concrete, and to try to convey the rationale for a more overt relationship to the study of humanities, I would like to turn to *Beowulf* (Klaeber, 1950). This will provide an example of ideation and show, more precisely, what a computer might emulate.

The *Beowulf* manuscript is divided into two distinct hands, and much discussion over the last century has been focused on the integrity of the two parts: whether they are both by the same author, whether they are even meant to be read together. This in turn has generated papers on continuity of style, theme, and the purpose of each part. It was when I began to write a book on medieval and classical epic that a simple yet remarkable parallel between the two sections became apparent.

Relatively early in the epic the evil of Grendel is made manifest in a deadly raid on Hrothgar's great hall and the sleeping soldiers within. The sequence of events is as follows:

- Arrival of a fiend (*feond*) [Gendel]

- A theft occurs (the lives of 30 men are taken)

- The footprints of the fiend are discovered

- Deliberation of how to retaliate follows

- The arrival of Beowulf

Much later in the poem an identical sequence of events takes place:

- Arrival of a *feond* (lone exile)

- Theft occurs (a treasure object)

- The footprints of the fiend are discovered

- Retaliation for the crime

- The arrival of Beowulf

Given the importance of this parallel, it should be noted that it would be very difficult, perhaps impossible, to discover these sequences by using a concordance program or any current text analysis software. Some words are similar in each passage, such as *feond* and *las* (footprint), but the length of text is quite different in each case, most of the words are not cognate, and my distillation of the sequence is itself an outcome of an intuited correspondence imposed upon the text. To generate this parallel with existing software could be done, but only *after* some intimation of the correlation was already in mind. In arriving at the correlation, although some word to word connection was apparent, the insight into the passages was the product of an act of ideation subconsciously performed; the meaning was derived by visually reconstructing the scenes and placing one upon the other as images.

Equally as important were the thematic implications of this juxtaposition in the light of *Beowulf* scholarship and many received assumptions about the epic. In the first sequence, Grendel, a dire monster of the night, appears and slaughters a large contingent of Hrothgar's men. The king and his council recognize the demon from the fen by his footprints, and painfully deliberate how to seek retribution. To their succour comes Beowulf, and the slaughter is avenged.

In the second sequence much later in the poem, it is a man, a lone exile, who stumbles upon the hall of a sleeping dragon, steals a precious object and departs, leaving footprints. The dragon awakes, and retaliates viciously by burning the countryside and the small towns around, including Beowulf's, with his dreadful fire. As the frames of these powerful images unfold, equations can be drawn: Grendel with an exiled human being; Heorot, Hrothgar's hall, with the dragon's dwelling; the dragon with Hrothgar. The one constant is Beowulf, although those familiar with the poem know that in the second part the once great warrior is old and will soon die in performing the identical act that he attempted against Grendel: avenging a crime. The implied equivalence in these passages between precious treasure and the lives of Hrothgar's men is obviously reminiscent of *wergild*, the giving of treasure to compensate for the loss of life in battle in order (ironically here) to prevent future bloodshed between the warring parties.

What the poet has done, if this analogy is accurate, is to collect characters into a particular class of events, conceptualizing them by narrative structures which then determine our understanding of those characters and, by extension, the poem at large. Here there is no explicit correspondence between one sequence and the other by the poet, nor do any of the human folk announce that they feel strongly allied to the monsters of the night. Great poetry does not work that way, and *Beowulf* is a great poem. Rather, the characters, especially Beowulf, continually define themselves in opposition to Grendel and the dragon, even while the poet subtly pictures them as corresponding in nearly identical ways one to the other. Wiglaf's famous concluding speech concerning Beowulf's complicity in the great suffering of his people thus takes on more poignancy. The idea of the hero and the heroic code is also strongly questioned in this ideated scheme. These revelations significantly changed the way I read and taught *Beowulf*, though it is still interesting to watch students' reticence to accept—and most of them ultimately do not—the possibility of a main character, so apparently heroic in stature, shaded by and reflecting Grendel and the dragon.

5 Conclusions

It has become almost commonplace that the most important application of computers is their ability to enable us to understand better how we think. To apply computers to the ideational aspect of literature may enable axiomatic statements about intellection to be generated. From the perspective of the humanities, such explorations may have something to say about the condition of being human, allowing us to get closer to the literary work—not to the definitive meaning of a text (if there is such a thing), but to the fantastic interplay between text and reader that in part defines us, defines the text, and helps define the culture in which texts originate and are received.

Tacit in this paper is the recognition that the application of computers to the humanities is by choice, however fanciful. The applications we have chosen for study in the humanities are perforce mostly limited to hardware and software that, over successive generations, has been predominantly number-based and quantitative in its operation. At the same time we are also guided by decades of accepted scholarly approaches, whose norms play heavily in teaching appointments, the granting of tenure, and the exams we devise for our students. Exploring a literary work by word, sentence, verse, or phoneme facilitates the kind of intellectual processes that seem to stimulate the discovery of new meaning, but it does not mimic or capture those processes. The small white box through which this paper was composed is a neutral tool, but an amazingly powerful one. We have yet, as humanists, to put it through its paces.

In writing this paper I was continually reminded of Wordsworth's conclusion to the 1850 *Prelude*, lines I read avidly as a younger student taken up as much with the workings of the mind as with the words that so powerfully express it. Speaking to his closest friends, Wordsworth declares that they shall go forth as prophets of Nature to teach others about that which has most inspired and moved them in the world:

Instruct them how the mind of man becomes
A thousand times more beautiful than the earth
On which he dwells, above this frame of things
(Which, 'mid all revolution in the hopes
And fears of men, doth still remain unchanged)
In beauty exalted, as it is itself
Of quality and fabric more divine.

Listening now at the end of the twentieth century, the spirited optimism and utter faith in the divinity of the human mind is perhaps less ringing, less assured, less defensible. The most incongruous word might be 'beautiful,' that which the mind possesses a thousand-fold above the still, unchanging frame of the natural world. Yet perhaps it is only the frame that is tarnished. This new age will undoubtedly bring to bear further confirmation of the elegance, the imponderable complexity, the quality and fabric of the mind, for which the humanities exist—but only if we are determined enough to exploit it. The proposition is ultimately moot, but I have tried to suggest that it is our obligation to do so, and to teach those who follow how we did it.

10

Introducing Undergraduate Students to Automated Text Retrieval in Humanities Courses

Edward A. Friedman, James E. McClellan III and Arthur Shapiro

1 Introduction

Until recently large electronic databases and high-speed full-text search software have been the exclusive province of advanced scholars in the humanities. Now, however, exciting possibilities present themselves for integrating the power and flexibility of available full-text technologies into the undergraduate classroom and offering beginning undergraduate students in the humanities easy access to detailed and high-level scholarly work in their own studies and research.

In 1988, with support from the Humanities Grant Program of the New Jersey Department of Higher Education, we experimented with the use of full-text retrieval technology in a humanities course at Stevens Institute of Technology. A machine-readable database of eight books of about 2700 pages by or about Galileo Galilei was incorporated into an existing history of science course on Galileo and the Scientific Revolution. In this chapter we report on the details of our experiment, student responses to it, and implications for the future of computers and the 'electronic' library in undergraduate humanities education.[1]

The project was motivated by a concern for the role of electronic libraries in humanities education. Since the establishment of the great Library of Alexandria by Ptolemy II in the Third Century B.C., libraries have been focal points of intellectual activity. Students and scholars have become accustomed to pursue their studies in library environments. Since the Renaissance certainly, the norm for teaching and learning in the humanities has centred on acquiring information from bound texts found in libraries.

[1] We wish to thank Richard Widdicombe, Director of the Stevens Library and Therese Joy Johnsen, Information Services Librarian for their participation in this project. Frederic Woodbridge Wilson, Manager of Data Processing of The Pierpont Morgan Library in New York served as evaluation consultant for the project and provided us with many useful suggestions and constructive critiques. Michael Lesk, Division Manager of Computer Sciences Research, at Bell Communications Research provided us with important insights and strong encouragement in the pursuit of this effort.

In recent years, however, the computer, scholarship based on the computer, and new possibilities of computer-based pedagogy have altered the nature of study and instruction in the humanities. As electronic texts become increasingly available, new access to scholarship promises to restructure humanities education. What happens or what should happen when a computer workstation or an extended computer network makes instantaneously available large numbers of volumes that previously rested on library shelves? With this potential for redefinition of humanities education in mind, we have set out to examine several issues involving student use of electronic texts. These are as follows.

1. How can electronic texts be incorporated most efficiently into an undergraduate humanities course? Our concern here is with independent texts that one would expect to find in a library collection. Our concern is not with structured interrelated collections such as those which have been orchestrated in various hypertext projects. Under what circumstances are unstructured electronic texts more useful and under what circumstances are printed bound texts more useful?

2. What search tools are required to facilitate access to collections of electronic texts by novice students? We do not anticipate that the concordance software that has been used by scholars during the past decade will be suitable for undergraduate students who are studying introductory courses. We expect that software capabilities that help students prioritize information found in searches and that help identify new relevant materials suggested by their initial searches will be important.

3. What are the variations in individual student performance in using electronic text retrieval systems? Will students with different backgrounds, computer experience, and cognitive style, respond with significant differences in their use of these systems?

The three areas of concern noted above are interrelated. It is likely that optimal strategies for a given student will depend upon personal characteristics of the student, the software tools that are available, and the subject matter that is being studied.

These issues are new for most humanities educators. Those who have examined questions of full-text search in undergraduate education have done so using either the techniques of advanced scholars or a carefully designed hypertext environment. In contrast, we are examining far more general usage of electronic text resources as might be applicable in a broad array of undergraduate humanities courses.

Until recently, scholars in the humanities have pursued database and electronic 'full-text' study on mainframe computers utilizing expensive storage devices. Rapid changes in technology have made it possible to utilize desk-top computers with relatively low-cost mass storage devices. A 40 megabyte hard disk can store 8 to 10 thousand pages of text along with the necessary software and files for search activities. A 5.25 inch optical disk can handle at least five times that number of pages.

Not only is economical mass storage now available, but also software designed to access stored information in a rapid and convenient manner for the humanities student is becoming available for use on desk-top computers. These storage and search systems function with IBM PC/AT or compatible machines. We have used and we are continuing to experiment with these technologies to create an enhanced learning environment for undergraduates to study texts in the humanities.

We did not substitute a full-text electronic capability for traditional textbooks and printed materials. Rather, we added this capability to an existing course and are studying its effects and impact on student learning. Thus, hard copy volumes of reference material are also available on the reserve shelves of the library. In addition, students purchase course texts as is generally done.

2 Educational Context for Galileo Project at Stevens

Stevens students have a background and orientation that are particularly appropriate for this innovative project in humanities education. We believe that this project entails one of the most comprehensive uses of full text computer-based methods in undergraduate education anywhere. Stevens students are able to engage in this activity as sophisticated computer users for whom the technology presents less of a barrier in implementing electronic search and research activities than it might to other students in other settings.

At Stevens Institute of Technology every student owns a powerful computer. All entering students in 1988 acquired an AT&T 6312 WGS with at least 20 megabytes of hard disk storage. Stevens has also implemented a high speed, state-of-the-art network which accommodates all academic facilities as well as dormitory rooms. Computing has become as much a part of the academic and living environment at Stevens as telephones.

Many Stevens students with superior academic ability are highly motivated in their humanities courses. The Stevens humanities program has received national recognition and support in past years by the National Endowment for the Humanities and the Andrew W. Mellon Foundation.

At its most general, the Stevens approach to this project is to experiment with an electronic library, and to create a setting with generic tools that are capable of assisting students in any independent study situation. Increasingly, students, professionals and scholars will be confronted by massive electronic library databases. All will be challenged to extract meaning and relationships in subject areas which are of specific interest to them. This project yielded some insights into the process.

3 Summary of Experience in the Spring 1988 Semester

During the Spring 1988 semester, 34 students were enrolled in the course Hu 361: Galileo and the Scientific Revolution. Almost all of the students were in their junior year. Students were required to purchase the following texts:

- Galileo, *Dialogue on the Two Chief World Systems*

- S. Drake, *Discoveries and Opinions of Galileo*

- G. De Santillana, *The Crime of Galileo*

In addition the following books were placed on reserve in the Williams Library:

- Galileo, *Discourses on the Two New Sciences*

- S. Drake, *Galileo at Work: A Scientific Biography*

- S. Drake, *Galileo Studies*

- S. Drake & C. O'Malley, *The Controversy on the Comets of 1618*

- W. Wallace, *Prelude to Galileo*

All eight of the above volumes (approximately 2700 pages of text) were entered into an electronic database by a service bureau in a format that created screen displays that closely duplicated the printed pages. Graphics could not be accommodated in this first phase due to cost and technical problems in integrating image and text files. The database consisted of about 6.8 megabytes of storage. 'Personal Librarian' search software was utilized to organize this information and to perform search activities. The expanded database including ancillary files was about 13 megabytes.

Students had access to two AT&T 6310 computers located in a public area of the Stevens library. A printer was available for their use. The computers have 20 megabyte hard disks and are IBM PC/AT compatible.

We experimented with the Galileo database and workstations to discover the pedagogical possibilities and limits of the system. Students were asked to utilize the electronic system in several ways. They had to respond to two homework assignments which asked detailed questions about the readings. They had to prepare term papers. And, they were encouraged to browse through electronic and hard-copy versions of the material.

The focused homework assignments were structured so that half the class was asked to utilize the electronic database while the other half of the class used printed texts. (A typical focused question asked, 'In Galileo's *Dialogue on the Two Chief World Systems* what does Salviati mean when he suggests 'a superior and better sense must take precedence over common sense and ordinary sensible experience'?') In the second assignment the groups were interchanged.

In neither homework assignment did the instructor know which group was which when the grading was performed. An examination of the grades received for these assignments showed that those who did well using the electronic database did not do as well using the hard copy texts and vice versa. It seemed to indicate that students were displaying two distinct cognitive styles—one that favoured electronic search and one that favoured hard copy. We consider this a major finding of our study and project to date.

Separate student essays were approximately 7 to 10 double spaced pages in length plus footnotes and references. Students selected topics and pursued their research in consultation with the instructor. In addition to the written report, students were required to make an oral presentation to the class. Not every student used the Galileo database in preparing their papers, but at least three-quarters did so, at least in part. Examples of some of the varied topics include: Galileo on Magnetism; Galileo's Concept of Fire; The Inquisition; Galileo and the Scientific Revolution; and, Another View of the Galilean Trial: A Review of *Galileo: Heretic*.

We were impressed and surprised at the high level of detail and the sensitivity to a range of issues with which many students pursued their topics. In addition to reducing the superficiality that is often the case in student reports, the use of the database carried over into class reports. Not only did each student become an 'expert' in his or her area of particular inquiry, but students also brought their expertise into the classroom both as rapporteurs and as an informed audience. That is, students were able to comment more critically and help guide their classmates more than is usually the case.

. Prior to initiating this project, concern was expressed by a number of scholars and teachers that students might be drawn into a preoccupation with minutiae or technical exercises such as word counting. We are pleased to report that such technical preoccupation did not emerge, but we are disappointed that no student took the opportunity for some kind of word frequency study of the Galileo material. ('Personal Librarian' software indexes and counts the number of times each word appears in the database, thus allowing for such a study. See Figure 10.1.)

Extended interviews were conducted with seven students. The student who studied Galileo's concept of fire did all of his research for his essay via the electronic database. He found 155 instances of the word fire in the database as well as up to 60 examples of fire within 20 words of light or heat or flame. He also found 22 'hits' for 'Aristotle' within 20 words of fire. He read through all of the examples at the computer terminal. (While not all of these 'hits' proved productive, they nonetheless quickly put the student in touch with the essentials of the question.) Other students doing similar types of searches preferred to obtain a listing of references and then sit with the hard copy versions of the books.

We were intrigued by a special, 'expand' feature of the software. Using this feature, one enters a key word, and, after a separate search of the database, the software returns other words that may be relevant to the initial query and which might merit further searching. Unfortunately, students did not make full use of the vocabulary expansion capability of the software. One example of its productive utilization occurred when a student asked for words associated with the word 'moon' and obtained the word 'crown,' an association which refers to the fringes of light that make the moon appear larger than it is.

Each student received a questionnaire at the end of the term regarding their perceptions of the Galileo database. Twenty-eight of thirty-four students (82%) replied to the survey, and their responses were overwhelmingly positive. Three-quarters of those replying said that the electronic search system provided more material more quickly than the ordinary use of books. Nearly 90% said that the system was very easy or moderately easy to use. 82% percent of the students said that the system simplified search for specific information, while 61% said that the system simplified their research on general themes. 39% percent felt that the electronic system provided them with more complete information in their research; 43% felt that printed texts and the electronic database provided about the same information; only 18% of the students felt that working with hard-copy texts provided more information than using the electronic database. Asked whether, distinct from searching for particular information, they found that the electronic system and its software encouraged browsing through the Galileo Library, a surprising 68% responded affirmatively.

There was an overwhelming response that the system was easy to use, fast, and effective. In one case a student volunteered the observation that he accomplished in two hours with the electronic database what would have take at least eight to twelve hours of analysis and review of the hard copy books. The student who stated this was one of the most conscientious in the course and was not simply trying to find short cuts to facile answers. His class report and his essay were judged to be of high quality.

Other information gathered from students in interviews and through question-naires reveals that enhancements to the software, expansion of the database and modifications in the way in which the system is introduced to the students promise to significantly enhance the effectiveness of this approach. Given the positive results of the initial implementation and the potential benefit to a wide community of humanities students and educators, we are seeking to enhance the system during subsequent academic years.

4 Example of Database Use: Galileo on Fire

Galileo's telescopic discoveries are well known. So is his work regarding falling bodies. And the world knows, too, about Galileo and the Inquisition. What if, perchance, one were interested in a less well-known aspect of this scientist's work, say his views on fire, how would one proceed?

Figure 10.1 shows a portion of the index file created by the Personal Librarian software. Here the word fire has been identified by the software, in pre-indexing the text, a total of 323 times.

```
FINITY          2
FINTE           1
FINY            2
FIORE           1
FIORENTINO      2
FIROENZA        1
FIORY           2
FIR             1
FIRCE           1
FIRE          323
FIREBRAND       6
FIREND          3
FIRENZE         2
FIRENZOULA      1
FIRENZUOLA     22
FIREPLACE       2
FIREWORK        2
FIRM           39
FIRMA           4
```

Enter command>

Fig. 10.1: Personal Librarian: Alpha word list

In Figure 10.2 a screen display indicates that a search for the word fire results in identification of 155 pages containing the word fire. The first nine 'hits' in order of frequency of occurrences of the sought after word are identified. The other 146 pages may be displayed as needed.

Figure 10.3 presents a screen display having 48 words that the software has identified as being related to fire by using the 'expand' function embedded in the software. These words suggest new search avenues for novices seeking to learn about Galileo's concept of fire.

Figure 10.4 lists the three 'hits' that occur when the words 'fire' and 'corpuscle' are searched for co-occurrence on the same page. Figure 10.5 then brings to the screen the page from 'hit' #1 for co-occurrence of 'fire' and 'corpuscle.' We see that using this search strategy students are led directly to Galileo's concept of fire and his remarkable theory of heat!

5 Conclusion

We believe that this project has demonstrated that full-text electronic search can provide undergraduate students who are novices in a particular area of scholarship with opportunities to easily access important information and to explore for themselves relationships involving multiple categories or concepts more effectively than with the printed texts. We feel that the open-ended and unstructured nature of full-text databases and related search software offer students greater independence in exploring new material than comparable hypertext systems.

Many questions remain, however. We need to know more about how exactly different students approach and utilize electronic databases such as the one created for this study. How do they conceive of the learning environment provided for

```
get Display Jump > < Quit Help Set List Bar Alpha Expand Past SOrt EDit Write
 Rank
 1)  page:  CONTROVERSY ON THE COMETS
            120                                               CONTROVERSY ON COMETS

 2)  page:  TWO WORLD SYSTEMS
                                      The Second Day

 3)  page:  CONTROVERSY ON THE COMETS
                                                                THE ASSAYER

 4)  page:  CONTROVERSY ON THE COMETS
                              DISCOURSE ON THE COMETS

 5)  page:  CRIME OF GALILEO
                                [93]

 6)  page:  CONTROVERSY ON THE COMETS
                                       THE ASSAYER

 7)  page:  CONTROVERSY ON THE COMETS
                              THE ASTRONOMICAL BALANCE

 8)  page:  CONTROVERSY ON THE COMETS
            296                               CONTROVERSY ON COMETS

 9)  page:  CONTROVERSY ON THE COMETS
            290                               CONTROVERSY ON COMETS

Query 1       Retrieved 155
Enter command>                         DB: galileo
FIRE
```

Fig. 10.2: Personal Librarian: list of documents retrieved

```
get Display Jump > < Quit Help Set List Bar Alpha Expand Past SOrt EDit Write


FRICTION                  RUN                     BURN
EXHAL                     HEAT                    KINDLE
MELT                      LEADEN                  IMPOSS
HARD                      CEMETERY                FLAME
CORPUSCLE                 PORE                    COMBUST
GRAZE                     LIGHTE                  EXCITE
IGNIT                     BREEZE                  MARIO
LIGHTNE                   ADHERE                  EXCIT
TOUCHE                    QUANTITY                HEATE
DRY                       CHANCE                  REPEAT
DENSE                     CANDLE                  READILY
STICK                     ARROW                   POET
SUMMER                    LIE                     NON
STATEM                    BLOW                    KNEW
ROCK                      PENETR                  COMMENT
LEAD                      CONDIT                  PIECE


Enter command>                         DB: galileo
```

Fig. 10.3: Personal Librarian: Expand list

```
get Display Jump > < Quit Help Set List Bar Alpha Expand Past SOrt EDit Write
    Rank
        1)   page:  CONTROVERSY ON THE COMETS
                                                            THE ASSAYER

        2)   page:  CONTROVERSY ON THE COMETS
             312                              CONTROVERSY ON COMETS

        3)   page:  TWO NEW SCIENCES
             48               Galileo, Opere, VIII (85-86)




    Query 2        Retrieved 3
    Enter command>
    FIRE AND CORPUSCLE                              DB:  galileo
```

Fig. 10.4: Personal Librarian: co-occurence document list

```
get Display Jump > < Quit Help Set List Bar Alpha Expand Past SOrt EDit Write
-page-
CONTROVERSY ON THE COMETS
                                THE ASSAYER
                                                            313
rest their operation would remain null.  Thus we see that a quantity of fire retained in the pores and
narrow channels of a piece of quicklime does not warm us even when we hold it in our hands, because it rests
motionless.  But place the quicklime in water, where the fire has a greater propensity to motion than it has
in air--because of the greater gravity of this medium, and because the fire opens the pores of water as it
does not those of air--and the little corpuscles will escape; and, touching our hand, they will penetrate it
and we shall feel heat.
        Since, then, the presence of the fire-corpuscles does not suffice to excite heat, but we need also
their movement, it seems to me that one may very reasonably say that motion is the cause of heat.  This is
that motion by which arrows and other sticks are burned and by which lead and other metals are liquefied
when the little particles of fire penetrate the bodies, being either moved by themselves or, their

Hit Enter for more

Query 2        Retrieved 3        Doc. #2466        Rank 1

Enter command>

FIRE AND CORPUSCLE                              DB:  galileo
```

Fig. 10.5: Personal Librarian: document display list

them? How do differences in cognitive style, tentatively identified in this study, make themselves manifest in using electronic databases compared to traditional research methods using standard bibliographic tools and techniques? Is the search software used by advanced scholars appropriate for beginning undergraduates, or are special modifications required? These questions will become only more pointed, as we move from separate computer workstations, described here, to on-line network access of databases in the future.

Our feeling is that the electronic learning environment is genuinely different from the one we have inherited since the Library at Alexandria and since Gutenberg. Doubtless as further work in this area proceeds, undergraduate instruction in the humanities will require significant restructuring in order to integrate optimal use of electronic texts along with optimal use of bound texts.

11

Computers in the Study of Set Texts

Susan Hockey, Jo Freedman and John Cooper

1 Introduction

The Oxford Text Searching System (OTSS) was developed under a grant from the UK government Computers in Teaching Initiative (CTI) scheme, which is intended to introduce computers into the teaching of undergraduate disciplines rather than to be part of a general computer literacy initiative. The grant for the Oxford project[1] was awarded in the final round of funding in December 1986. This two-year project began in September 1987, and was thus one of the last to start. The primary aim of the project was to provide a simple interface through which users could gain access to already existing mainframe text analysis tools, without the need for training in the use of these tools or in the preparation of texts. This has been achieved through step-by-step screen menus and a simple text encoding scheme, both of which have been designed to apply to as wide a range of languages and texts as possible.

The kinds of analysis made possible by OTSS are already familiar to researchers in language and literature who have used computers. The main issue presented by the project has been to determine which tools are likely to be of most use to undergraduates, to develop software to meet their needs, and provide documentation which will help them to obtain interesting results with the minimum of frustration.

OTSS was designed in the first instance for the use of undergraduates studying at Oxford University. Thus a brief outline of the way in which undergraduate teaching is organized at Oxford may be useful as a guide to understanding some OTSS features.

2 Teaching at Oxford University

Oxford University has a teaching system whose roots go back many centuries and which is unusual by modern standards. Apart from Cambridge University, where more or less the same college system operates, no other university in

[1] The project wishes to thank various people who have given their time to developing the software and experimenting with OTSS in the classroom. Mr Lou Burnard's assistance has been valuable particularly in connection with BASIS and the Oxford Text Archive, and Dr Don Fowler and Mr David Robey have shown remarkable patience in the teething phases and have given stimulating advice on the academic aspects.

Britain or North America organizes itself in quite the same way. In the first place, although there are Faculties and departments as in any other university, there are also colleges, which are the original institutions out of which the University grew in the late Middle Ages. Not all the colleges date back that far, of course, as their number has been added to through the centuries. Each undergraduate (or graduate, for that matter) must be a member of both a college and the University. Undergraduates reside in their college for most if not all of the time they spend in Oxford. But unlike a hall of residence, the senior members of the University (the professors, lecturers, readers, etc.) also belong to the college, where most undergraduate teaching for arts subjects takes place.

Teaching is based on the tutorial, which is virtually a one-to-one teaching session, although lectures and seminars also form a part of the teaching programme. However, it is the tutorial which is the compulsory element and which is therefore at the centre of the undergraduate's education. Attendance at lectures and seminars is very rarely compulsory.

Every student has a tutor, who is usually from the college to which he or she belongs, and although it may be necessary to be taught by different tutors for different parts of the syllabus, the college tutor will be in overall charge of the student's progress. It is on the basis of the tutorials that a student's termly work is assessed, but such assessment is used only to steer the student through his or her studies; it does not contribute to the grading of the final degree. This is awarded entirely on the basis of the results of the final examinations, in which papers, usually consisting almost entirely of essay questions, are sat for over a two, or sometimes three, week period.

The major part of undergraduate work in language and literature subjects (English, Modern Languages, Classics, Oriental Languages) at Oxford is based on the close study of texts. Such study may also enter into other undergraduate humanities courses, such as philosophy. The lectures, which are generally optional, as mentioned above, are intended to cover both the compulsory sections of the syllabuses and those subjects which may be given as special, or optional, papers in the final examinations. The tutorials may number one or two per week, and can be taken alone or with another student (although the number is rarely more than two). For these the undergraduate is required to write essays on subjects set by the tutor, on the basis of reading lists consisting of books and articles that can be consulted in the college or university libraries.

The aim of the Oxford Text Searching System (OTSS), was, in the first place, to make important texts readily available in machine readable form to undergraduates, and then to consider how these texts might be used in an undergraduate's studies. The undergraduate may wish to access them in the same way as he or she has access to library volumes; the lecturer may wish to have a searching program and texts available for demonstration purposes during lectures or a tutorial; or the lecturer may wish to incorporate the computer more directly into a course, with the aim of acquainting the undergraduate with the use of computers in specific areas of research. For all these purposes, the OTSS software had to be able to provide access to the texts with a minimum of computer expertise being required from the user.

Undergraduates at Oxford can work in a number of different places: in their colleges, in their faculties, and in one or more of the various departmental and central libraries. The OTSS software has been designed to run on IBM-PC and compatible workstations. These communicate with the University Computing Service's mainframe VAX computer through a network which runs parallel to the University telephone system, so that the facilities of the project are available from almost anywhere in the university. The only requirement for the PCs is that an EGA card should be installed if any characters other than the standard IBM keyboard characters are required. The software will run without an EGA card, but texts with non-standard characters appear in transliteration. The texts are held, and the searches run, on the mainframe computer.

Computer searches of texts are intended to be used as supplementary aids to existing teaching methods, not to replace them. The ways in which they have been integrated into undergraduate teaching during the pilot courses given as part of the project can be summarised under three broad headings:

1. The undergraduate can use the searching facilities, etc., on his or her own initiative, having received basic instruction in the use of the software during a teaching session;

2. Computer work can be incorporated by tutors into tutorial assignments, so that the undergraduate is encouraged to use the computer as part of the preparation for the tutorial essay;

3. The computer can be used as an adjunct to classes and lectures, so that those who attend can be given the option of examining the texts under discussion in more detail and corroborating the lecturer's claims.

Work on OTSS has proceeded on two fronts: the creation and refinement of the necessary software, and the preparation of texts. The OTSS team consists of a full-time programmer and a part-time text handler. The project is a collaborative one between the Computing Service and the Faculties of English Language and Literature, Literae Humaniores (Classics), Medieval and Modern Languages, and Oriental Studies, and it began in one area of study in each of these Faculties. The University's Computing Teaching Centre is involved in the project, and several members of the Oxford University Computing Service, where the project is housed, have contributed to its development. The Theology Faculty is also now joining the project.

3 Software

The system which has been implemented in Oxford is simple in that it uses existing software as much as possible, while the OTSS software provides an easy interface for the undergraduate environment. It is intended that the OTSS user should be completely unaware of the workings of the mainframe computer to which OTSS gives access. The usernames on which the searches are run are unknown to the user, as are the ways in which the texts are stored. This means that the texts cannot be altered by anyone except the project staff, and that they cannot be accessed outside OTSS. Although it would be possible to mark up the texts so that morphological analysis and lemmatization could be incorporated into OTSS, it was decided that this would involve a great deal more time than was available to the project. The main part of the interface has been written in Turbo Pascal, while the browsing facility to view the results uses the Turbo Editor Toolkit.

The two mainframe packages which OTSS gives access to are OCP and BASIS. The Oxford Concordance Program (OCP) makes word counts, concordances, and word indexes. Normally a user would be required to write a command file in order to execute one of these procedures, but the OTSS software will compose its own command file from the answers given by the user to menu options. BASIS is a data management system with extensive options for storing, retrieving, and manipulating textual data. It is extremely useful for the type of work done using the OTSS system because it is able to access long texts rapidly via indexes. In a full BASIS session on the mainframe computer the user must type in the BASIS commands, but it is also possible for screen menus to be composed using the BASIS command language, and this was done for the OTSS project by the Computing Service's BASIS expert.

The user enters OTSS on the PC, and is then logged on to the central University VAX cluster, the login procedure being hidden from the user. The screen asks which language is required (at the moment Middle and Old English, modern English, Greek, Italian, German and Latin are offered; Arabic, Hebrew, and Russian (Cyrillic and Old Church Slavonic) will soon be available). Then the user is asked whether OCP or BASIS is wanted. If BASIS is selected, the screen then displays a series of menus which offer a limited selection of BASIS search options. An option also exists at the moment for the user to enter a full BASIS session directly from OTSS.

If OCP is chosen, the user selects one or more texts, and can request bibliographical details on the screen. Then, if the user has asked to make a word list, an index, or a concordance, the OTSS software displays menus and composes an OCP command file from the answers given. The menus are subdivided logically into choosing which portions of a text are to be examined, which words are to be studied, and how the analysis is to be performed. A subset of OCP options is offered including: words ordered by their endings or frequency, subset of words to be included or excluded, frequency range, phrases, collocations, and subsets of texts for analysis. The command file is then sent to the VAX and the job is run. The results file is sent back to the PC and this is manipulated by the software, depending on whether the display is required for screen or printer. At the moment the software provides output for dot-matrix printers, but it is hoped to be able eventually to provide for output to a laser printer. OTSS also has a basic screen editor allowing modification of the output file.

The Duke University Toolkit is being used to generate non-standard characters for the PC screen. A full Greek font is available with all accents, and Russian and Hebrew fonts have also been obtained and modified; an Old Church Slavonic font has been created. OTSS can also display most languages which use a form of the Roman script, since many of the extra accented and otherwise modified characters have been designed (several are of course available through the extended IBM character set). Languages which have so far been made available in this way include Old and Middle English, Turkish, and Italian. An Arabic screen font has also been developed by the project, but its implementation has been delayed while a printer font is being sought. For exotic scripts a keyboard mapping diagram is displayed when the user replies to a menu option requiring a word or words to be typed in those scripts.

Various printer fonts have been created using the Fontgen program, which is part of Vuwriter. The project chose to use the NEC P-6 as the standard printer; other printers can be used but they will only print using their own latin character sets. Old and Middle English, Greek, Hebrew, and Russian were adapted for the project from fonts already in use.

4 Texts

Oxford seemed ideally situated for this project because of the presence of the Oxford Text Archive, and many of the texts used have come from this source. Of course, one of the problems was that a uniform encoding system had to be used and the texts in the Archive use a wide variety of formats. The project started with Greek and Latin texts for a Classics pilot course and renaissance Italian texts for an Italian pilot course.

The advantage with the Greek texts is that the Archive holdings come from the Thesaurus Linguae Graecae (TLG) corpus tapes, and are thus uniformly encoded, although largely with orthographical rather than syntactical or semantic markers—the latter might have been more useful for the project. The Latin texts in the Archive were not so uniformly encoded, some being so old that they had practically no encoding and were entirely in capitals. Fortunately more up-to-date versions could be read from the CD-ROM prepared by the Packard Institute and Robert Kraft (PHI-CCAT disk), in which we were assisted by both Professor Kraft and the members of the Construe project at Manchester University.

Most of the Italian texts had already been obtained from the Italian language collection of electronic texts at Pisa by David Robey of the Medieval and Modern Languages Faculty, or had been prepared by him for his own research. The texts in the Old English Corpus are also being made available for the project. Several other teaching members of the University who are interested in the OTSS project have machine-readable texts on which they have been working, and these can be called upon when the project moves on to other languages.

One large and one fairly short Italian text were input on the Computing Service's optical scanner, the KDEM, by the project team, as were a couple of Middle English texts, but Faculties are now being encouraged to provide their own funds for inputting from printed texts in this way.

The basic encoding system is a fairly simple set of COCOA references, which divides up the texts into major sections and discriminates between speakers in dialogue and drama. Where the texts are prepared from already existing machine-readable forms which contain a more complex encoding system, the extra features are retained, but in a form which is transparent to the OTSS system, thus leaving room for the addition of any of these extra features should they be required.

The COCOA references can be easily converted into a form suitable for BASIS. There are certain limitations on the subdivisions of a text in BASIS, which means that when converting from COCOA format the overall structure of the text must be taken into account and modified where necessary. A BASIS database consists of a large number of documents, each of which corresponds to a natural division in the original, large enough to be free-standing, small enough to be focused. In the Italian poetry texts, for example, each canto is a document; in the Latin texts, each poem or oration, or each book of a long work is a document. For the purposes of search-evaluation, each document is further subdivided into context units. In verse texts, these correspond with the verse lines; in prose texts, with a sentence or other division in the text. Searches involving more than one term can be carried out such that the two terms are found (a) anywhere within the same document, (b) anywhere within the same context unit, (c) anywhere within a specified number of context units, as well as (d) adjacent to each other. Searches however, cannot be carried out across document boundaries. BASIS uses its own index to locate documents containing a given term. The 'number of hits' taken from this index refers to the number of documents containing at least one occurrence of the term concerned. The current version of BASIS is not able to give the total number of occurrences of the term.

It will be observed that texts must be stored twice, the first for use with OCP, and the second in a BASIS database.

In the case of the TLG texts and the PHI-CCAT Latin texts, it was felt that proof-reading was unnecessary, and similarly in the case of texts which had previously been used for analyses. Other Archive texts and those input via the KDEM have been proof-read against the relevant printed edition. The award of a Larger Personal Research Grant by the British Academy to David Robey has enabled him to engage a graduate student to proof-read the Italian texts thoroughly with the aim of using them to produce micro-fiche concordances.

Another point about the text preparation, especially in relation to the distribution of OTSS throughout the University, concerns copyright. Users of OTSS are not able to download complete copies of texts to the PC. Several of the texts already in use have been licensed only for use at Oxford University. Others have been obtained from different sources and the position of the project with regard to the copyright of these texts is still under review. Some investigations on copyright have recently been carried out by the Oxford Text Archive team, who were naturally even more concerned by this issue. We have recently been informed by the University solicitor that the 'Copyright, Designs and Patents Act' of 15 November 1988 places new restrictions on the copying of texts, which includes storage 'in any medium by electronic means,' and this new legislation is being studied.

5 Pilot Courses

After preliminary work on the software and the texts, two pilot courses were run in the Trinity term of 1988, one using renaissance Italian texts and the other a number of classical authors. Both were run in a computing room specially set aside by the Literae Humaniores and Modern Language faculties for the project and equipped with seven PCs and two dot-matrix printers. Only OCP was available within OTSS in Trinity Term at this time.

The first pilot course, which was given by David Robey of the Modern Languages Faculty, took as its subject a compact corpus of four major Italian Renaissance narrative poems, all written within a single century, all in the same metrical form, and all drawing in varying degrees on a common set of literary traditions and conventions: Ariosto's *Orlando furioso*, Boiardo's *Orlando amoroso*, Tasso's *Gerusaleme liberata*, and Poliziano's *Stanze*. The students first used the software in relation to questions of thematic interest, for example searching for key terms such as 'fortuna' in the *Furioso*. They then moved on to compare type/token ratios as indices of lexical range of richness, to compare counts of certain conjunctions as indices of syntactic complexity or the use of simile, to make counts of certain kinds of sound repetition with a view to investigating alliteration, and to produce rhyming dictionaries with a view to identifying borrowings by one poet from another.

The results of this pilot project largely confirmed the accepted views of the relationships between the texts. As noted above, there are good historical and prosodic reasons for considering these texts as a single corpus. The computer analyses provided confirmatory evidence from a stylistic approach, but also drew attention to the individual differences between the poems. The course consisted almost entirely of hands-on work by those attending, and it was felt that such a method was best suited to initial introductions to the facilities at a level which is immediately relevant to undergraduate essay topics.

In Michaelmas term 1988, David Robey also gave four lectures on the language and style of Dante's *Divine Comedy*, followed by an introduction to the use of OTSS facilities in relation to this topic. The computer sessions examined aspects of vocabulary, prosody, key terms, and themes in the *Divine Comedy* using both OCP and BASIS. Emphasis was laid on encouraging undergraduates to use OTSS as a resource for essay writing, with the treatment of actual essay topics being given considerable attention. The more successful topics were those such as

'Discuss the importance of Dante's address to the reader' which can be identified by specific terms such as 'lettor,' 'pensa,' etc.

The other pilot project was run by Dr Fowler of the Literae Humaniores faculty using Latin and Greek texts. This was run as a general introduction to the different possibilities which the use of the system offered: the students were shown how to search for words and phrases, how to use wild-card options in such cases as searches for phonetic features, and how to search for collocates. These techniques were then used to solve two kinds of problem. Alongside exercises such as 'Examine the occasions in Catullus where one word ends and the following begins with the same consonant,' there were other questions such as: 'Examine the explicit references to "anger" in the *Iliad*', or 'Examine "love and death" as a motive in Catullus.' These latter questions were designed to help students to understand that to move from a desire to investigate a question to a formulation precise enough to put to the computer involves a large element of analysis and choice. The results of this course showed that, if the software is going to be used to give students a broad based and comprehensive practical introduction to the use of the computer in literary analysis, a large number of texts needs to be made available.

6 Preliminary Findings

The two pilot projects demonstrated the effectiveness of the menus, and the ease and speed with which students can familiarize themselves with the basic practicalities involved. When it comes to considering how computer text searching can be best integrated into the undergraduates' courses, however, each shed light on a different aspect.

If the emphasis is on the students' learning a basic set of text-searching skills, then applying these as they see fit to the texts their curriculum requires them to study, increasing these skills as they progress, we have seen that an extensive library of texts must be made available. To support the OTSS on this scale would require considerable resources for text preparation and probably a full-time text preparer.

The machine-readable texts that the project has used employ a wide variety of encoding principles. This means that there is no one way that these texts can be converted automatically, or semi-automatically, to a single format suitable for the project by writing, for example, a SNOBOL program. Each text has to be considered separately, and examined in detail for its quirks and inconsistencies. Very few of the texts taken from the Archive have accompanying documentation on editions, mark-up conventions, special character coding, etc. This is largely a question of the constraints under which the Archive was put together, and much work is now being done under a British Library grant to improve this situation. In most cases it is necessary to go back to the printed texts to establish both the conventions used in a machine readable text, and to determine which edition was its source.

Even when many texts come from a single source with a consistently applied encoding scheme, as is the case with the TLG material, the mark-up reflects the characteristics of the printed text from which the electronic text has been prepared, thus concentrating on features which are not immediately relevant to the kind of work which undergraduates would want to do. For example, one of the first experiments was to mark up the *Iliad* for occurrences of proper names and speakers. No information for this could be gathered from the TLG text beyond a list of all the words beginning with an upper case character. It took several days to accomplish this mark-up for just the first book of the *Iliad*, and the experiment was accordingly abandoned.

When, however, the text-searching facilities were directed towards solving specific problems within a supervised course, there was not such a need for large quantities of texts, and the students could start to obtain interesting results fairly early on. Whether this kind of motivation induces students to continue using the facilities for their own work is something which it is as yet too early to say, but it will be interesting to note if OTSS continues to be used after David Robey's integrated course on Dante's *Divine Comedy*.

The software has now been sufficiently tested so that it can be distributed to anyone within the University who has the necessary hardware. The rapidity with which undergraduates were able to master the menus indicates that only a very minimum amount is needed in the way of written documentation on the actual operation of OTSS. A small HELP facility is available.

The project is considering providing some basic documentation which would introduce undergraduates to the kind of analysis in which the computer can play a useful role, since it seems that this initial phase is the one in which they need the most help. This does not appear to be the case for graduates and researchers, however, who already come to the computer with ideas, practical or not (but that is another question), of what they want to do.

The pilot courses have suggested that matters of lexis, syntax, and phonology are those most likely to profit from computer-assisted study. The heading of lexis comprises such topics as: the examination of type/token ratios in a text, which can suggest conclusions about the richness or originality of a writer's vocabulary; and the closer investigation of an author's vocabulary, both key terms and common terms, which can illuminate the author's use of topoi and themes. Word counts and concordances can also help in the study of sentence structure or of, say, an author's use of simile; searches with wild card options can pick out alliteration and rhyming patterns. Some of these analyses obviously need an OCP approach, but others, especially where specific terms have to be examined in context, can be more usefully done by browsing through the text on screen using BASIS.

One of the basic problems in all of these operations is how to eliminate useless material, and, although this can be learnt by experience, it would seem necessary to give the beginner some examples, suggestions, and hints to illustrate how time spent initially thinking carefully about the details of the search, etc., can save a great deal of time when it comes to analysing the results. Areas in which computers are not likely to provide any interesting results should also be pointed out. This again comes back to the point about stimulating the undergraduate's motivation at the very beginning to try to ensure that disappointing initial results do not discourage him or her from continuing beyond the initial stages—an important point when teaching a new technique.

So far, OTSS is not able to make use of more sophisticated software, such as lemmatization programs, or retrieval aided by a lexical database, to refine or expand search requests. Thus it was not possible to study vocabulary at the level of the lemma, or syntax through parsed text, although the use of wild-cards in searching through BASIS word lists and examining patterns with OCP ensure that these topics can be tackled at a simple level.

It is hoped that by demonstrating OTSS to the members of the various Faculties concerned, they will be stimulated to use it themselves and then to encourage its use by undergraduates. At the moment it still seems that those who have already used the computer for research, through the OCP for example, are those who are keen to use OTSS in undergraduate teaching. Others are more reluctant to embark on the electronic path. The simplicity of the OTSS software should encourage teachers to experiment with the computer as a general tool, one which can stimulate the interest of their students. Only when the results of these experiments are analysed (as we are doing in this project) can such tools can be refined, and more definite suggestions made concerning the use of computers in the teaching of literature.

More recently methods of studying text such as hypertext, the advanced scholar's workstation, the literary database, etc., have been proposed. While these hold great promise, they are still at an experimental research stage, and until we know exactly how a scholar studies a text we cannot model it very effectively on a computer. For a project involving undergraduates it is perhaps better to concentrate on those aspects which are more readily understood and whose limitations are known. Thus we can avoid the dangers of either simplifying the problem to suit what the computer can do easily, or attempting to use the computer for things which are perhaps better done without it.

12

Text and Hypertext: Reflections on the Role of the Computer in Teaching Modern American Poetry

John M. Slatin

1 Introduction

In this paper, I will discuss the principles underlying the creation of hypertext-based materials for a course in modern American poetry, and the design decisions implementing those principles. I will then go on to discuss the role of the computer in the transmission and transformation of cultural values.

What is Hypertext?

Ted Nelson introduced the term *hypertext* into the discourse of computing in the mid-1960s, a few years before Julia Kristeva (1969) introduced the term *intertextuality* into the discourse of literary criticism. *Hypertext* then entered critical parlance through Gerard Genette's attempt (1982) to extend and refine Kristeva's notion of intertextuality. Genette uses *hypertext* as the name for a particular type of intertextual relationship. Nelson (1987), however, defines hypertext as *non-sequential writing*. That is, the hypertext (or hyperdocument) is one whose component parts are not meant to be read in a particular sequence. Nelson's definition incorporates many familiar things—encyclopedias, for instance, or the Talmud, or seventeenth-century emblem books, or texts with footnotes. Disrupting the flow of the text, these are all instances of what Nelson means by non-sequential writing. But Nelson was not thinking only of printed matter: he specifically had in mind material that would be both composed and published electronically, by means of a computer.

Nelson is quite right in pointing out that a great deal of printed matter forces the reader to depart from strict linear sequence. But he underestimated the consequences of introducing the computer as a tool for composing and disseminating hypertext. As I have argued elsewhere (Slatin, in press), hypertext is vastly different from traditional text, and it is the computer that makes the difference. *True hypertext exists and can exist only on-line, only in the computer.* This difference is crucial, and not just because it substitutes monitors, keyboards, and mice for the customary physical apparatus associated with the book. The difference is crucial because, as Douglas Hofstadter (1985) has said, 'It is the organization of memory which defines what concepts are'—and hypertext uses *machine memory* in a way that has no precise analogue in the traditional text environment. The shift to machine memory may be as significant as the shift from orality to literacy, whose implications are so brilliantly probed in Eric Havelock's account (1962) of Plato: Plato's attack on the poets, in *The Republic* and elsewhere, is rooted in the need to replace the rote memorization and recitation of Homeric narrative with ethical and philosophical thought at a level of abstraction that was dependent upon the (then) new technology of alphabetic writing (see also Ong, 1982, and Bolter, 1984).

At first glance, it may seem that Nelson and Kristeva are talking about two very different things. Intertextuality, for Kristeva (and Genette, 1982), displaces meaning from the individual text to a *metatext* constituted by the relationship(s) among texts. Harold Bloom's (1973) contention that 'the meaning of a poem can only be another poem' nicely sums up one possible implication of a position like Kristeva's (which is not without its own historical antecedents: cf. Frye (1957), 'Poetry can only be made out of other poems. . .'; and T. S. Eliot, 1928). Such notions seem to have little in common with Nelson's sort of hypertext, but only because the formalist emphasis of Nelson's terminology obscures the *relational* character of hypertext.

A hypertext (also sometimes called a hyperdocument) consists of *nodes* and *links*. A node is a unit of information (which may be anything from a single point on the computer screen to a book-length text, though such extremes are generally impractical) which is electronically connected—linked—to one or more other units of information. Like other postmodern 'narratives,' both literary and scientific, described by David Porush (1989), hypertext replaces the modernist concern for 'objects, positions, order, and stability' with an emphasis on 'processes, relations, chaos, and instability as the foundations of reality.'

Poetry and Intertextuality

Computer scientist and polymath Douglas Hofstadter (1985) puts the postmodern view sharply when he writes that 'Nothing is a concept except by virtue of the way it is connected up *in the mind* with other things that are also concepts.' In other words, as Hofstadter goes on to say, a mental object becomes a concept because it is connected in our minds with other mental objects that we recognize as concepts: its 'concepthood' is a function of relationality.

What Hofstadter says about concepts is equally true of poetry. Nothing is a poem except by virtue of the way it is 'connected up,' in the mind, with other things that are also poems. A poem is a poem because it is linked in our minds with other mental objects that we have already come to recognize as poems. As Kristeva and Genette (and Eliot, and Frye, and Bloom) have taught us, the 'poeticality' of a poem is a function of intertextuality, which may be crudely defined as the notion that all texts are bound up with a multiplicity of other texts, in such intricate ways and to such an extent that any given text has to be described as being constituted by its relations with other texts. In practice, this means that we know a poem as a poem because, when we see it, we associate it with other things we have read, which we have already recognized as poems.

What I have just said may seem too obvious, or too trivial, to bear saying. But every teacher of poetry knows how much trouble students have in forming such connections. Confronted by a new text—especially if it is a twentieth-century text which (like *The Waste Land* or Wallace Stevens' 'Of Modern Poetry') takes its relation to literary tradition as its central subject—many undergraduates will be unable to perceive it as being connected with any other poetic texts. Or, what is equally unhelpful, they may find that the new text resembles *all* the other poems they have ever read and can remember in any way. In other words, they are more likely than not to miss the 'pointers'—the quotations, allusions, and echoes by which the poet refers to or remembers other poems, whether consciously or not. In missing these textual 'pointers' and thus failing to recognize both the text's relatedness and its uniqueness (since the perception of uniqueness depends, again, on relation), the untrained reader misses the very identity of the text as a poem: it is not accidental that many students still respond to works by Ezra Pound, William Carlos Williams, or Marianne Moore by saying 'That's not a poem.'

There are really several problems here. First of all, these students simply have not read enough poems to recognize the moments when poems refer to other poems. Second, from the discovery that a given poem is related to one or more other poems, they do not generalize to see that all poems are related to other texts. To put the matter more broadly still, they do not conceive of texts as being in dynamic relation with other texts.

2 A Hypercourse in Modern American Poetry

The foregoing account of what happens (or rather, what doesn't happen) when undergraduates confront a new poem has certain pedagogical implications: it implies that we must not only help our students learn to 'explicate' in the now-traditional New Critical manner (which remains a powerful instrument); we must also help them to discover and explicate the poem's relatedness, both to other poems and to other cultural phenomena. This is among the guiding assumptions of the most ambitious effort to use hypertext (and hypermedia) in literary instruction, the Intermedia project at Brown University (Yankelovich, et al., 1988). However, we might go further still and argue that we must help our students learn to *construct* the relationships by which poetry is constituted.

I shall now describe my efforts to exploit the power of hypertext, and specifically of Apple Computer's HyperCard, in addressing the problems outlined above. HyperCard runs on Apple Macintosh computers with at least 1 megabyte of Random Access Memory (RAM) and two 800 kilobyte floppy disk drives (a hard disk is strongly recommended, however). The program is based on the metaphor of the 3 × 5 inch file card: a screenful of information is called a 'card.' Related 'cards' are grouped together in 'stacks' and linked together by 'buttons' (a button is a 'live' area on the computer screen); stacks, cards, and buttons (as well as the 'fields' containing text) can be programmed by a 'stackware' author.

Hypertext and Intertextuality

HyperCard (like hypertext in general) provides the instructor with the ability to *simulate* intertextual relationships in a dynamic, interactive environment. Each 'card' in a poetry 'stack' contains the text of a poem plus one or more 'buttons' linking it to other cards. Quotations, allusions, and other phrases calling for explanation are overlaid with buttons linked to explanatory materials, related poems, and so forth. These buttons are transparent at first, so that (as may also happen in Intermedia) the student will initially perceive the text as freestanding, isolated. Pressing a button labelled 'Buttons' (see Figure 12.1) reveals the location of all previously hidden buttons on the card; thus the student is led to understand that the apparent separateness of the text is only a kind of optical illusion: in fact the text reaches out in many directions to incorporate and be incorporated by other materials.

Hypertext as a Medium for Instruction and Learning

The ability to simulate intertextual links, and to establish electronic links between otherwise discrete bodies of material, makes hypertext a powerful medium for instruction. To the extent that hypertext provides both a wider range of material than might otherwise be available, and that it allows the student to explore relationships independently of the instructor—to the extent, that is, that it encourages the student to *act* upon the material she or he is exploring, experimenting with different sequences and arrangements—hypertext is also a powerful medium for learning.

Conceptions Underlying the Hypercourse

The hypercourse is based on a series of propositions. The central proposition is that *poems are defined by their connections with other texts*. This formulation is fleshed out metaphorically, thus: *Poetry is an ongoing conversation within and across culture*. The conversational metaphor is important, because it emphasizes the dynamic, responsive, and *social* nature of the poem and its relations with other texts. It is also meant to suggest that poetry engages the whole culture, and that many different relationships may obtain between individual poems and the larger culture to which they belong. Finally, the conversational metaphor is meant to include the students themselves as active participants in the ongoing conversation by which poetry constitutes itself: thus the third proposition, that *understanding begins with the recognition and articulation of 'conversational' relationships*.

Implementation: Designing the Hypercourse

Taken together, these underlying notions have important implications, both for the nature of the materials to be included in a course so conceived, and for the manner in which those materials are to be organized. That poems are defined by their relationships with other poems implies, of course, that a good many poems should be included. That poetry more generally may be understood as a 'conversation' within and across culture implies that other cultural phenomena—both in the arts and elsewhere—must have a place as well. That understanding depends upon the ability to recognize, articulate, and construct significant 'conversational' relationships implies that the materials must be organized in such a fashion as to foster the perception and formation of such relationships.

Course materials should be presented in clear, attractive, and above all readable formats which make the different types of materials readily distinguishable. (The student should never be in doubt, for instance, about whether she is looking at a poem or at some kind of explanatory material—unless of course the poem itself is playing upon such confusion.) In addition, the course should be designed in such a way as to accommodate the different needs of students taking the introductory literature course on the one hand, and of graduate students doing more advanced work on the other. The course and its procedures must be intelligible in the absence of an instructor, and the computer has to be as unobtrusive, as transparent, as possible, so that the student is free to concentrate on the material without being distracted by the mechanism of the presentation.

Materials

The initial offering of the hypercourse will present a limited selection of work by the following poets: Ezra Pound, Robert Frost, T. S. Eliot, William Carlos Williams, Wallace Stevens, Marianne Moore, Langston Hughes, Elizabeth Bishop, Robert Lowell, and Sylvia Plath. Poetic texts are supplemented by visual images, sound recordings, and a variety of explanatory and other materials.

Individual poems are presented as discrete, individual texts, one poem per 'card.' All poems by the same author are grouped together into 'stacks' identified by the author's name. Thus there is a 'Marianne Moore' stack, an 'Ezra Pound' stack, a 'Langston Hughes' stack, and so forth, and the student can easily read through all the available works by a given author. (This is simply a matter of pressing the arrow-shaped 'Next' button at the bottom of the screen, which takes you to the next card in the sequence, or the 'Previous' arrow, immediately to the left, which takes you back one screen. To look for a specific poem, you can either press the 'Scan' button, which lets you flip quickly through all the cards in the stack—you click the mouse button when you see something you want to examine more closely—or you can click on the author's name and, when prompted to do so, enter the title of the poem you wish to see; the 'Search' button may also be used: see Figure 12.1 below.)

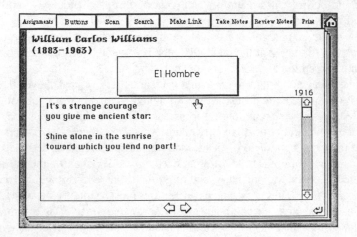

Fig. 12.1: HyperCard screen showing William Carlos Williams' 'El Hombre' as it first appeared to the students

So far, HyperCard has no particular advantage over the ordinary printed book, which has served us so well for so long, and indeed reading in this way is perhaps less convenient (as various studies have shown, it takes about thirty per cent longer to read a screenful of text than it does a printed page: Shneiderman, 1986). HyperCard's power begins to make itself felt, however, when we look at the following sequence, which approximates what a student might see and do during a typical session.

Demonstration

The first goal is to create what Michael Joyce (1988), in a recent article, calls an 'exploratory' hypertext or hyperdocument, in which the student explores linkages established by the instructor who designs the course. The examples that follow will represent such an exploratory sequence; the hypothetical student will follow a *structured pathway*, in which the choice of texts and explanatory material follows a syllabus assigned by the instructor. After completing such a session, the student would go on to participate more actively as a co-author or collaborator in what Joyce calls a 'constructive' hypertext, representing multiple understandings or constructions of the course materials.

Let's make the following suppositions. We're studying the work of William Carlos Williams (1883–1963). The student would begin by reading through a large number of poems by Williams—just beginning at the beginning of the stack, perhaps, and going on through to the end, as one would in reading a selection of poems in a more conventional anthology. Having read through the poems once—thereby building up at least a subliminal sense of characteristic features and so forth, the student would then go back to specific poems for more detailed exploration.

Introducing the Idea that Poems are Related to Other Poems

We want to reinforce the core notion that poems are defined by their relationship to other poems. The student is invited to look first at a short early poem, called 'El Hombre' ('The Man'), first published in 1916.

'El Hombre' is not an especially distinguished poem. The star is treated in an obviously symbolic manner which helps to identify this as an early poem: Williams will later repudiate such 'crude symbolism' (Williams, 1923/1970). At the same time, though, 'El Hombre' displays a characteristic attitude: we see a kind of defiant sense of separation, for the star coexists with the sunrise without actually contributing to it; in the same way, Williams believes, the poem and the world coexist in a complementary rather than a mutually constitutive relationship. As I say, however, 'El Hombre' is not an especially distinguished poem—or rather, it wouldn't be one if Williams' friend and slightly older contemporary, Wallace Stevens, hadn't singled it out as a point of departure for a poem of his own.

The press of a button overlaying the title brings up the relevant information and offers the student a choice: to continue reading Williams, or to look at the Stevens

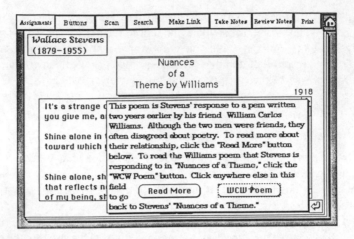

Fig. 12.2: HyperCard screen showing Wallace Stevens' 'Nuances of a Theme by Williams' with explanatory note

poem that responds to 'El Hombre.' Let us assume that the student has chosen to look at Stevens; pressing the appropriate button brings up a card displaying the text of his poem 'Nuances of a Theme by Williams' (1918).

The relationship between this text and the previous poem by Williams is direct and relatively straightforward. While there is no way to predict the Stevens poem from the fact that 'El Hombre' exists, Stevens announces that his poem is related to something by Williams—and he even reproduces Williams' text as part of his own. The student can verify this by selecting the appropriate button; or the student may choose a fuller discussion of the relationship between the two poets (see Figure 12.2).

Introducing the Idea that Poems may be Related to Other Arts

The student's attention is now directed to Williams' poem 'The Great Figure,' of 1921, which will serve as an instance of another central idea: that poetry 'converses' not only with other poetry, but with other arts as well.

As with 'El Hombre' and 'Nuances of a Theme by Williams,' the title field is again overlaid with a button that brings up a text field. In this case, the text reproduces Williams' own account of the circumstances under which 'The Great Figure' was composed, and notes that, like 'El Hombre,' this poem also provoked a response—this time not by another poet, but by the painter Charles Demuth, Williams' friend and fellow Rutherford (New Jersey) resident. Clicking the mouse as instructed, the student brings a reproduction of the painting onscreen.

It would be possible to describe at some length the considerable differences in what the two artists have chosen to emphasize: Williams concentrates on the act of following the firetruck's movement 'among the rain and lights' and through the city, while Demuth attends to the heraldic quality of the emblematic number 5. Even so, the relationship between Williams' poem and Demuth's painting is a relatively straightforward one, and it is time now to introduce the student to more intricate relationships.

Introducing the Idea of Polyvocal Conversations

The next stop along this structured pathway is Williams' 'The Pot of Flowers,' as it appeared in an important book called *Spring and All* in 1923. The aim now is to help the student discover that a poem may be related to one or more other poems *and* to other works of art as well.

Again the title functions as a button, bringing up a text field explaining that, as part of *Spring and All*, 'The Pot of Flowers' is one component of Williams' effort to answer what he felt as the urgent challenge of Eliot's *Waste Land* (1922). Clicking on the title of Eliot's poem brings up a brief description of *The Waste Land* and offers the student the option of continuing with the explanatory note on 'The Pot of Flowers' or branching out to examine *The Waste Land* itself before returning to the Williams poem.

We'll suppose that the student chooses to continue reading the explanatory material. Next she learns that 'The Pot of Flowers,' which had at first seemed to be a vivid but straightforward description of flowers in a pot, is in fact based upon a painting by Charles Demuth (just as Demuth's *I Saw the Figure 5 in Gold* was based on Williams' 'The Great Figure'). The painting is called *Tuberoses*; pressing Demuth's name brings it up on the screen.

After looking at the painting for a few moments, the student continues reading, and learns that there may be yet another element in the increasingly complex web of relations to which this apparently simple poem belongs. Williams' first love, his first poetic model, was Keats; perhaps, then, 'The Pot of Flowers' stands in some sort of ironic relation to Keats' *Isabella; or, The Pot of Basil* (1820). Pressing the title of Keats' poem brings up yet another field, this one providing a brief summary of *Isabella* and transcribing the last few stanzas of the poem (see Figure 12.3).

This in turn might be connected to a more general discussion of Williams and Keats; and that discussion might be linked to an even more general essay on the relationship of modernism to romanticism—a problem of considerable interest to scholars, and one that students tend to find interesting as well.

Encouraging Student Responses

We have now seen something of what might be done with a structured pathway through a portion of the course materials. We must point out some potential dangers, however. The student has looked at a fairly large array of material; there is a good deal to remember, not only about Williams and his relations with his fellow artists, but also about the student's own path through the materials; this is what hypertext researchers call the problem of *cognitive overhead*. The

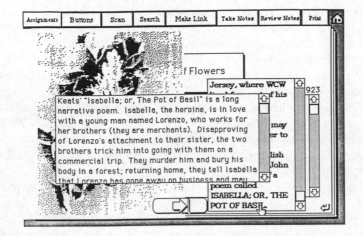

Fig. 12.3: Hypercard screen showing Williams' 'The Pot of Flowers' with explanatory note on Keats' *Isabella* and the reproduction of Charles Demuth's watercolor *Tuberoses*

problem is compounded because it is difficult to tell exactly where one is in a hypertext environment (whereas with a book one always knows how far one is from beginning or end), and because there are so many possible ways to get from one point to any of a number of other points: the risk of disorientation is quite real.

These problems are not trivial, but they may be turned to instructive advantage. A mild sense of disorientation and confusion may spur students to enter a more actively 'constructive' relationship (to use Michael Joyce's term again) with what they have seen and read, as a way of clarifying their understanding. Of course, this won't just 'happen:' students must be actively encouraged to enter into this new relationship, to become what I call co-authors of the hypertext. (It is not implausible to think that students are willing to enter such relationships. Students who have used Intermedia at Brown University have complained that they are not free either to add new materials or to create new links among existing materials: *IRIS video, 1989*; and my own experience in my department's computer classroom at the University of Texas indicates that students are eager to collaborate in constructing a body of knowledge.) This means that the hypercourse must offer various means of participation.

The first necessity is for *free exploration*, in which the student pursues any and all links that interest him or her (this also entails some sort of 'bookmarking' feature which enables the student to return to his or her point of departure). Next, students must also have access to a method of *annotation*, in which they attach their own notes and comments to particular poems (or images, or any other element of the course) as if in the margins of the page. Pressing the 'Take Notes' button that appears on each card opens a scrolling text field and places the cursor on the first blank line; when finished entering the note, the student presses the button again to close the field and store the note in a separate location for later review and possible 'export' to a word processing program. A 'mapping' facility will also be provided—that is, a set of tools for diagramming relationships as the student understands them.

The next step calls for the *construction of links*, in which the student creates new links between a given text and other course materials. The 'Make Link' button allows the student to tap HyperCard's linking facilities without requiring knowledge of the mechanisms that create the links; here the student is also given 'space' (in a text field) to justify the linkage. Equally important, the courseware must permit the expansion of the knowledge base. The student must be given the opportunity to add new materials, creating and explaining links between such new materials and what already exists.

And finally, all student-produced materials (except for individual annotations, which are private unless the student wishes to 'publish' them) will be available for inspection by the entire class; thus students will be involved as active producers, and not merely consumers, of course materials.

3 Conclusions

Some readers, having come this far, may feel that in trying to exploit the power of the computer as a tool for helping students to perceive intertextual relationships, I have created more problems than I have solved. Some may feel, for instance, that using the computer to present poetry deprives students of one of poetry's very real pleasures—that of handling the pages of a well-made, handsomely printed volume. Others may feel that using the computer—and especially the Macintosh, and especially HyperCard—for teaching poetry builds a fundamental distortion of the poetic medium into the very design of a course which proposes to teach people what poetry is and how to read it. That is, the Macintosh and HyperCard might be said to distort the nature of the poem by presenting it as an essentially *visual* object rather than a structure of words; this apparent distortion is exacerbated by the combination of text and visual images (as in the examples above), which blurs the distinctiveness of both media.

These are by no means trivial objections. On the contrary, they speak directly to the uneasy relationship between the print culture—in which we have all grown up, and upon which depend not only our livelihoods but also our professional, and often our personal identities—and the culture whose defining technology is the computer (Bolter 1984). It is not enough to answer someone who insists that poetry is a verbal medium by pointing to such visually oriented poems as Herbert's 'Easter-Wings' (1633) or Blake's 'The Sick Rose' (1794) or Emmett Williams' *Anthology of Concrete Poetry* (1967). For the issue is not whether poetry is verbal or visual: the issue is literature itself. As Richard Lanham (1989) has pointed out, the shift from page to screen, from print to the digitized word, entails a major change in the status of the book as a privileged cultural icon. There is no way to dodge this: the change is upon us, in the humanities and elsewhere, and we will have to wrestle with our knowledge that to put literature into the computer is to transform it in fundamental ways. For some, this transformation must appear as a disaster of almost unprecedented proportions. What Lanham describes as the democratizing effect of digitalizing text will for some readers mean that to enter poetry into the computer is to treat it not as poetry but rather as mere *data* of neither more nor less value than any other data, and thus to devalue it entirely. My final anecdote is meant to offer a degree of comfort.

When I first bought a word processor in 1984, I made many unsuccessful and utterly frustrating attempts to create a 'style sheet' that would automatically format long verse quotations. I had reached the point of enraged despair, when suddenly it came to me that the computer neither knew nor cared anything about poetry—that from the standpoint of the computer, or more precisely of the word processing software, all that mattered was that poetry's margins are not right-justified, and that one doesn't want automatic wordwrap. From the computer's point of view, poetry is simply a species of text in which the *user* determines the length of each line.

Solving that particular problem eliminated one source of irritation, and made my work easier from a mechanical standpoint. But it did much more than that. Rather than draining the value from the poem's words, and from the intricate formal arrangement of those words, the discovery that the computer knew nothing about poetry forced me to realize that it was I, and not the computer, that invested those words and arrangements with such a heavy burden of meaning and value. Poetry is above all a *human* thing: the values attached to it are precisely the values that *we* attach, neither more nor less, and that we attach not just individually and idiosyncratically but collectively, *culturally*, as well. Viewed from that perspective, hypertext becomes a mechanism for demonstrating and exploring, and indeed for creating, cultural attachments. It is a machine that both helps us to endow marks on a page (or patterns of phosphor on a screen) with value and to understand more clearly what we have done.

13

An Examination of Hypertext as an Authoring Tool in Art and Design Education

Alan Dyer and Kate Milner

1 Introduction

Many people working in humanities education now know something about hypertext and how it works. We have seen demonstrations of hypertext systems where the mouse is clicked and new images and bodies of text appear on the screen like rabbits appearing out of a hat. There is considerable novelty value in such demonstrations. There is also considerable interest in the idea that elements within a hypertext system can be endlessly linked and cross referenced. However, teachers are beginning to ask, 'How are such systems being used in practice?' and 'What is their potential in particular educational contexts?' This chapter, based on research carried out over a period of four years at Coventry Polytechnic, attempts to address these questions as they apply to undergraduate art and design education.

In the Faculty of Art and Design at Coventry, teaching staff are considering whether hypertext software might stand alongside painting, sculpture, film, video, etc., as one more creative medium available to students. They are also considering the idea that hypertext authoring methods might form a bridge between the studio-based practical aspects of art and design courses and the more theoretical components of such courses.

Production of essays and theses in art history and complementary studies might involve the creation of interactive 'knowledge structures' which in their construction will exploit and stimulate the two-dimensional and three-dimensional skills fostered in the studio.

2 Hypertext

Producing a hypertext document is not like writing a conventional essay or thesis in which a fixed linear narrative is presented to the reader. The creator of the document does not prescribe a fixed route which must be followed by the reader in order for the document to have 'meaning.' The author designs the document in such a way that users can plot their own route through the text and images. The author is responsible for initially installing text and images into the document and also has to design the structure in such a way that multiple pathways can be taken through the document without causing the user to become lost. The author, then, must devise navigational systems or 'maps.' In doing so the author is having to exercise a multi-dimensional view of the 'knowledge structure.'

It is this characteristic of hypertext authoring which is of interest for those teachers who are currently supervising theoretical research projects in an art and design context at Coventry Polytechnic. The skills which this type of authoring can exercise when used in the context of historical and theoretical studies are those associated not only with research and scholarship but with the ability to devise two-dimensional and three-dimensional structures—that is, with design and visualisation skills.

The reasons for constructing a hypertext document can be as varied as the reasons for writing a book. The document could be intended to convey information, tell a story, express a reaction to a group of images, or simply function as an informative database relating to a given subject area. However, although the intentions might be different for each author certain basic problems remain constant: how to install in a computer-based document a particular body of information on a given topic and how to design a structure and a navigational system with appropriate maps which will enable readers to access the document freely and choose their own pathways through the information.

3 Hypertext in Art and Design Education

Much of the current work on the introduction of hypertext into humanities education involves the creation of interactive databases which provide a learning environment for the student. The teacher, or 'expert,' first decides upon the data to be installed in the system and then designs the mechanics by which the student interrogates the database. The Art and Design Faculty at Coventry Polytechnic has not followed this path. Hypertext has been introduced as an authoring tool for students rather than as a teaching aid for the institution.

In art and design education attempts are constantly being made to identify new media which have genuine potential for creative authoring and to introduce such media into the coursework and projects. The new medium must possess the features traditionally associated with art and design practice and should show a high degree of flexibility so that it can be moulded and shaped according to the intuitions, flights of fancy, or communication needs of the individual. Staff responsible for supervising students' creative work also need to understand the potential of the new medium, its limitations and its capacity to stimulate and extend creative thinking. Thus the Coventry research has been designed to examine hypertext as a potentially creative authoring medium and to address the following questions:

1. Is hypertext a creative authoring medium?

2. In what educational context might hypertext be appropriate and in what context might it be counter-productive?

3. What effect might hypertext have on traditional assumptions about scholarship and the authoring of research material?

4. What educational benefits can be derived from the use of hypertext as an authoring tool for art and design students?

5. Is hypertext heralding new forms of authoring appropriate to the so-called 'electronic age' or the 'information society'?

The present chapter cannot, of course, begin to answer all these questions. However, it will attempt to describe how the questions are being approached in an art and design education context.

4 Hypertext and Creative Practice

Within the field of art education the manipulation of visual imagery in relation to perception, appearances and the representation of reality has been extensively explored over many years. The picture is both a window onto a world of appearances and, at the same time, stands as an interface between the artist, the audience and various models of reality. It is in this context that the potential of hypertext is currently being explored.

It is being explored not simply as a technical tool but as a 'painterly' medium for creative artists. The term 'painterly' refers to the degree of fluidity or malleability of a medium, its capacity to be shaped or moulded until it becomes a faithful representation of the author's creative vision, and the subtlety with which it can be modified to represent an idea or network of ideas which the author wishes to communicate. Since hypertext is being examined within the educational context we are also exploring its potential for expanding a student's capacity for creative (lateral) thought, involving not simply visual elements in a design system but also conceptual elements in an information system or 'knowledge structure.'

Theoretical work at Coventry, over some fifteen years, has included the modelling of graphic images for representing conceptual worlds. Unlike the traditional pictorial realisms the new representations function as models or maps. They are windows onto an abstract world of information, or knowledge structures. Throughout this period it has become increasingly clear that paper-based graphic maps could function as strong and informative images, but as interfaces they were often inflexible, limited by the number of graphic elements it is possible to display at any one time on a single surface.

Developments in computer systems and low cost hardware and software have made it possible to extend the modelling of such interfaces beyond the limitations of conventional paper-based media. On the electronic interface graphic elements are not fixed and static. The electronic interface permits graphic elements to be endlessly replaced, mixed or superimposed until the medium which is being modelled takes on the characteristics of both two-dimensional and three-dimensional structures, with an added time-based dimension. The software which seems to lend itself most readily to this type of authoring, or modelling, is hypertext.

It is an implicit feature of art and design education at undergraduate level that struggling with a painting, sculpture or design project is not simply a struggle to craft a usable, functional, and ultimately marketable artifact. Studio practice presents the student with a medium and a set of problems. The student might try to give visual form to a set of technical or theoretical problems or try to give formal expression to personally held beliefs or perceptions of reality.

Ideally, the particular medium should be flexible enough to play its part in an 'ideas processing' dialogue with the student or practitioner. A tutor is able to observe, comment on and influence the nature of the dialogue by observing its progression both in the development of the picture and through conversation with the student. In art education this process of creative authoring is well established; it is one of the educational methods used to foster creativity and conceptual development.

The traditional essay format offers less variety in its manipulative characteristics because of its strict formatting rules and its essentially linear nature. New forms of knowledge manipulation and presentation employing hypertext can offer a middle ground between studio based image manipulation skills and the text based theoretical components of courses. At present there is much speculation about hypertext and its potential. Research at Coventry seems to suggest that it might be a system which allows theoretical material to be manipulated in ways which have much in common with the techniques of pictorial and sculptural representation.

The most obvious application of hypertext in the theoretical part of the art and design course is in the graphical representation and organisation of ideas and information. This involves not simply the use of visual images for illustration, but the creation of 'maps' or 'models' which describe a particular aspect of reality, organise information in relation to the development of a particular theory, or create and plot multiple pathways through a knowledge structure. Figure 13.1 shows a typical example of the division between studio practice and the historical/theoretical studies component of art and design degree courses. Hypertext is shown as a potential bridge between the characteristics of the two areas listed.

In an educational environment, where students are exposed to a wide range of visual media and where courses involve the development of creative design skills, the construction of graphic models provides students with images of 'wholes' that might not otherwise be perceived. This makes students' graphic constructions valuable aids to perception, learning, data organisation, concept manipulation and communication. These are also processes fundamental to the construction of hypertext documents. The use of such teaching and learning techniques in the context of art theory allows students to engage in, and to develop, techniques and

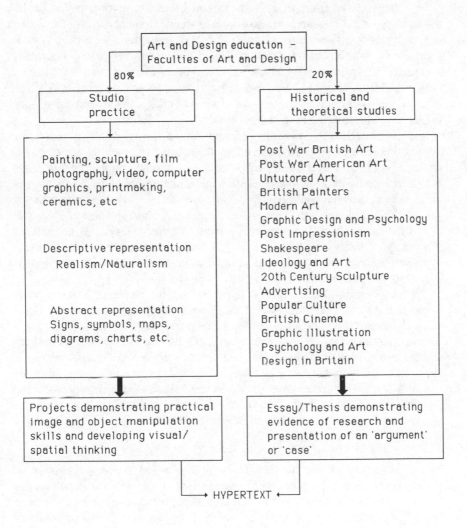

Fig. 13.1: Potential function of hypertext incorporating visual design and theoretical components of course

processes which have many formal similarities with their studio-based practical projects.

Problems of navigation, mapping and management of multiple pathways, intrinsic to hypertext systems, are also central to art and design practice. The ability to create pictures, three-dimensional constructions, diagrams, symbols, graphic signs, even simple box/arrow structures should give art and design students a ready purchase on the processes by which theoretical material is organised in hypertext systems. Furthermore it should enable tutors to approach students' theoretical material in ways which, from the point of view of critical discussion, have much in common with tutoring in the studio or workshop.

It might be argued that even in documents which consist wholly of text-based information the devising of navigation routes relating to potential meanings becomes a problem of overview or map-making. Although graphic images might not be included within the body of information, the design and manipulation of the system as a whole could be dependent upon the type of image manipulation skills described earlier and which are an integral part of art and design education. If it is the case that information management in hypertext systems necessitates plans, maps, charts or diagrams for navigational purposes, then clearly a fruitful relationship exists between theoretical research presentation in hypertext and the characteristics of art and design practice.

The construction of documents in hypertext systems develops students' visualisation and design skills in ways that are not encountered in the conventional essay or thesis. Theoretical studies departments in colleges of art and design, as with many humanities courses, usually demand that students present their ideas, and the results of their theoretical research in the form of strict, linear narratives. However, with the advent of electronic interactive documents opportunities are available for the author to develop approaches to knowledge manipulation and presentation which can draw upon non-linear modes of thinking. The new forms of authoring also lend themselves to collaborative authorship.

5 Hypertext in Theoretical Studies

In the early days of art education teaching was based almost exclusively on studio and workshop practice, with students pursuing an interest in painting or sculpture assisted by tutors with a professional background in the area. The aim was to give students a training which would allow them to become professional artists and designers in their turn. Before the 1960s such courses taught little history and theory. However, as art and design courses were granted degree status by the CNAA during the 1960s it was felt that they needed a more formal theoretical component. This development led to the establishment of departments of art history which provided the student with a historical context within which they could better locate their own practice. The departments of art history also added a range of 'complementary studies' options such as philosophy, psychology, anthropology, cultural studies, etc., which allowed art and design students to explore a range of theoretical perspectives and research methods in relation to their practical studio-based work.

For some institutions this broadening of studies has worked well but for others it has proved problematic. The two separate elements of the courses, theoretical studies and studio practice, are often seen as mutually exclusive so far as good educational practice is concerned. This apparent division between theory and practice can also be perpetuated by the staff whose teaching (and training) is located on one or the other side of this divide. Studio and workshop tutors usually have a background as practising artists or designers, while lecturers in complementary studies usually have a university background in one of the humanities disciplines.

During the late 1960s and early 1970s developments occurred in art practice which began to cross the boundary between theory and practice in art. Conceptual Art and the Art Language were movements concerned primarily with the manipulation and representation of theory rather than with the manufacture of aesthetic artifacts. Artists began to produce creative work which was intended as a more direct communication of conceptual material and as an expression of theoretical research. The Faculty of Art and Design at Coventry Polytechnic was one of the first to introduce conceptual art into the undergraduate curriculum and has remained highly sympathetic to the blending of theory and practice on its courses. Currently eighty percent of an art and design degree course at Coventry Polytechnic is assessed on studio work and twenty percent on the presentation of essays and a thesis representing work in complementary studies (this is probably typical of most British art and design degree courses). Clearly, any way in which these two elements could be better integrated would be of value to the students and the institution. It is in this light that the Faculty is considering the introduction of hypertext into the theoretical studies component of its courses.

As described earlier in this chapter, hypertext has already found a place in the studios and workshops. Hypertext certainly is not seen as a replacement for traditional art and design media. However, its ability to bring together the qualities of a number of different media in one piece of work makes it exciting to students. There have been instances where students who have already come to appreciate the potential of this new medium in the studio have asked if they could submit a hypertext document in place of an essay or thesis. It is evident from their work that analytical and theoretical work can be contained within hypertext, but no formal criteria currently exist for the assessment of such documents.

At present work in complementary studies is usually assessed through the presentation of essays and a thesis. This procedure, however, has certain limitations for art and design students. Approximately eighty percent of their time is spent in the studios and workshops learning how to manipulate essentially visual media to express their ideas, feelings or perceptions. The skills which they are trying to develop (and for which they were initially offered places on art and design courses) often have little in common with the skills required to pursue theoretical research and to write a thesis. This does not mean that art students have no interest in the communication of ideas, or that art education does not foster an ability to structure thought. It is simply that these educational aims are pursued through different media. What has come to the attention of certain members of staff at Coventry Polytechnic is the realization that hypertext as an authoring medium has much in common with studio based media such as paint, sculpture or film. Moreover, because hypertext permits the organisation of text and images in elaborate and variously structured networks, it can be used by art and design students to organise and present theoretical work in the complementary studies context while using the design and visualisation skills which are more typical of their creative work in the studios.

With reference to the section on hypertext at the beginning of this chapter we must consider how the characteristics of this new medium can relate to the educational objectives and requirements as set out in the theoretical components of art and design degree courses. Initially the design and construction of a hypertext document means dealing with two different problems of organisation. That is, deciding what should make up the elements of the document and deciding how those elements should be linked together. There exists the additional problem of indicating to the reader where the links are and where they might lead. This is usually referred to as the problem navigation. The new hypertext software, particularly HyperCard and Guide, places few constraints on the user. There are few restrictions on the sort of material which can make up the elements of the document and no particular structure predetermined by the medium.

Deciding on the elements of a hypertext document might be equivalent to organising notes for a thesis. An element might be a description of an idea, a particular view of the subject in question, a relevant quotation, an illustration or a diagram, all of which might be contained in a thesis. However, since hypertext can allow the creation of an inclusive network of material we might go one step further and allow the inclusion of expressive material. A student dealing with the work of an artist might include analyses of particular examples of that artist's work, but they might also include examples of their own work made in response to the object of their study. The expressive work does not replace the analytical work, it stands alongside it as another way of responding to the subject.

Organising material for a thesis means finding the most appropriate sequence for that material. However, although the thesis is invariably presented as a linear narrative it is not always logically linear. References are made backwards and forward in the document, illustrations are referred to at different points, footnotes and appendices are contained in separate sections. An author could break down this type of structure into component parts and reconstruct it in hypertext so that material referred to in different parts of the document is more easily available, or a hypertext thesis could involve the construction of a relational database about a particular subject. There is no doubt that to understand the relationships which exist between the various components of a branch of knowledge is much the same as understanding the subject itself. There is clear educational benefit for the student undertaking this sort of task.

Both the above structures allow the inclusion of expressive material but imply working in a way which is significantly different from the way the student works in the studio. Both approaches require the author to first decide upon a structure and then slot material into the appropriate position. To work creatively is to keep the relationships between the various components of the piece fluid. The final pattern is only fixed at the point where the artist feels the work is finished. It might be possible to allow the hypertext author to work in the same way thereby mirroring, in a more fundamental sense, the ways of thinking developed in the studio. An author might work on elements of the document, creating links as they occur and breaking others. The work is only finished when he or she feels satisfied that the links made between the elements of the document properly express the relationships found between them.

This leaves the problem of navigation. Producing a thesis does not only require that a student has the ability to organise thoughts about a particular question: it requires that he or she should be able to communicate those thoughts to a third party. The clarity of the structure of a hypertext document depends upon the clarity with which thought is organised. If the means of navigation is sufficiently obvious, clarity of thought can be demonstrated to an assessor. As described earlier art and design students are accustomed to making visual models and representations. Because of this they may be better placed than many students to find ways of aiding navigation by giving visual expression to the types of networked knowledge structures made possible by hypertext. There is, therefore, the distinct possibility that the work of art and design students in this area could be of benefit to hypertext authors and users in general.

The examples illustrated below show the basic structure of two hypertext essay submissions by students in the Faculty of Art and Design at Coventry. Figure 13.2 shows the structure of an essay by a second year fine art student. The essay deals with the decentering of authorship. It uses the architectural structure of the 'Panopticon' (a design for a prison in which all cells can be observed and controlled from a central tower) as a metaphor for centralised authorship. The essay both argues for and, through its own mode of hypertext presentation, demonstrates the transfer of control from author to user.

Figure 13.3 is an analysis of a poem 'Andromeda' by Gerard Manley Hopkins. The document was produced by a student on the electronic graphics course. The map shows the basic routes which a user may take in examining the various sections within the document.

In spite of the highly demanding nature of these projects both from the point of view of researching the theoretical source material and designing the hypertext structure, hypertext documents are not readily acceptable as alternatives to the traditional 'scholarly' thesis. This is not because hypertext is incapable of effectively handling research material but because adequate criteria for student assessment

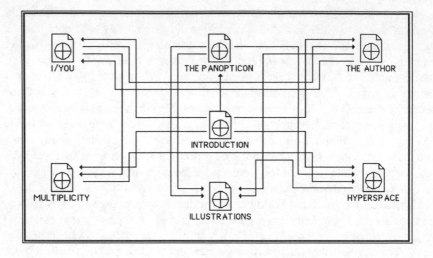

Fig. 13.2: Panopticon

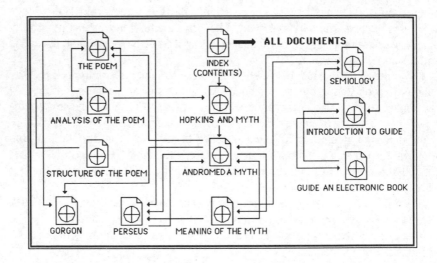

Fig. 13.3: Andromeda

in this medium have not yet been established. At present a central requirement for the submission of essays and theses in the Faculty of Art at Coventry is the presentation of a particular 'case' or 'argument.' This in turn necessitates a strict linear narrative and a high degree of author control over the reader. The formal examination of this requirement (the extent to which an argued case through a strict linear narrative is an indispensable requirement for the demonstration of scholarship) is a matter of ongoing research. Because of the novelty of this new medium and its potential for undermining traditional assumptions about scholarly authorship there are very few teachers who feel confident to judge hypertext documents alongside traditional research presentation media.

This will probably change. Even if hypertext does not become a widely used medium for student authoring in education, computer-based presentations of some sort are bound to become more common. If we are asking students to gather information from computer based systems, if we are allowing them to organise and edit their work on computer, then the requirement to produce print-outs on paper at the end of a project might be unnecessary.

In the meantime, for reasons described above, it is very difficult to set down hard and fast rules for the assessment of hypertext documents. The structure the student develops for a particular work in an art and design context is likely to be both a personal response to the material under investigation and a product of creative intuition rather than a slavish adherence to a standard presentation format which might be easier for institutions to assess. Perhaps the basic requirement ought to be that a document should be the work of an individual student, that the links made in the document should be rational and defensible, and the means of navigation should be clear enough to allow the assessor to follow a path which makes sense. This does not exploit all of the possibilities inherent in hypertext authoring but it does allow students to construct documents in a way that makes use of their creative skills.

6 Conclusion

It remains to be seen, as more art and design students are introduced to hypertext, whether it will indeed form a bridge between the skills developed in the studios and workshops and those required for the theoretical components of art and design degree courses. However, the examples produced so far by students at Coventry Polytechnic seem to indicate that there is reason for optimism. If hypertext documents are constructed which show that students are able to use this medium to develop a rounded, inclusive view of a subject then perhaps other disciplines might consider handing over this new software to their own students. If it is feasible that students might gain some educational benefit from producing their own hypertext documents, and if there is a demand from those students to be allowed to submit such documents in the place of the traditional essay/thesis, then the academic establishment must find adequate criteria for assessing them. In the early stages it seems unlikely that these criteria can allow for all the possibilities of hypertext. The potential challenges it makes to the way we view undergraduate education are too complex to be assimilated quickly. However, academics would do well to consider how they might include hypertext among the other media and presentation models they make available to their students, since its potential educational benefits seem too numerous to be ignored.

14

Teaching Computer-Based Document Design

Alison Black

1 Introduction

Technological change has meant that the writing, designing and production of paper documents can proceed seamlessly in electronic media, from the author's initial ideas to the production of formatted camera-ready copy. Research has isolated some of the consequences of computerisation for the cognitive processes of document writers and readers (Gould & Grischkowsky, 1984; Hansen & Haas, 1988). However, more specialised issues relating to the *designing* of documents on screen have received less attention. Document designers manipulate the same text that writers create and readers use, but focus on the visible form of that text. A change of working medium that alters both the techniques for manipulating text and the visible feedback resulting from those manipulations is likely to affect both designers' working method and the solutions to design problems that they produce.

In this paper I consider the impact of working in an electronic medium on novices' problem solving in designing. Drawing on two studies of students using desktop publishing technology for document design tasks I shall illustrate how working on screen is not a simple translation of paper-based processes to a new environment but brings both new freedoms and new constraints that must be catered for in teaching. The constraints that are of most concern are those that distract students from full exploration of problems, drawing them into a narrow method of working dictated by the software they are using. Such subtle changes may be obscured by the need for students and staff to get to grips with the technology, but I shall suggest that it is necessary to make the constraints explicit in order to incorporate the technology into teaching in a manner that enhances rather than limits the development of students' skills.

2 Learning the Processes of Document Design

Giving Visible Form to Ideas

Document design is a process of planning information. To make good design decisions, students must take into account constraints such as the pragmatics of written language, historical precedents, socio-cultural trends, cognitive ergonomics and the technologies and organisation of production. But above all, they must be able to distil their understanding of design problems into the production of documents that have good visible form.

Right from the earliest stages of tackling a problem, students' thinking is likely to be mediated by sketches or visible notes, made to familiarise themselves with the material they are manipulating. These notes may be very rough to start with: possibly just 'thumbnail' sketches that indicate the structural relationships between elements of a document without focusing in detail on any particular elements. Then as a design problem becomes more familiar, these rough sketches are worked up to more precise drafts that may culminate in a simulation of the document representing final design decisions. Like language, the sketches have different inflections depending on whether students are using them for their own records and reflections, or for communicating ideas to colleagues and clients, or for communicating with tutors.

One obvious consequence of moving designing from paper to screen is that designers are one step removed from the marks they are making. Many screen-based design systems have WYSIWYG interfaces that allow direct manipulation of entities on screen (Shneiderman, 1983). Nevertheless, the engagement between users and the paper on which their marks will eventually appear is not direct, and the repertoire of marks that can be made is restricted by the software being used. There are some designers who believe that the only tool to give the tactile sensitivity required for designing is the pencil; even the range of marks that a 'technical pen' can produce is considered too limited (Mackie, 1988). But generally designers use a wide range of tools including brushes, pens and pencils and are willing to place screen tools alongside more traditional devices.

The limited sensitivity and articulatory range of screen tools can be traded off against the labour saved compared to hand-rendering drafts. Marks that can be made on screen have the advantage of being clear and consistently reproducible. This might be especially helpful for novice designers who often find the manual preparation of drafts laborious. It could be argued that screen tools might allow novices to attend to the development of ideas without over-concern for their physical execution and so could improve the quality of their decision-making.

However, moving from paper to screen may affect the visible processes of document design beyond the actual making of marks on paper. Many designers respond to design problems by generating a range of solutions and exploring them all before commitment to any particular solution (Jones, 1981). Encouraging novices to withhold judgements about a range of potential solutions and to experiment with each solution methodically is always difficult. A flexible approach can be fostered in teaching by emphasising the decision-making processes leading to a particular solution and by comparing the chosen solution with other possibilities. Discussions about decisions and comparisons of alternatives are always mediated through the visible evidence provided by students' sketches and drafts. Students sometimes pin up part-finished solutions around the area in which they are working. These act as prompts both to the students' own reflections (even at times when their attention is not specifically directed to those particular drafts) and to responses from other students and members of staff. Ideally, then, the medium in which students learn problem solving in designing must primarily be a medium that supports the generation and comparison of alternative visible forms.

Exploring Visible Form on Screen

The generation of draft solutions on screen is technically straightforward. New files can be opened, worked on, stored and printed out. However, there is a striking difference between the appearance of screen-generated and hand-rendered drafts. All screen drafts look very finished. Both on the screen itself and when printed out on paper, the text elements look as though they might be in their final form. This contrasts with hand-rendered drafts which, as I have discussed above, vary in appearance from very provisional to very final, depending on the stage of problem solving and the amount of care and skill invested by the student. On paper, the focus of attention during the initial stages of planning a document can therefore only be structural form, since producing a draft solution that looks finished requires so much work. On screen, the immediate finished appearance of draft solutions may be a distraction from structural issues. The 'rhetorical significance' of the proposed solution has changed: since the text looks so finished so soon, it appears that no further work is needed. Consequently students working on screen may not experiment fully with the visible form of the document.

Even if they are not distracted from experimentation by the finished appearance of their draft solutions students may be diverted from a systematic and comparative approach to designing by the linear interface that most document preparation and graphics software presents. It is usually easy to create and work on a series of draft solutions. Nevertheless the assumption underlying the software is that drafts are worked on one at a time. In some more powerful systems it is possible to display more than one draft at a time, but multiple comparisons of a range of draft solutions are never a starting point for the software. Students who do not have well-established working methods are perhaps more likely than experienced designers to adopt the linear working method implied by the interface: they may confine their work to the development of one particular design solution rather than exploring a range of possible alternatives.

A further distraction from the preparation of a range of alternative solutions may be the ease with which any single solution can be altered. If screen tools did not allow the alteration and manipulation of marks, they would not be of any use to designers. However, the facility for erasing marks and revising individual drafts indefinitely may mean that no concrete record is made of the progress of an idea. Experienced practitioners who understand the importance of making records may interrupt their screen working in order to record stages in the preparation of a document, but novices are unlikely to do so. Interfaces that can play back the stages of a user's interaction may, in the future, be one answer to this problem (see Makkuni, 1987). In the meantime working on screen demands conscious record-making in a way that is not necessary in paper drafting where a record is an inevitable by-product of drafting itself.

3 Studies of Students Designing on Paper and on Screen

The two questionnaire studies described below were conducted at the University of Reading to investigate the effects of working on screen on the design decisions of students using desktop publishing software. The studies are presented in some detail in order to draw links between students' responses to the questionnaires and the factors discussed above: the change in visible feedback and the implied linear working method in screen-based designing.

Study 1: Visible Feedback and Design Decisions

Twenty-nine first-year students of typography and graphic communication were questioned after they had completed their first exercise in text design. Before the exercise the students had been shown how to manipulate the style, size and spacing of textual elements to reflect the relationships between them and how to represent these relationships in thumbnail sketches. In the exercise itself the students planned the same text twice, working once on paper and once on screen: half the students worked on paper first and then moved on to screen, the other half worked in the reverse order (a section of the text is shown in Figure 14.1). The exercise was carried out in two regular studio sessions, each of two hours.

The students completed the questionnaire immediately after the design exercise, when they had had no formal feedback from staff about their final drafts, and then a second time, after a review in which students displayed their final drafts and a colleague, Andrew Boag, led a general discussion of their work. The students responses to a selection of the questions are shown in Table 14.1. Since there were no significant differences between the responses of students who had worked on paper first and those who had worked on screen first the data have been collapsed across the two groups.

When the students first completed the questionnaire, their ratings showed they were more satisfied with their final screen drafts than their final paper drafts. They also felt it had been easier to make design decisions on screen, to implement those decisions on screen and to work with text provided in electronic form rather than on paper. The students felt that if they were presented with the task again they would be happier to work on screen than on paper.

When students answered the same questions again after their review, their ratings of satisfaction with their screen-produced drafts dropped. In contrast, their ratings of their paper-produced drafts increased significantly. Furthermore, whilst ratings of the ease of making design decisions on screen did not change, ratings of the ease of making decisions on paper increased so there was no longer a difference in the ratings for the ease of decision-making in the two media. Students' ratings

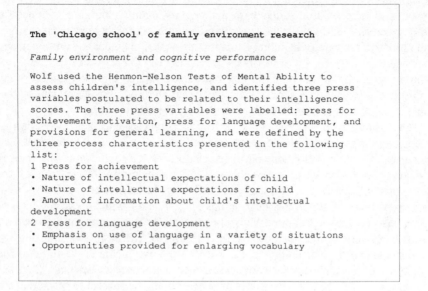

The 'Chicago school' of family environment research

Family environment and cognitive performance

Wolf used the Henmon-Nelson Tests of Mental Ability to
assess children's intelligence, and identified three press
variables postulated to be related to their intelligence
scores. The three press variables were labelled: press for
achievement motivation, press for language development, and
provisions for general learning, and were defined by the
three process characteristics presented in the following
list:
1 Press for achievement
• Nature of intellectual expectations of child
• Nature of intellectual expectations for child
• Amount of information about child's intellectual
development
2 Press for language development
• Emphasis on use of language in a variety of situations
• Opportunities provided for enlarging vocabulary

Fig. 14.1: Text presented to students in Study 1

Table 14.1: Mean ratings given by students in response to questions presented in Study 1.
The variance for the ratings are given in parentheses. The probabilities of the differences
between media (Mann-Whitney u) are given for each question

Time:	After design exercise			After design review		
Medium:	Paper	Screen	p	Paper	Screen	p
How satisfied were you with your finished work? (5 indicates very satisfied)	2.48	3.59	<.01	3.07	2.77	n.s
	(1.04)	(0.75)		(0.84)	(0.58)	
How easy was it to make decisions about the design of the text on each medium? (5 indicates very satisfied)	2.55	3.00	<.05	3.04	3.07	n.s.
	(0.39)	(0.57)		(0.49)	(0.53)	
How easy was it to implement your design decisions in each medium? (5 indicates very easy)	3.03	3.83	<.01	2.74	3.48	<.01
	(0.89)	(0.71)		(0.66)	(0.64)	
How easy was it to work from initial text supplied in each medium? (5 indicates very easy)	2.33	3.28	<.001	2.33	3.30	<.001
	(0.76)	(0.85)		(1.08)	(0.91)	
How happy would you be to work again in each medium? (5 indicates very happy)	3.38	4.44	<.001	3.70	3.96	n.s
	(1.32)	(0.32)		(1.29)	(1.19)	

of the ease of implementing design decisions dropped after the review for both paper and screen, but in neither case significantly, maintaining the preference for the screen as a medium for implementing ideas. Similarly there were no changes in ratings of the ease of handling initial text presented on paper and on screen and the preference for screen over paper was maintained. Finally, students' ratings of the prospect of working on paper again increased slightly and their ratings of the prospect of working on screen again decreased slightly after the review so that there was no longer a significant preference for screen to paper.

The pattern of changes in students' ratings suggests that their evaluation of their work was not simply depressed overall by the review, but rather that they were basing their evaluations on different criteria before and after the review. Students were consistent across the two questionnaires in their ratings of the ease of implementing design decisions and of the ease of working from text in electronic form. Furthermore their ratings of satisfaction with the end-products of their work on screen decreased whilst the ratings of their work on paper increased; and there were similar patterns for their ratings of the ease of making design decisions, and of their willingness to work in the two media in the future. The pattern suggests that before the review students' opinions were swayed by the ease of producing finished-looking drafts on screen, to the extent that they felt that the drafting decisions had been better on screen than on paper. But when the students' attention was drawn to structural issues concerning their drafts their ratings of the screen-produced drafts and the decision-making underlying them fell. In contrast, the students took a more generous view of their paper drafts and the decisions underlying them once they judged them in terms of their structure rather than their finished appearance.

Working on screen appeared, initially at least, to be a more satisfying experience for these students, presumably because it relieved them of the labour of hand-rendering drafts. But working on screen did not produce design solutions which, in the long term, the students found satisfactory. This switch of attitude suggests that before the review students' exploration of ideas may have been curtailed by the finished appearance of the visible feedback from their screen drafts.

Study 2: Linear Working and Design Decisions

The task that students carried out in Study 1 was, to some extent, artificial, in that it involved working exclusively in one medium at a time. In real life, however, designers might expect to work across both paper and screen at different stages and for different tasks during the planning of a document. Given students' initial preference in Study 1 for working on screen, it remained to be seen whether, in a more realistic situation where there was freedom to work across the two media, they would opt to work exclusively on screen. Study 2 investigated how students divided design tasks between screen and paper and the consequences of choosing to work in a particular medium for the planning processes underlying their work. Eighteen second-year students were questioned. They had some experience of designing, but were relatively new to working on screen. The students had just completed a two-week exercise in which they had designed a leaflet for desktop publishing, using text supplied on disc (there was a choice of two texts: one about housing benefit and another about environmental health).

The students were asked initially to estimate what percentage of their time had been spent working on paper. Their responses were distributed bimodally, with modes at 10 per cent and 70 per cent. The students were then presented with a list of the tasks they were expected to have performed during drafting and asked whether they had carried out these tasks predominantly on paper or predominantly on screen. All but two students claimed to have prepared their initial rough ideas on paper and all students claimed to have carried out 'adjustment' tasks on screen. But there was less consensus over the medium for carrying out the intermediate tasks of 'copy-fitting' (the calculation of how many characters the text includes and how much space it will take up in different formats) and finalising the document 'grid' (the overall positional plan within which the elements of the document are coordinated): ten of the students copy-fitted on screen and, of these, nine finalised the grid on screen. All of the students who had finalised the grid on screen had estimated that they had spent less than 50 per cent of their time working on paper.

Finally the students were asked to rate their level of agreement with four statements about the impact of the screen environment on their work (see Table 14.2). There was a trend for the students who had worked more than 50 per cent of their time on screen (S group) to feel that they compromised their initial design ideas in accordance with the limitations of the software they were using more than students who had worked more than 50 per cent of their time on paper (P group). There was a trend for the P group to give higher ratings than the S group of the degree to which they had pushed their knowledge of the software in order to put their initial design ideas into practice. The P group were also more convinced than the S group that both their working method and the end product itself would have been different had they worked entirely on paper.

Taken together, the responses suggest that the students had at least two different approaches to the division of work between paper and screen. There was an overall progression from paper to screen that might have been expected, considering that the students' training to that point had been mostly paper-based, yet they were expected to produce final drafts on screen. But within that progression, some students showed a far greater commitment to screen working, to the extent that they only spent 10 per cent of their time working on paper.

The differences in students' working methods were most obvious in the choice of medium for copy-fitting and adjusting the grid. Copy-fitting on paper is a tedious process that, nevertheless, gives designers a command of the material with which they are working. On screen, text can be 'fitted' by trial and error, simply by choosing a particular format and seeing how far the text goes when it is produced in that format. The finding that all but one of the students who copy-fitted on screen also finalised the grid on screen is not coincidental. Without a clear command of the material to be included in a document, it is difficult to specify the document's structure. If text is 'fitted' ad hoc on screen then the structure of the document can only be arrived at in response to the different fittings.

It could be argued that the students working predominantly on screen had adopted a much more fluid, intuitive working method than students working on paper, which might be beneficial to the development of their design ideas. However, such a position would not take into account students' rating of the four statements about the impact of the screen environment on their work. Students working predominantly on screen appeared to have compromised their initial ideas

Table 14.2: Mean ratings given by students in Study 2 of their level of agreement with statements about designing on screen. The range of rating for each statement is given in parentheses

| | Mean ratings of agreement | |
| | 5 indicates complete agreement | |
Statements:	Students working predominantly on paper (n=9)	Students working predominantly on screen (n=9)
I compromised my initial design in accordance with what I found I could produce with the available software.	2.4 (1–4)	3.9 (2–5)
I pushed my knowledge of the software in order to put my original design ideas into practice	4.1 (3–5)	2.6 (1–4)
Generally speaking, if I had designed this work on paper my working method would have been similar	2.6 (2–5)	3.7 (2–5)
Generally speaking, if I had designed this work on screen my working method would have been similar	2.1 (1–3)	2.9 (2–5)

more and to have made less of an effort to push their original plans forward in the screen environment. They were also less prepared than students working predominantly on paper to accept that either their working method or end-product would have been different on paper. Moving to work on screen early in the design process may have limited the students' exploration of the design problem so that they pursued the first solution that appeared workable on screen without admitting the possibility of alternative solutions. It appears that screen-based working is less flexible than paper-based working, although this speculation needs to be supported by observational studies of the actual process of designing and by assessment of the qualitative differences between work produced in the two media.

4 Promoting Appropriate Computer-Based Practice in Teaching

Even though the present studies suggest that working on screen may, for some students at least, limit the development of ideas during designing this need not necessarily be the case. Study 1 showed that although students' initial evaluation of their drafts was influenced by how finished the drafts appeared to be, their evaluations altered after a general discussion of design criteria. Given a wider experience of drafting on screen and more contact between tutors and students, it might be expected that novices would develop a more questioning appraisal of screen-generated drafts. Study 2 showed that half the students confined their drafting largely to the screen and, consequently, may not have fully considered the range of possible design solutions. Nevertheless, the remaining half of the students divided their work between paper and screen in a manner that may have been more appropriate to the tasks they were performing.

If students are to develop an appropriate working method in any medium they need to understand the advantages and limitations of that medium in relation to their own strengths and weaknesses as practitioners. There is a tendency in designing (as, possibly, in other creative activities, such as writing) to focus attention on products at the expense of the processes leading to the generation of those products. However, practitioners involved with text design have discussed design tools in the past (Tschichold, 1932) and now they must add screen-based tools to their discussion (Hewson, 1987; Miller Rubin, 1989). This kind of discussion can be taken into the teaching setting: the design exercise in Study 2 was subsequently used as a basis for a discussion of working method in desktop publishing. The aim of the discussion was to encourage students who had not already done so to make conscious choices about the medium in which they carried out particular tasks and to be aware of the potential consequences of working in a particular medium for their design decisions.

If students choose to use screen-based design tools then they need to know how to get the best out of those tools. To do this, they need to know how to 'work the system' or environment in which the tools operate. In the case of designing, working the system may involve understanding file management within the operating system and considering how to name and identify draft solutions so that stages in the development of an idea can be traced. Since, as has been suggested, design tools themselves tend to support a linear method of working rather than the parallel, comparative processes that underlie graphic planning, working the system may include using other, related software, such as databases, to make the storage and retrieval of drafts more efficient. Time and budget pressures often confine the use of software in teaching to that established specifically for a particular domain. But this narrow focus may also be a consequence of simply not considering the relevance of other less specialised software (Wright, 1988). Breaking through this restricted use of software involves cultivating a wider interest in the capabilities of the system, an interest that many teaching staff will consider an imposition when added to their existing teaching and research responsibilities. Furthermore there is a danger that fostering such an interest in students may lead to a 'cult of the machine' that is a distraction from the specific design purpose for which the technology was intended.

Perhaps the best way to ensure that students know both how to use the system and when not to use the system is to integrate the technology into working life alongside other studio tools. Computers cannot be secreted away in special rooms (which often become identified with particular students and staff members) or used only in particular projects or teaching sessions. Screen-based designing must take on the visible and social attributes of paper-based designing. It must be socialised so that it becomes what Illich (1973, ch. 2) would have called a 'convivial' as well as a congenial design technology.

15

Bridging Disciplines: The Example of Music Science

Paul Davis

1 Introduction

This chapter is concerned with the matter of interdisciplinarity. Although most of the examples are drawn from the discipline of Music Science, the arguments put forward are addressed to a wider audience than academics in the creative arts. The aim is to show the need for a more positive attitude to be taken towards interdisciplinarity in humanities subjects generally; also to signal the increasing demand for academics capable of working within and across the boundaries of what are traditionally regarded as separate disciplines. Ideal case studies are to be found in disciplines where information technology, especially the use of computers, now underpins a significant part of the work in the subject area. Music Science, as a relatively new discipline and one that is interdisciplinary by definition, is able to provide examples of the gains brought about by such a widening of scope and of some possible pitfalls. The reader will be able to identify parallel instances in other disciplines.

The establishment of the CATH conferences has highlighted one very important aspect of the growth of interdisciplinary work in Higher Education. Most of the delegates to our conferences are presently engaged in both teaching and research within their 'home' disciplines whilst at the same time being actively involved in the use of computers and calling upon the skills of some other discipline(s) to further their work. Another clear indicator is to be found in the (not that recent) appearance of 'thematic areas' such as American Studies, Media Studies, Area Studies, Urban Studies, Cultural Studies, etc. These and other multidisciplinary study areas, whilst still clearly having the need for the expertise of specialists in the relevant discrete disciplines, also rely upon the experience of some academics who have worked in two or three different disciplines. Without such minds, aware of links of concepts and ideas across disciplines, it is not possible to give a full coherence to the picture which would otherwise be fragmentary—a jigsaw puzzle with missing pieces.

It is important to underline the distinction between the terms 'multidisciplinary' and 'interdisciplinary' as they are sometimes confused. Multidisciplinarity implies the meeting of academic areas within a wider thematic context, each area remaining essentially discrete in terms of teaching. In such cases it is the student who is expected to forge the links across subjects. By contrast, interdisciplinarity implies extensive experience gained by a single teacher/academic of two or more distinct areas of knowledge at a level where professional expertise and judgement can be brought to bear on the conjunction of those disciplines. Here the process of linking is initiated in the teacher.

Teachers who move into interdisciplinary work inevitably come into contact with those from other disciplines who are following the same path. In many cases they discover common ground: they come to represent a human parallel of the classic Venn diagram. If sufficient numbers find a common set of objectives, a new subject grouping is the likely result. Such intersections of interdisciplinary work may lead to the establishment of a new polydiscipline. The idea is by no means revolutionary: many now well-established academic disciplines, notably in the sciences, came into existence in this way—for example, radio astronomy and molecular biology.

The move towards interdisciplinarity can prove problematic for the individual. The acquisition of a reasonable level of expertise in a second or even third discipline is an extremely time-consuming, not to say demanding undertaking. It inevitably leads to a notable reduction in the time spent working in the 'home' discipline. This gives some foundation for the view held by many academics that such activities can only result in a dilution of the specialist nature of the discipline. But herein lies the true central issue. Are academic disciplines truly 'specialist' in the sense of being totally discrete? In one sense clearly they are, but any discipline ultimately suffers from total isolation.

Musicians in Higher Education are placed in a potentially more extreme position with regard to information technology than their colleagues in other humanities disciplines. A new form of music industry has appeared in the past ten years which is based almost entirely on digital technology. Furthermore, it has grown with such rapidity, being backed by powerful commercial forces, that it has taken many music academics unawares. However, this new digital technology has provided hitherto unattainable powers of sound synthesis and processing which have given access to a world of sound unimaginable twenty years ago. Likewise, the use of computers by music analysts and music psychologists has made it possible to venture into critical areas of music study which were literally impossible to enter previously.[1] The lessons being learned by musicians in the new technological developments in their subject may well be of value to those working in other disciplines as new technologies appear in the coming years.

[1] Any issue over the past five years of *Journal of Music Theory, Computer Music Journal, Music Psychology, Music Perception*, etc., contains one or more articles in the various fields of Music Science.

The expansion of music technology and of the use of computers in many branches of music analysis and research has resulted in the need for the involvement of a number of additional disciplines to unite and cohere research, which in turn has led to the creation of an overall polydisciplinary grouping that has become known (principally in the United States) as Music Science. In order for an individual to venture into this discipline it is regarded as a prerequisite to possess a good undergraduate or graduate qualification both in music and in computer science. In addition a sound knowledge of musical acoustics and digitised sound is expected, plus a respectable working knowledge of one or more of the 'adjuncted' disciplines. The list of these is comparatively long and includes musical analysis, psychoacoustics, psychology of music, linguistics, artificial intelligence, and electronic engineering. Clearly this is attainable only by the individual being willing to devote much time and effort over a period of some years.

Such are the demands of any polydisciplinary area that great determination is needed on the part of the individual to make any headway. In any such undertaking, further study supplants research as the primary activity for considerable periods of time. All those academics who have educated themselves in the use of a computer in order to achieve a subject-oriented objective will be well aware of this fact. But in so doing, the teacher also regains the experience of being a student in an unfamiliar area of study, at the same time exercising the primary process of student-centred learning: discovery of the essentials of a subject, with little or no tutorial assistance.

This chapter will thus concern itself with three main issues:

1. the perception of interdisciplinarity within academe and the identifiable need to consider it as being the remit of some academics in the future, together with the implications of this for arts and humanities disciplines;

2. the impact of the technology of the music industry upon musicians and music academics;

3. changes brought about by new digital technology upon some aspects of teaching and research in Higher Education, the sheer diversity of potential disciplines involved, and the need for the return by some academics to the once widely accepted role of polymath as exemplified in the recently created polydiscipline of Music Science.

2 Attitudes to Interdisciplinarity

Much of academe still seems to harbour a very real suspicion of interdisciplinarity. The idea of gaining expertise in selected aspects of several disciplines is often seen as being beneficial to students but not to teachers/academics. As has been stated earlier, this is often perceived as a dilution of the potency of an academic in the principal 'home' subject. In other words, multidisciplinarity (achieved by con-joining discrete disciplines under the umbrella of a course outline, but still keep-ing them essentially isolated) is often preferred to interdisciplinarity (achieved by gathering and correlating facts, ideas and concepts across disciplines that in 'real life' do have substantial effects upon and relationship with one another), especially when the latter requires individual academics to step firmly outside their own declared disciplines. It would appear that a dual standard is being applied. According to this viewpoint, students may be actively encouraged to stretch their minds across and between disciplines, but the academic must remain chaste in the purity of the discipline—better still if it is further refined to a sub-discipline.

This dual standard at times exhibits an almost nineteenth century Romantic admiration of great breadth of capability, exemplified by the salutary description of a colleague as 'a true Renaissance man,' whilst at the same time advocating (often narrow) subject specialism as the major (perhaps only) path to the furthering of universal knowledge and the academic success of the individual. A similar dualism of attitude condemns the person who shows shifting but absorbed interest in a variety of traditional disciplines (applying labels such as 'grasshopper mind'), whilst at the same time showing great respect for someone capable of identifying links both within and across disciplines which others have simply not been able to see due to the narrow viewpoint of their own particular specialism (describing such a person, after de Bono's term, as a 'gifted lateral thinker'). Until the late seventeenth century the highest praise for any well educated man was to be described as a polymath. Any day-to-day reference to da Vinci, Galileo, Newton, Locke, or Descartes still calls forth no little respect, yet how many happily identify with da Vinci the engineer or Newton the music theorist?

Likely Origins of Attitudes

Let us briefly examine the provenance of the single subject specialism ideal. Perhaps the attitudes relating to subject insularity began with the splitting of the Seven Liberal Arts and Sciences into the Quadrivium of Sciences (Arithmetic, Geometry, Music, and Astronomy) and the Trivium of Arts (Grammar, Rhetoric, and Logic) during the late Renaissance. Notably here, Music is categorised as a Science whilst the Arts are, interestingly, all word-based disciplines. However, it was still expected that any educated man would acquaint himself with the essentials of all these disciplines during his lifetime. The seventeenth century re-classification of disciplines into Arts and Sciences was based on concepts very similar to the Primary and Secondary qualities of Descartes—i.e. the exactly quantifiable versus the non-quantifiable. One interesting by-product of this was that Music moved into the classification of Arts.

Francis Bacon, in his re-classification of areas of knowledge and of academic disciplines, produced a re-vitalisation of attitudes to the pursuit of knowledge. His insistence upon the need for the 'operative' as well as the 'speculative' approach was no small factor in the establishment of empirical approaches and of scientific method in general. The images presented in his fantasy of Salomon's House (in *New Atlantis*, 1624) led to the formation of the Royal Society in London and to the adoption of the idea of research institutes. It is often said that Bacon invented the idea of division of labour, but this is to overlook a vitally important part of his vision: the concept of the 'common culture.' In this view, each individual should be encouraged to contribute to the total culture by exercising a specialism, but also to be versed in a variety of other skills and disciplines. This, he argues, leads to a society where knowledge is shared in a way which encourages the fruitful interaction of ideas, as well as to a society full of awareness of the world around it.

The compilation of encyclopaedias in the eighteenth century, as well as having the explicit objective of demystifying knowledge, reflected the belief that at least the greater part of human knowledge could be set down in a single book, albeit in many volumes. In the event it led to the realisation that no one man could ever hope to encompass even the essentials of the major disciplines in a single lifetime: the adoption of absolute subject specialisms was then perceived as being inevitable. This is not to say that specialisation was a new phenomenon: clearly it had been common practice for centuries. The important change lay in questioning whether any variety of disciplines should be encompassed by one scholar. By the early nineteenth century the science of Physics had become so extensively developed in content and so complex in its concepts as to call for total devotion to its study in order to master the science.

It is generally acknowledged that the science of Physics was the first discipline to demand total specialisation. Throughout the nineteenth century it led, perhaps dominated, first the sciences and then all academic disciplines in terms of attitudes to study and scholarship. Other sciences, such as Chemistry, Biology and Astronomy, together with Mathematics became regarded in the same light by the end of the century. From the middle of the century there was a gradual escalation of specialisation accompanied by the creation of subdisciplines within the sciences. This was soon echoed in the arts, not so much by an actual necessity as by a perceived necessity in order to maintain some kind of parity with what had become regarded as the inherently more 'revered' sciences.

In parallel to this gradual realignment of the more traditional disciplines, from the mid-seventeenth century an increasing number of more practical (i.e. 'artisan') disciplines have been admitted to a position of academic respectability, including such strange bedfellows as Art History, Music Analysis, Literary Criticism, various forms of Engineering and latterly Business Studies and the Social Sciences. Each has consciously built its own tradition of scholarship and has followed the trend towards specialisation, often echoing the external trappings of the 'hard' sciences in the apparent belief that the application of 'scientific method' legitimatises a discipline.

The growth of subdisciplines of considerable size means that now, more than ever before, no one person can hope to be fully versed in even a single discipline.

A Contrary View

Admitting this to be true, it is also a fact of life that we all, as human beings, acquire partial ability in a great variety of knowledge and skills in order to make sense of life and to survive. It is surely not defensible to argue that we have the need to acquire the full 'content' of any particular body of knowledge in order to make use of it in other circumstances. Specialists in every discipline will always be needed in order to ensure the stability and progress of human knowledge, but we must not infer from this that single subject specialism should be the norm. The object of study at undergraduate level need not (and perhaps should not) always be single-subject based. The number of our graduates who today move on to pursue postgraduate work in a discipline that is largely, even totally different to their first degree is on the increase, the traditional D.Phil being replaced by a Masters in a second discipline plus publications in two or more fields. It hardly needs stressing that the demands of industry and the enterprise culture of our time call for some substantial rethinking, in which an interdisciplinary approach needs must play a significant part.

The Impact of the Music Industry on Educational Needs

Musicians, like their colleagues in art and design, have been faced in the past ten years with a whole new technology that has changed radically the very nature of certain areas of their subject. The popular music press stresses the large turnover of the world music industry (especially in the United States and Japan). Though some of this is accounted for by tape, black disc and compact disc recording, it is nevertheless clear that one major area of the industry is the production of microprocessor driven systems for composition and performance of pop/rock music: on the one hand, the ubiquitous synthesiser and drum machine and the associated new technology for sound sampling and manipulation (represented by the latest keyboards and effects units); on the other, the development of highly sophisticated software packages and of new hardware music add-ons for low-cost microcomputer systems. The relation of this to the rapidly growing music leisure industry largely accounts for the great commercial success of the products. However, there are problems in the industry which arise from shortcomings in the prior education of its personnel.

The implementation of MIDI (Musical Instrument Digital Interface) from 1983 brought digitally controlled music into very wide currency. Yet even at a comparatively early stage, problems with the MIDI system came to light.[2] Its extremely low clock-rate of data transmission (31.25 KBaud) has already been found to be unequal to many musical tasks in performance. More importantly, the keyboard-based event/data structure of keypress transmission is quite unsuitable for many musical purposes. The cause of this was almost certainly a lack of foresight as to the long-term implications should the system be taken up by the wider community

[2] As examples of specifically identified problems see Jordan (1986) or Moore (1988).

of musicians. Being originally designed as a quick and easy 'communications system' for the electronic instruments used by rock musicians, its designers sadly failed to foresee the implications of the new 'electronic rock' and the demands that it might place on the technology. In addition, certain fundamental musical shortcomings, such as the inability to transmit legato playing and note-slurring, are evident and tend to indicate an over-simplistic approach to the musical needs of rock in the 80s. The subsequent enthusiastic adoption of MIDI by musicians outside the rock world placed a further burden upon the implementation of the system which it was unable to support. One may well argue that the system was never designed to meet such needs: one can only wonder why. This might well be used as an example to highlight the need for a greater involvement of practising trained musicians in hi-tech fields.

Computers as such have also come into their own in the pop/rock music field in yet another guise, that of sequencing packages – a composing tool for non-literate musicians. (The latter term is not used in any way pejoratively. It refers to those musicians who have no use for traditional music notation, nor the concepts that arise from it, in their music—and such musicians are in the majority.) These often highly complex and expensive software packages, running on microcomputers such as Atari ST, IBM PC, and Apple Macintosh, offer elaborate composition tool-boxes which are currently being used by a very large market of player/composers. A significant number of these have been designed by musically aware persons in the industry, but their total reliance on the MIDI transmission system weakens the potential power of these systems considerably. The training of a new breed of 'music technologist' is an immediately identifiable need for the new music industry.

Digital recording has rapidly become the accepted norm for high quality sound reproduction. The arrival of PCM and digital mastering (sometimes using the latest generations of totally digital sound processing consoles—such as the highly complex Neve mixing desk system in use at CTS, BBC, Tape One, etc.) has set a new standard with the CD (compact disc) that no part of the industry can now afford to avoid implementing to the full. Yet even in this area of the music industry there are still far too few technically trained musicians available to exercise their skills where they are greatly needed. This is especially true in the design and operation of facilities in both hard- and software.

This list represents only the main features of the multi-million dollar music industry, and identifies the significant shortage of technologically expert music personnel. The present-day music industry is formidable in its power to remould the very content and performance style of music. It is therefore reasonable to argue that it ought to be the responsibility of the institutions of Higher Education to provide the major share of such personnel.

Reactions in Higher Education

Some academic musicians have made the effort to come to terms with the processor-based systems that now dominate the music industry. Others, in some ways understandably, have shied away from any involvement with the digitally-oriented side of music, seeing it as having the potential to depreciate musicianly values and the human qualities of their art. True, it does have such a potential, but all the more so if well trained musicians fail to involve themselves in it.

It is true that the more esoteric areas of digitally produced music have gained substantial ground in the universities, as have analysis of music by computer and computer-based experiment and analysis in music psychology. This, however, is not a wide enough basis to prepare future graduates to deal with the demands of the music industry and profession. Yet the music industry is in need of real musicians with some substantial technical understanding in order to be able to develop existing music hardware and software along the best possible artistic lines and to take a proper part in the evolution of new and musicianly-oriented concepts in processor-based music systems.

The fact that much of the new technology is associated with vernacular musics (primarily with rock and 'pop') has served to widen the gap between many of our musicians in Higher Education and the developments within the industry. As has long been the case, the more 'traditional' music departments frequently regard these musics as being beyond their remit, though even this view is in the process of change.

However, a positive side to this is now emerging: discussions are now to be found in the pop/rock technology journals[3] couched in surprisingly similar terms to those in the 'learned' journals. It would seem that the nature of the problems may now bring previously disparate and mutually distancing musicians very much closer together in outlook, thus forming a common set of objectives based on the exploration of the full capabilities of processor-controlled music systems and on overcoming the limitations imposed by them.

3 Interdisciplinarity in Music: The Case of Music Science

Recognizing this difficulty, the fact remains that significant numbers of academic musicians have become involved in a variety of computer-based aspects of music and have then found the need to venture into other disciplines (notably certain areas of psychology and linguistics, as well as computer engineering) in order to achieve their ends. In the same way, some psychologists have chosen music as their primary target for the investigation of perception and cognition. This partial merging of disciplines is not a new phenomenon, but is one that seems to be steadily on the increase. In the United States the establishment of Music Science in some Universities as a recognised polydisciplinary area[4] indicates some

---

[3] For example, *Sound on Sound, Music Technology, Guitarist, Keyboards Today.*
[4] For example, University of California at San Diego and Cornell University.

acceptance of the idea, but also reflects a certain uneasiness felt by academics at being seen to be involved in several disciplines. At the Second International Conference for Science and Music (City University, London, September 1987) the topic of interdisciplinarity was raised and led to some very pointed discussion. It was clearly the experience of colleagues, in the UK, the USA and elsewhere, that lip service seems to be paid to the concept by encouraging teachers to 'seek links with other disciplines,' but that any suggestion that academics might possess (or gain) additional expertise straddling two or more disciplines tends to be regarded with some suspicion and may even meet with marked hostility. This has led like-minded academics to draw together in an attempt to form new polydisciplines, of which Music Science is an example. Such developments call for serious consideration of the matter of interdisciplinarity by academics generally.

4 Other Uses of Music Technology in the Universities

Looking towards the use of microprocessor-driven music systems in the world of electroacoustic music, extremely expensive systems have been put together in the professional music studios (such as those at IRCAM in Paris). Most music departments in universities now attempt to provide reduced (ie., resource led) versions of such studios for electroacoustic composition purposes, using some kind of admixture of analog recording with digital sound creation and manipulation. Those with extensive budgets tend to employ the (in)famous and costly Fairlight sound synthesis system or the even more costly Emulator or Synergy machines.[5] It is an ironic fact however, and a spur to re-examine some of our attitudes, that the majority of these very expensive and highly versatile music machines are owned by successful rock musicians.

Many music departments in Higher Education are at work with a whole variety of computer tools for other musical purposes: music composition and analysis, music psychology, sound synthesis, sound analysis (both spectral and event-led) etc.

Regrettably there also appears to be a fairly widespread use of computers simply to reinforce more traditional aspects of the music curriculum. It is of concern that in some cases little use is made of the computer in some departments beyond

[5] The three systems mentioned here are all in a price range in six figures (Pounds Sterling). As such, their use has become somewhat divisive in that they mark off the 'haves' from the 'have-nots' among departments of music. The Fairlight system was the first large-scale computer synthesis and composition machine and as such has always been strongly oriented towards a 'computer scientist' approach to sound. This, combined with the high cost, has tended to give the system an elitist image. The development of moderately powerful systems on microcomputers in recent years has led to a gradual increase in the use of low-cost computer music systems by academic departments and by composers. One attempt to universalise and standardise a system for practising electro-acoustic musicians has been the establishment of the Composers' Desktop Project at York. This independent group is gradually building up a complex but low-cost system based around the Atari 1040 ST intended to give composers a home-based system which is capable of handling the formative stages of a new piece. The resulting material is then carried on disc to a professional computer sound studio for completion at the necessary higher quality.

music theory drills, 'harmony exercises' which are now virtually irrelevant to music training needs, and the almost equally questionable task of aural training and testing. In this there is a sobering reminder of the early use of computers in Computer-Assisted Language Learning where it was often remarked that the introduction of computers had taken modern language teaching back thirty years.

The enormous capability of microelectronics to provide music composition tools is being ignored in some institutions. Three causes might be posited for this: lack of finance, lack of expertise and deliberate resistance. The low cost of musically valuable systems hosted by standard microcomputers (such as the Hybrid Music System with the BBC Master) must dismiss the first of these in all but exceptional circumstances. The other two suggested causes indicate the need for education, albeit in a different sense in each case.

If one accepts that the true functions of music are, de facto, creation and performance, with analysis and theoretical and historical studies supports to the art rather than its substance, then this fact is (or should be) of the deepest concern to the music educator. This latter statement would be readily accepted by all musical academics in 'traditional' musical contexts. It is not yet accepted in relation to the use of digital technology.

5 Music Information Theory

The rapidly evolving area of Music Information Theory calls for multiple skills in its practitioners that at present are rare—in other words a specific grouping of a number of the disciplines identified above as comprising Music Science. In Britain there already exist a number of music psychologists who devote much time to research into music perception, cognition and the like, using computers and employing either artificial intelligence or music control languages.[6] But there are still very few instances of truly interdisciplinary academics who possess the combination of a professional music training (including acoustics and psycho-acoustics) with computing, who also have competence in psychology of music, audiometrics, or linguistics. Yet such combinations of discipline are necessary to follow these lines of investigation. If this is not realised, research will have a tendency to fracture into discrete areas with minimal contact between them in terms of understanding. We now have the tools and techniques to expand the understanding of the art of music in ways never before possible. We are more deficient in human resources than in technological resources to carry out the task.

Music Information Theory is presently striving towards a deeper understanding of the two principal acts of music: composition and performance. The nature of the prescriptive and descriptive score[7] is being closely examined in relation to live

[6] For example, Eric Clarke (City University), Ian Cross (Oxford University), Robert West (London University)

[7] 'Prescriptive Score' refers to a music score written down in order to lead to a performance. The music comes into existence after the act of notating. 'Descriptive Score' refers to the notation of music that is created by the performers (most forms of folk, jazz and rock exemplify this in Western music).

performance with the assistance of digital technology. The concept of quantisation in traditional Western music notation is being thoroughly re-examined, as it has become a central issue in the digital translation of live performance and in the encoding of pre-composed music for digitally based instruments. This area of Music Science has almost unlimited possibilities for those willing to make themselves capable of venturing into it.

Thus there are two important reasons for us to encourage those who wish to venture into Music Science. First, it has the potential for significant advances in the understanding of the art of music that are not otherwise attainable. Secondly, the possibilities for industrial employment of such a 'product' of our future Higher Education system justifies the time and effort spent in terms of the enterprise culture.

6 Wider Contexts of Interdisciplinarity

These general concepts needs must apply to other disciplines too. The rapid growth of the application of digital technology to almost every form of academic and industrial advance must call for the same breadth of abilities from at least a proportion of the practitioners of every discipline. For a considerable time there existed a belief that 'pure' computer scientists could (and perhaps should) provide for the needs of other disciplines that needed computer applications. The greatest difficulties always arose in communicating the needs of a wide range of disciplines to the computer specialists.

In recent years, isolated academics from almost every humanities discipline have become involved in computer-based work and have soon found it necessary to come to terms with the technology themselves rather than to rely on others. At the same time there has been a need in many cases to venture into other facets of computer use, such as artificial intelligence. Some parts of every discipline also have recourse to quite dissimilar disciplines in order to fill out a part of the total picture. With so much activity across what can only be regarded as the artificial boundaries of 'subject areas' it is now essential to re-examine these boundaries in the light of all the foregoing arguments and to positively encourage those who are already engaged in the broadening of subject horizons. This in turn calls for two things: an understanding of and empathy with those who wish to become polymaths, and the enthusiasm of a number of people to accept the challenge of mastering several disciplines in turn.

This is an attempt to record the events of the music on paper post hoc, either for others to play or to allow analysis of the music. The music exists before the notation, which itself provides an inaccurate record due to the rigidly quantised nature of Western music notation. The comparison of the two forms of score with the live performances associated with them leads to deep and complex questions about the nature of both composition and performance.

7 Teaching, Learning and Research

The implications for teaching and research are very positive. Specialists will continue to work in discrete areas to advance and transmit detailed knowledge. Polymaths will be able to effect links between disciplines and bring relevant advances of one discipline to bear on another. New polydisciplines are a likely consequence of this.

The generation of students now entering Higher Education will contain a noticeable number of computer-literate, if not computer-expert individuals. This, in fact, has already begun. In many cases the students will know more than their mentors: most of us have had some evidence of this already. In Britain the concepts behind the GCSE and behind patterns of A/S and A Level choice are already pointing to a greater breadth, but not dilution, of study perspectives. Increasing numbers of mature students are entering Higher Education, bringing wider experiential backgrounds into the learning/teaching situation.

Modularisation, unitisation and semestrisation of courses is on the increase and promises to be the principal pattern in the greater part of Higher Education for the next decade and beyond. In this scenario, at least the underlying objectives of the 'University Without Walls' movement that was current in the mid 1970s may well become a reality in the mid 1990s. Perhaps individuality of knowledge groupings from person to person will characterise higher learning in the coming century as it did in the seventeenth century. We shall need as diverse a pattern of thinking among academics as will become the norm among students.

16

Modern Studies of Modern Languages

Frank Knowles and Agnes Kukulska-Hulme

1 Introduction

The modern languages, or foreign languages (FL) teaching scene was probably
the first discipline in the arts and humanities to be affected in a mass way, over
a quarter of a century ago, by technology for teaching purposes—in the shape
of the language laboratory, with its dual profile of hardware and software. Such
devices became more or less ubiquitous in tertiary, secondary and, to some extent,
even in primary education. Unfortunately, they also rapidly came to be seen as
enslaving rather than liberating agents, primarily because of their almost universal
use as rigid skills-trainers. This is a danger which continues today to confront
methodologists and those who design and author instructional materials which
utilise a specific and, prima facie, 'alien' delivery system. What is, of course,
important is how to achieve smoothly the necessary transition from pencil and
paper, plus chalk and talk, to a learning environment which is perceived as natural
and stimulating by those using it, both teacher and taught.

It is very clear on all counts today that there is enormous scope for the involvement of computers and IT more generally in the business of foreign-language
teaching and research. Even talk of a 'redefinition' of the whole field is no longer
merely hyperbolic—it has already taken place, at least in a technical sense: new,
more expansive boundaries have been set and new scope has been created. It is
now up to those directly involved to mark out this new territory and make it arable
and capable of bearing the fruits which need to be cultivated on it. This challenge
is already finding its champions.

As is well known, computers have been assisting FL teachers and scholars in
their work for some very considerable time. Now, however, this minority stands
to become the overwhelming majority as the ergonomics, economics, appropriacy
and cost-effectiveness of using computers are accepted by the FL confraternity
at large, with all the multifarious activities it pursues and the profiles it assumes.
It would be wrong to claim, however, that all is over bar the shouting! There are
many legitimate questions which need to be asked and which are being asked. The
grand lines of this debate can be summarised as follows: does the involvement of
computers lead to new insights, to qualitatively and substantively new techniques,
in fact, to a paradigm shift? What are the 'before and after' pictures of the

discipline like? Are the computational methods being used not just new in the domain of their application but also, perhaps, innovative from the point of view of computer science itself? If so, then both the donor and receptor disciplines stand to be affected in terms of their own evolution to fuller maturity.

2 Computers and Language Studies

In the field of research computer techniques were applied to language-oriented problems very early indeed: the commissioning of electronic devices—the progenitors of today's computers—and the use of algorithmic, statistical and pattern-matching methods in the field of cryptology, notably cryptanalysis, is attested as far back as 1942. In the early years of peace after the Second World War significant programmes of research into machine translation were initiated and pursued, with a seemingly impossible mixture of ingenuousness and disingenuousness on the part of the researchers involved—these particular efforts have experienced their troughs and crests ever since then and are today finally assuming a more realistic posture. This comes at a time when the pace of hardware and software advances has quickened and when translators and other 'language mediators' have shown themselves much more willing than previously to espouse the rough-and-ready working practices the use of such machine aids entails. Computer-assisted textual studies (Cameron, et al., 1986), ranging from 'straight-up' concordancing to stylostatistic investigations, are now regarded by many linguists and literary scholars as routine working methods—computer assistance here has origins dating back well over a generation. The methods themselves, of course, antedate by a considerable period the advent of the technology that now makes the business of using them so unencumbered by logistic constraints. Information Science has in like manner long been in the business of designing and implementing computer software and systems involving natural language processing for the important purposes of information search and retrieval systems.

Let us, however, come back centre stage to FL: the study of modern languages—we must not forget that English is a foreign language for millions and millions of people, by the way!—is, like any other academic discipline, an amalgam of three components: firstly, intellectual reasoning and general cerebration; secondly, a database, in this case, that which is particular to the language involved; and thirdly, the need to develop a set of very specific but nonetheless multifunctional skills. One is strongly tempted to add in an affective dimension in view of the fact that it is impossible to undertake the long-term and committed study of a foreign language without simultaneously developing feelings of affection for the object of study. In the ultimate, this process is, of course, referred to as 'going native'! However, the relativities between the above three main components are rather different in FL learning than is the case in most other subjects.

Firstly, the skills effort is a major undertaking: for progression in language skills alone, ab initio to interpreting standard, something of the order of 3000 hours of systematic instruction (75 weeks at 5 days per week, for 8 hours per day), coupled with extensive practice and private study, is necessary. In the framework of university studies, such a regimen is not really feasible and recourse is taken to passable alternatives, such as an aggregate of, say, 1000 hours of concentrated instruction alongside a 'year out' plus two long vacations abroad for the students: the 'stage' overseas yields something like 8000 waking hours (70 weeks at 16 hours per day) of 'exposure' which is episodic, rather than systematic. Pedagogically, these two learning styles are at opposite ends of a spectrum: the ideal case would be a much more integrated and judiciously planned mixture of the two approaches. Secondly, the database of a language is—to use modern parlance—'hairy:' the ratio of system to data is small. Thirdly, the intellectual component too has three dimensions to it: the language itself; the people who speak it; and the country or countries where it is spoken. One ought perhaps to add the value derived from deliberate or involuntary—often the latter—comparisons and contrasts of the unfamiliar with the familiar. Analogies with other subjects are not easy to adduce but one of the more successful ones would liken the study of foreign languages to that of music: students of foreign languages must, on this analogy, be both expert instrumentalists and composers.

The aims of foreign language teaching can be expressed on both a lofty and a utilitarian level. On the one hand, the task is to impart to students such cognitive knowledge and skills as will enable them to function not only as effective communicators but also as authentic and empathetic partners in their dealings, professional and personal, with citizens of foreign countries. On the other hand, it is necessary for students to learn how to focus their aim, often how to narrow their 'field of fire,' so to speak, and how precisely to optimise the returns on the effort they expend. Along with the grand strategy must go a set of severely practical goals—these are to some extent a matter of quite deliberate personal choice and such choices can lead to the exclusion or severe 'deprioritisation' of areas which might, prima facie, be considered absolutely essential: is an oral command, or translating, or area studies a high priority or not, in given circumstances? Although the foreign-language arena can thus appear to be very diversified, often tempting students to dissipate their efforts, there is a growing call for an appropriate focus to be created and emphasis placed today in higher education on the various professional contexts for which students need to be intellectually and practically prepared.

The abiding tasks of FL research are expressible in terms which, mutatis mutandis, are equally valid for other subject disciplines: capturing new data; transforming such data into utilisable information and systematic results; developing new methodological tools; demonstrating applications and applicability; extending the power of analysis; facilitating the process of synthesis; and (re-)evaluating the paradigm, both internally and in terms of its interstices and interface with other areas of academic endeavour. One particular effort which may be more characteristic of FL work—although ready comparisons with mathematics are possible—is the definition and elaboration of useful FL subsets for 'outsiders.'

Some remarks about postgraduate research seem apposite at this point. Humanities research, never properly supported by a designated research council, is under very considerable pressures at the present time. Symptoms of these pressures are, for instance, the '36-month Ph.D' and the recent suggestion by the British Academy that undergraduate degrees in the humanities may no longer be preparing students for immediate entry into postgraduate research work. One corollary of the present situation—irrespective of how substantive and substantiated the British Academy's worries may be—is that attention needs to be urgently devoted to the design and the implementation of suitable, comprehensive and systematic research methods courses for postgraduate students in the humanities. Such courses will involve computers in a dual way: as important objects of attention in their own right and also as delivery vehicles for much of the content of these courses.

The working and study world of foreign languages has always been extensively variegated along two dimensions. The first dimension is, of course, dictated by the fact that there are many different foreign languages: the universals of language study, carefully distilled by linguists from all of these tongues, can act as a framework and reference point, but often such an approach is, effectively speaking, submerged in the structure and data of individual language systems. The other dimension is that of the chosen focal point: is the aim to retain a strictly linguistic, almost introverted, focus, or is it to explore a given speech community's cultural manifestations, phenomena which are sui generis, idiosyncratic, holistic and resistant to generalisation? Or is it to examine in detail the realia of the countries involved, their organisation and infrastructure, their economic, political or geopolitical significance? Linguists would aver that activities of this last-mentioned variety can themselves only be truly understood and mastered via the language in which the given society operates and formulates its collective wisdom. One quite visible trend today in higher education centres concerned with foreign language teaching, learning and research is a reduced degree of introversion and a commensurately growing tendency, proceeding via cross-disciplinarity, to interdisciplinarity—this is being accompanied pari passu by the espousal of cross-national contrastive studies and by the emergence of internationalist methodologies. This is a very important role for the humanities to play.

3 The Development of Computing

It is now apposite to say something about computers themselves: since their advent in the 1940's computers have progressively revolutionised very many areas of human activity. For scholars of the natural sciences, engineering, medicine, as well as the social sciences and humanities the computer has, in varying degrees, transformed working methods. In some cases, such as meteorology, the transformation is what might literally be called cataclysmic: professional methods used prior to the deployment of computers are antediluvian compared with what they are today. There is, quite simply, no real basis of comparison. In other disciplines, particularly in linguistics and its satellite activities, the desirability of calling on computer assistance has been a more gradual process of perception and movement, and the effects have been commensurately less pervasive in their scope and inexorability. Today, as noted above, more and more scholars in the humanities are coming round to the conviction that they too have a definite stake in the information technology (IT) revolution; they are increasingly amenable to the idea of using computers, not just for the purposes of logistic efficiency—in teaching, for instance—but also in order to be less vulnerable to the dangers of subjectivity in their research findings and analyses. Humanities scholars, including linguists, have necessarily been affected too by the more general process of mathematicisation, or at least formalisation, which has, over the thirty to forty years, exerted such a far-reaching influence on scholarly thinking about economic and sociological phenomena.

What then is the nature of this machine, the technological device called the computer, which has transformed so many areas of life? In its essentials, the computer's importance derives from two simple, easily understandable and easily feasible notions: firstly, the possibility of coding utterly diverse types of data in an electronically reliable and uniquely identifiable manner; secondly, the ability to submit such data to programs, to process it—whatever that term may mean in the actuality of many different applications and contexts—and to output 'results' with a consistency and a speed which are far in excess of the capacity of the human brain aided by human motor skills. The use of the word 'data' in this formulation needs to be glossed further: there is a special and crucially important type of data without which computers would be virtually emasculated—data in the form of operational instructions which are intended to be applied to 'real' data, in the normal sense of that term. This feature is often referred to as the 'stored program' concept: if the word 'program' designates, as one of its meanings, an ordered sequence of activities, viewable as an entity, then it is clear that in computer parlance such a definition is especially apt. Computer programs, at least in their 'classical' guise, are indeed ordered sequences of steps, either commands or conditions, which are executed according to the logical flow of the programmer's intentions. Programmers must predict, if their programs are to be useful, certain logical options which can be selected according to given criteria testable within the processing environment itself, that is, at a remove in time and space from the programmer's original conception. This is the essence of the so-called algorithmic method. In other words, the aim of those who use computers to assist them with their work is quite literally to analyse problems, to break them down into sub-problems and discrete steps so as then to be able to synthesise solutions in such a way that no further human intervention is required because the human, preferably algorithmic thought-process and problem-solving strategy have been captured and can be perpetuated at will in a computational environment.

At the present time an important evolution is taking place, as we all know, with regard to the methodology of computer programming. Although traditional methods which have withstood the test of time, are still predominant, many efforts are under way to develop further and to enhance programming languages which have a radically different philosophy. If traditional languages such as FORTRAN, AL-GOL68, PL/I or PASCAL, are characterised as 'imperative' languages—because the individual program statements give orders—then languages of a more recent design, such as PROLOG, can be classified as 'declarative and interrogative:' the essence of programming in such languages is to establish a set of entities, to assign their attributes as appropriate, to declare relationships holding between the entities, and subsequently to interrogate the resulting environment in order to elicit relationships not declared contiguously or not even declared at all, all as part of an analysis of truth-values and an enquiry into presuppositions and entailments. This is an important development in the humanities, not least in computational linguistics, because it dispenses with many of the constraints and artificialities of imperative language programming in favour of intuitively more satisfying and better matched methods for heuristically formulating and solving problems.

A further aspect of the always welcome evolution of computer programming techniques concerns the design of software tools and their functional appropriateness for particular types of user. There was a time when it was a reasonable assumption that anyone making use of a computer would have familiarity with standard software techniques, would even have a respectable grasp of the functional and technological details of machine architecture, and would possess programming skills of some sophistication. In other words, the computer's power was, by and large, accessible only to experts and aficionados who were, in their turn, made to put up with poor ergonomics, arcane software and atrocious documentation. Fortunately, such times are rapidly on the wane: there has been a major reorientation in the way software tools are designed—now a very high premium is placed on 'user-friendliness,' involving clear menus, pull-down windows, fail-safe procedures, etc. The so-called 'end-user' no longer needs to know how to program in order to make highly sophisticated use of most of what the information technology revolution has to offer. Developments of this sort have crucial benefits to offer FL specialists and it is to be hoped that they will soon enjoy an *embarras de richesses* as far as suitable and attractive hardware and software options are concerned. This happy situation is not with us yet, however. In order for it to transpire, some attitudes must change and some inhibitions must be overcome: IT must be courted rather than flirted with, and the engagement must lead to wedlock.

The mention of hardware is a pointer to the statement that hardware itself has undergone a process of rapid technological advance and diversification. It is still, of course, true that so-called mainframe computers are every bit as important as they always have been, even if they are in the nature of things bound to suffer from being available only to those with a certain amount of institutional support and personal determination. The real change has been the design and marketing of powerful machines of small physical dimensions which can be put to work on surprisingly realistic tasks against a capital outlay which is constantly decreasing. In other words, value for money gets better and better. This appears to be a trend which may well continue for the next decade at least. Hand in hand with the increasing power and sophistication of these so-called personal or desktop computers (PCs) has gone a commensurate enhancement of ancillary hardware such as visual display units (VDUs) and laser printers. The very logistics of work have been transformed by developments such as networking and distributed systems. It is true to say that today there are virtually no problem-solutions, known to be technologically feasible, which cannot be implemented on devices of the above sort. It is indeed a tenable view that computers—be they of the maxi, midi, mini or micro variety—have assumed a pre-eminence in technologically advanced societies which permeates those societies through and through, both predicating future prosperity and exercising a major influence as a new mass medium, not just on professional life but also on education and leisure. This facet of societal computerisation has great relevance to both the pragmatic and the cultural role of language outside the realm of higher educational institutions.

4 Information Technology and the Student

Let us now try to take a snapshot of the position of foreign-language staff and students insofar as they are actively able today to profit from the IT revolution. Obviously, almost everything depends on institutional support and that varies very much from institution to institution, and from country to country. The general picture in the advanced world is very encouraging, however. In the UK statements from bodies such as the University Grants Committee and the Computer Board are on record to the effect that there are specific and entirely valid computing requirements in the humanities area and that these requirements need to be accorded a proper priority in financial plans and budgets. From a resourcing point of view it must be remembered that one is always dealing with the threesome of hardware, software and humanware. The next question down is concerned with how whatever resources are available are partitioned and allocated—this has particular relevance to the perennial question of whether an institution should provide a central computing service alone, or encourage a distributed approach which, in its turn, gives rise to the option of going for non-mainframe solutions if they commend themselves. It is very clear that both approaches need to co-exist in most institutions, depending—obviously—on the portfolio of activities adjudged to have a high priority.

One of the abiding—and currently very topical—questions is differentiation of research and teaching, the former still quite largely mainframe-oriented, the latter profiled more towards multi-station workshops. The research infrastructure nearly always needs to be underpinned by suitable staffing levels, with a due complement of computer officers knowledgeable about and specialising in applications software. Another underpinning mechanism is, of course, electronic mail which makes feasible the sort of inter-institutional research effort and scholarly collaboration which is so characteristic of the humanities. A number of UK institutions of higher learning—notably universities of technology—now have

PC procurement policies based on the principle of a 'one-per-desk' provision for members of academic staff. This type of policy may, in its turn, be complemented by a 'one workstation per four or five students' approach, translated into suitable physical terms by extensive local area network facilities. Moreover, the days are surely not far off when it will be virtually de rigueur for all types of undergraduate students to acquire—at a suitable price—PCs for the duration of their courses.

What has just been said is probably a valid prescription or description for any humanities student—what, then, are the special factors which may apply to FL students? Firstly, FL students need and want to do FL word processing as well as working through the medium of English. 'Word processing' is, incidentally, a 'weaker' term than its French or German counterparts, 'traitement de texte' and 'Textverarbeitung,' respectively. What is really implied and striven for is an advanced L1/L2 (mother tongue/foreign language) writing environment of the sort now becoming commercially available and permitting a full range of text-based activities such as: full dictionary consultation (not mere 'spell checking'); indexing, concordancing, frequency tabulation; structuring ideas; text de- and re-construction, such as summarising and stylistic 'transposition,' for instance; document revision; on-screen text comparison; draft translation; stylistic monitoring, such as checking cohesive ties, etc.(Britton and Glynn, 1989). This amounts, of course, to the integration of the various tools needed at the 'writer's and translator's workbench.' The design of the physical bench itself, so to speak, needs much care and attention too. It is an unhappy accident that in so many respects—and in a wider sense too—computing software is so very Anglo-centric. This means that, in our local environment, it is necessary to go to great lengths to provide students—many of them actually from EEC countries—with facilities for working with foreign character-sets, with FL menus, with FL spelling-checkers and so on. In fact, they accumulate a lot of experience in doing that, not only at their university base but also in the professional placements which constitute an integral part of their programme of studies—in this instance it can amount to over 3000 hours of professional working time. It should, of course, be borne in mind that the majority of FL students at technological universities are studying on joint or combined honours programmes involving other disciplines, such as business studies, biology, or computer science.

However, there is more than mere word processing to the computing experience which FL students acquire (Chesters and Gardner, 1988): three other types of computing are involved. Arguably, the most important of all is database work. FL students are easily taught—via 'mini-dictionary' simulation—the fundamentals and the significance of database computing. They learn to appreciate why it may be significant in a special way that the modern French word for a computer is now 'ordinateur' rather than the previous term 'calculatrice'! In many cases students develop their own personal databases for use in other areas of their studies—the fact that more university libraries are by now fully computerised, offering electronic retrieval and title browsing, is an added bonus. In the very near future

FL—and other—students will be able to gain ready access to local and remote, proprietary and public-domain databases of a professional orientation to assist them in the extensive project work of a sociological, business studies or economics profile which forms an essential part of their studies. Such a development is already very much in train at Aston, for instance. Plans are also in hand there to introduce volunteer students to appropriate statistical packages and to provide them with the necessary training in statistics, in an attempt to open up yet further desirable professional options for them once they graduate. In all these areas of their work, FL students, for instance, can take on board more readily than most others the fact of life that there are important cross-national and cultural differentials in professional fields which might at first sight appear to be 100%-shared 'universes of discourse.' FL students can, moreover, even profit from acquainting themselves with spreadsheet software which can prove very suitable for project work on opinion polls or demographic and sociolinguistic studies, as well as in the orthodox areas of national and international accounting studied, for instance, by Aston students following a joint honours programme in International Business and Modern Languages.

The last type of computing—who is to say whether it is the most important or distinctive?—is computer-assisted language learning (CALL), particularly audio-enhanced computer-assisted language learning (AECALL: Hainline, 1987). Remarks earlier about whether the effect of computers or technology is to enslave or liberate are topical again here. Early CALL software was virtually vitiated by its severely didactic but anti-educational character and by the rigidity with which the computer remained 'in charge' of the learning session. Further drawbacks were the artificiality of the exercises and the ergonomically and pedagogically hampering effect of 'short response' drills, specifically designed to minimise the need for extensive keyboarded responses, given the error-proneness of that way of working. Today the so-called WIMP ('windows, icons, mouse, pointer') environment has removed that latter obstacle and the evolution of audio enhancement stands to see off the former problem as well. The synchronisation—a term used somewhat loosely—of video, audio and machine-readable material is a major qualitative jump in this type of software. The advent of flexible animated graphics software, of voice input and output is a culminating transformation which is yet before us, hopefully not too far into the future. One major application awaiting rapid development is the computer-assisted enhancement, for pedagogical purposes, of satellite TV broadcasts in foreign languages. These advances appear to be only just over the threshold (Stevens, Sussex, and Tuman, 1988).

It is a potentially contentious step to dwell on the detailed obligations placed on non-computer scientists such as FL students by reason of their involvement with computers and IT. Is it permissible, so to speak, to teach students of this profile how to use applications software without also informing them of the bases on which such software is actually engineered—or indeed without going the whole hog and teaching them how to program, at least on the level of prototyping solutions to linguistic and language-related problems? Human nature appears to dictate that one of the earliest reactions most people have to packaged software is an urge to test it to destruction! Moreover, there is an irresistible temptation to profit from the facilities offered by the host programming language of a database management system; programming suitable 'end-user macros' in spreadsheet software is also a natural desire for most users of such powerful and serviceable tools. It is a question that cannot be addressed properly here but there is scope enough to make the point—we base this on several years' experience of teaching programming to FL students—that between ten and twenty percent of such students have innate skills in this area which might otherwise remain latent in the absence of such instruction. The fact that a cadre of people versed in natural language applications programming thereby evolves may be seen as a bonus, given the pressing need for the development and codification of a linguistics or natural language processing (NLP) equivalent of the National Algorithms Group (NAG) in the field of computational mathematics, statistics and engineering etc.!

5 The Next Step

It is easy to enumerate, in outline, other important desiderata: software for assisting in and also investigating the twin processes of document generation and revision—if inferencing, coherence and the sequencing of both explicit and implicit cohesive ties can also be modelled, so much the better. The notion of language spreadsheets also needs to be pursued: changes to a 'formula cell' in such an environment could trigger off—or could call for interaction on—consequential changes of a morphological, syntactic or even stylistic nature in the linguistic material subordinate to or associated with that 'controller cell.' For example, a sentence presented to students for transformation—the students might even choose what sort of transformation!—would be accompanied by a separate cell containing details of the way in which the sentence is to be changed. In the simplest possible instance, say, of number concord students would then commence their task: the point is that the spreadsheet approach would then highlight and draw to students' attention, either immediately or in the appropriate sequence, all the points at which intervention was required.

On a higher level software tools to permit or to scrutinise reasoning by analogy or reasoning on the basis of incomplete information—so common in the humanities—is urgently needed; even a powerful and flexible ability to detect and examine the premises to arguments would be a great step forward. On the 'static' side of humanities computing the search should be urgently continued for methods to operationalise for on-line use reference works such as dictionaries, encyclopaedias and thesauri—methods should be evolved for building into such repositories a multiplicity of learning paths, adaptive ones if possible. In fact, in order to support language learning, particularly the productive use of language— whether the language involved is the mother tongue or a foreign language is neither here nor there—more must be known about the components of these activities. If computers are involved then it must be realised that they too are caught up in what we perceive to be the dilemma of language learning v. language acquisition. To what extent can an ostensibly holistic process like writing really and realistically be viewed as consisting of several aspects or be broken down into stages—which then somehow need to be re-aggregated? One has to keep looking beyond the mechanisation of old methods, e.g. traditional dictionary look-up, to new ways of supporting language use, such as conceptually-based dictionary organisation methods, integrated into text-processing software. Above all, it must be remembered that studying a language is to enter a process of learning about communication. Computers, of course, highlight certain aspects of communication, notably:

- interrogation skills: the way you ask a question determines the answer you get;

- relationships between entities: what turns data into information?

- the rigours of the written word: accuracy and logical organisation count a great deal;

- the complexity of linguistic skills: why can computers not translate fiction?

- conceptual difficulties: languages differ in the way in which they divide up the universe;

- presentation: the delivery of the message is as important as its content.

How many of the acknowledged achievements in computer-assisted FL work deserve to be called innovative in the sense that they have, in one way or another, redefined the FL area of the humanities? How many of the changes in prospect will have that effect? There is no doubt that the FL field is in the throes of a major transformation with respect to the ethos and the practicalities of its teaching, research and professional modalities. The sophisticated use of computers—and, rather more widely, of IT—has made possible significant qualitative advances: the ability to examine large quantities of intricately structured data, the ability to reduce the danger of subjectivity and unsupported value-judgement, the ability to conduct large-scale experimentation, the ability to detect structures and patterns in data which would surely have otherwise remained hidden, the ability to profit from algorithmic and statistical methods in the description and modelling of linguistic processes. These developments are now beginning to lead to the design and implementation of integrated utilities, such as the translator's and/or author's workbench and to the elaboration of lexical databases, configurable either as specialist's tools for the office or as public-domain utilities for the lounge.

The pace of development in innovative FL teaching at tertiary level—'modern studies of modern languages'—is very swift: those involved in it are clear that the FL paradigm has shifted, and not at all to the detriment of the foreign languages themselves. Computers have shown that they can be of enormous assistance with what was earlier referred to as the 'hairy FL database' and the skills acquisition exercise—work must obviously continue on both of these fronts. But should not attention be now focussed on how IT may be properly deployed to enhance the intellectual quality of FL and humanities work, and to promote the values to which all the humanities subscribe? One should not overlook the 'spin-off' benefits for academics in terms of a more sure-footed professionalism and the motivating awareness of the vital and exciting contribution to educational life which can and should flow from a new humanities, operating in tandem with information technology and, hopefully, hand in hand with other academic disciplines.

17

The Cognate Language Teacher: A Modern Approach to Teaching Medieval German

Felicity Rash

1 Introduction

The Cognate Language Teacher (CLT) is a computer program developed at West-field College, University of London. The project was funded by the Computer Board under the Computers in Teaching Initiative scheme. Its aim was to develop computer software which will assist a student to gain a reading knowledge of a language (the *target*), using a related language (the *cognate*) as a point of departure. The program is designed for use by students with or without previous computing experience. In the first instance, the two language pairs selected have been Catalan/Spanish and Middle High German/Modern German.

An *Authoring Package* has been designed to facilitate the preparation of new courses. In designing and preparing a course the tutor has full control over the way in which the various facilities are used. The program can be adapted for use at various levels of secondary and higher education. New texts can be read into the authoring program from a wordprocessing file or created directly onto the CLT. Within the authoring program the author creates the help details for each text by typing in details as they will be seen on screen by the student. On calling up the various types of help the author will be presented with an empty window in which to type. The help information can be recalled and edited at any time. Special characters can also be created.

This paper[1] will describe the Cognate Language Teacher, its aims and design, the facilities it provides and its use in the teaching of Middle High German. It will attempt to point out some of the major advantages and disadvantages of the CLT's features and record student reactions for each of these. It will address the question of the acceptability and effectiveness of the program—these do not always go hand in hand—and, finally, it will consider the scope of the CLT: its possible application

[1] I would like to thank Brian Murphy of the Computer Unit at Westfield College for his help in preparing this paper for publication.

to a wide variety of language combinations and its potential as a teaching aid in secondary and higher education.

2 Developing the CLT

The idea for a cognate language teacher originated at a research seminar in Westfield College's Department of Spanish. A need was felt for a system that would relieve lecturers of some of the time spent teaching the rudiments of a medieval language, which was related to a known modern language, when the ultimate object was to study the texts for their literary merit. It was thought that the computer could simulate the situation where the student proceeds through a text (perhaps an annotated edition) and seeks help from a dictionary, and where the lecturer intervenes from time to time to give information that illustrates the essential features of the language.

The CLT was developed with little reference to existing computer assisted language learning programs. No program was known that would solve the problems as perceived. The departments of Spanish and French use a number of CALL programs for remedial, reinforcement or revision work. In essence these are exercises that reinforce lessons taught in class. The programs normally require a considerable amount of interaction between the student and the program: the student types in answers to a variety of questions or fills in gaps in sentences and the program may mark the work and supply correct answers where necessary. Such programs are well suited to the revision of grammar and vocabulary and are ideally authored exclusively in the target language. Computer games, for example adventure games, are also popular, and are enjoyable to use as well as testing the student's ability to solve problems in a foreign language.

Most existing CALL programs assume students are learning a second language rather than a language which is cognate to one already known. The method of learning a cognate language is, in fact, quite different: teaching is highly specialized. It involves leading students on by deduction and inference to an understanding of the cognate language and its features. The student does not need to learn a totally new set of rules and vocabulary, but rather learns to compare the two cognate languages and work out the linguistic differences and similarities.

The CLT had to be quite different from existing programs that were in use in the College. The design team involved in the project had to grapple with the technical, pedagogical and linguistic aspects in isolation from any other known developments. Considerable thought was given to how much student interaction was required. It was felt that the program should be attractive enough for there to be no need to create any artificial requirement for interaction. Students should be allowed to work independently but be able to ask for help, make notes, copy information and take away a copy of the results.

When it was time to prepare two pilot projects, after the award of the CTI grant, the researcher who had initially shown interest in a program for teaching medieval Spanish had left the College. It was then decided to choose a different modern to medieval pair: Middle High German and modern German. Although the idea for the CLT derived from a need to teach a medieval language, it was realized from a very early stage that there was scope for other than modern to medieval combinations of languages. Two related modern languages were therefore chosen as the second pair for the pilot project: modern Catalan and Castilian Spanish.

A pilot scheme was initiated in October 1987 and taken by 18 first year German undergraduate students who were required as part of their course to gain a reading knowledge of Middle High German. It was hoped to assess some of the implications of the CLT for the teacher and the student and to estimate its effectiveness in relation to the traditional methods. One hour-long supervised session per week was included in the timetable over a period of two terms. Students were closely observed, reactions noted and questionnaires given in the hope of evaluating student responses. Written tests were given before and after the CLT course in order to monitor actual achievement on the part of the students. I have since used the program with a second group of first year undergraduates and demonstrated its use to postgraduates and lecturers. Reactions were universally favourable. At a Sixth Form Open Day at Westfield College the CLT was demonstrated to a group of 19 school students and staff. The response from pupils and teachers was again very favourable.

3 The Aims of the CLT

Traditionally Middle High German grammar has been taught from text-books in order to give the student a reading-knowledge of the language. Although students are expected to have a thorough grounding in modern German before coming up to University and some are native speakers of the language, they are often intimidated by the prospect of learning a cognate medieval language. There is an ever-present dilemma suffered by most lecturers of medieval languages—how is one to equip the students with sufficient linguistic knowledge to read the language in its original form without putting the class off the language altogether. Middle High German grammar classes can be extremely tedious. Traditional teaching methods include: detailed instruction on historical phonology, morphology, syntax and lexicon; translation of texts into the mother tongue or the modern cognate; supervised reading of texts in class and, occasionally, grammar exercises. It is difficult for tutors to think of innovations in teaching methodology for a medieval language. Modernist colleagues can make use of audio-visual techniques to bring their languages to life and acquaint them with the language community whose language they are learning. Of course medievalists try to fill in on socio-cultural aspects of the medieval world, but the modern student increasingly expects more colourful and exciting teaching methods.

In the past students have frequently resorted to translations into modern German or English in order to study literary texts. Their overall appreciation of the works has therefore been limited. The CLT aims to make use of modern technological resources, and thus a fresh approach to the learning of the language, to help the student gain necessary linguistic skills and to improve academic performance. As a lecturer I welcomed the opportunity to use what promised to be an exciting new teaching method. Student reactions were nearly all positive. After initial alarm on the part of some 30% of the students (questions such as 'Why do we *have* to use a computer?'), all took to using the CLT very happily. Only one second year student, offered the use of the program for revision purposes, refused to use a computer for any purpose at all.

4 The CLT Program and its use

The CLT presents the student with a number of graded texts to be read on an IBM compatible microcomputer and a range of help options. On calling up the program the student is first given an introduction which summarizes the features on offer. It is possible to recall this introduction at any time and it is up to the student to inform him or herself of the facilities available. I prefer to schedule at least one supervised session to guide the class through the program's features.

The computer screen is divided into three sections:

1. The text to be read takes up the major part of the screen;

2. The basic menu is positioned at the bottom of the screen. It summarizes the types of help available and the function keys to be used. Once a help facility has been called up, a new menu appears and gives the options available within the type of help selected;

3. Directly above the bottom menu is a space for additional information about the current phrase or sentence, for typing in search strings, and to display special messages, for example, that Phrase Help is available on request.

Pearls of Wisdom

In the Middle High German course the first feature to appear on screen for each text is what has been named a 'pearl of wisdom.' Windows containing Pearls of Wisdom can be programmed to open up from time to time without the student having requested them. In this way, certain essential details can be forced upon the student, such as vital linguistic data; or interesting background information can appear, to lighten otherwise purely linguistic material, for example an explanation of the concept of feudal loyalty or a note that the motif of a lime tree symbolizes love. For the Middle High German version of the CLT it was decided to provide a pearl of wisdom for each of the major phonological differences between Middle High German and modern German as they are illustrated by words in the text. Pearls of wisdom do not have to be used quite as forcefully as in the Middle High German course and, through the authoring package, tutors creating new courses may choose to request a time delay before pearls of wisdom are released or may decide not to use the pearls at all.

Student reaction to the pearls was very positive. In the evaluation questionnaire, which was completed by 13 of the 18 students in the trial, 10 thought that there were 'just enough' pearls and that these were 'mostly interesting and stimulating,' 2 students thought the pearls excellent and 1 found that there were too many of them. In answer to the question: 'which type of pearl is most helpful,' 7 students found the linguistic information most helpful, 8 found the background information most useful and 5 found the explanations of difficult concepts most valuable. This adds up to more than 13, indicating that some students ticked more than one box when asked which feature they found *most* useful!

Word Help

Once the first pearl of wisdom disappears from the screen, the sentence currently being read is highlighted in a contrasting colour. Within the sentence the student can pick out the individual words by using the cursor key. On pressing the appropriate function key a dictionary entry for the word appears within a help window. The first level of help provides:

1. The text word;

2. The lemmatized form of the word in the text;

3. The cognate in modern German.

The second level of help gives the part of speech and the third level, if this is used, may provide additional semantic or etymological information. The authoring program provides for a fourth help level if this is required. The menu at the bottom of the screen displays a list of features that may be used within the Word Help, for example, the dictionary entry may be 'saved to the notepad' for future reference. All the students who completed the questionnaire found the Word Help useful.

Sentence Help

The Sentence Help highlights the current sentence using different colours for each part of speech (or, with monochrome monitors, different shadings of the same colour). A key to the colours used for highlighting is displayed at the bottom of the screen. The sentence is split into a number of syntactic units, for example: subject, verb, direct object, indirect object. Again the author has total freedom as to the number and type of units chosen. This feature is particularly useful in helping the student make sense of a very long or syntactically complex sentence. However, when questioned, students said that they had made less use of this facility than of others.

Phrase Help

As the student moves through the text messages may flash below the text, offering the chance to request help on the current phrase. This help provides extra linguistic information about the more complex phrases within a sentence. It explains difficult constructions and may offer more examples of the same construction type. The Phrase Help may of course be considered too important to be limited to an optional help type. It is up to the author to decide whether to force information on the student or whether data should be offered more discreetly, as with the Phrase Help. One disadvantage I experienced with the Phrase Help offered in this way was that the students frequently failed to notice the message flashing on the screen. It may be advisable to let the message appear on screen for longer. One problem associated with the program which was particularly noticeable with the Phrase Help is the tendency on the part of the student to look straight ahead at the main text and fail to notice what is happening on the periphery. Those students that made use of the Phrase Help found it very useful.

Clause Display

The clause display functions in a similar way to the Sentence Help. It highlights any sub-clauses within the current sentence. This feature can be a great aid in the comprehension of Middle High German sentences, where clauses may be ordered quite differently from those of modern German.

Notepad

The Notepad allows the user to create and edit notes about the current sentence. This feature, if used, can prevent the use of the CLT from becoming a totally passive exercise. The notes can be recalled and read or edited by returning to the relevant sentence or by implementing one of the CLT's search functions. It is also possible to read Word Help entries and Pearls of Wisdom into the Notepad using the Grab Word Help and Grab Pearl functions. During the trial session of 1987 students made extensive use of the Notepad facility, sometimes translating each sentence into English. Although it is not the aim of the Cognate Language Teacher to teach translation as an exercise, rather to enable the student to read the cognate language by relating it to another known language, I did not discourage the students from translating but merely told them that they did not have to do so. Many students said that they felt comfortable if they continued using some of the more traditional methods for learning a language, alongside the use of modern technology. Many felt that translating the texts helped them check if they had fully understood them. Furthermore, translation from Middle High German into English is still an option for examination on the University of London syllabus and I felt that the practice could do no harm.

Help

The Help function has two options. It will recall the instructions for using the CLT or it will present the student with a guide to the abbreviations used for the various parts of speech. It is possible to redefine these help functions using the authoring program.

Other Features

There is a search facility which enables the user to search backwards through text already studied. The Bookmark function returns one to a specified point in the text after, for example, completing a search operation. It is possible to print the current text along with any notes which may have been made. The student can review the previous five Pearls of Wisdom and also review previous Phrase Helps.

5 Assessment of the CLT

It was established that the CLT was a useful aid in the teaching of Middle High German. The students enjoyed using the CLT, which they found straightforward to operate and linguistically informative. They gained confidence in the language and progressed more rapidly than students using traditional methods only. The enjoyment they experienced whilst using the program encouraged them to use the CLT in their own time and to persevere with Middle High German despite its difficulties.

In the First Year examinations for the Session 1988/89 students were required to translate a passage of Middle High German into English. This exercise was at this time still a compulsory part of the University of London B.A. examination syllabus. The performance of the students involved in the CLT trial was, on average, 15% higher than in previous years. When assessing the significance of the results it was, however, necessary to bear in mind that the group of students who participated in the initial trial were particularly conscientious and enthusiastic. They had made the best possible use of the CLT, yet may have succeeded equally well if learning from text books alone. Some of the students who have subsequently used the program appeared less interested in using the CLT's full potential. Candidates examined since the CATH 88 Conference have nevertheless attained higher standards than in the past.

Thus, although the CLT appears to be universally acceptable, its effectiveness, whilst showing an improvement over traditional methods, depends on the attitude of the individual user. The program is designed for independent use, but, even in supervised tutorials, it is possible for students to ignore the facilities on offer. It was noted that the CLT could not be used as a total substitute for text-book based language classes for complex languages such as Middle High German. The amount of linguistic data available is naturally limited by the nature of the texts to be included in the course. Some of the systematic teaching is, therefore, lost, but students gain by an overall appreciation of the language and thus of the literature. The only complaint from users was that there was too little printed material for them to take home. Many students feel comforted if they can cling to some of the more traditional teaching methods alongside the modern technological system.

6 The scope of the CLT

The scope and academic implications of the CLT have yet to be fully explored but these are potentially boundless within the spheres of secondary and higher education. An Old French course is due to be completed at the University of Hull in Autumn 1989 and Westfield College has received suggestions for other courses in the following language pairs:

- Irish Gaelic and Scottish Gaelic

- Dutch and German

- Middle English from modern English

- Ukrainian from Russian

- Swiss German dialects from modern Standard German

- Rhaeto-Romance from Italian

- Spanish and Italian

- Spanish and Portuguese

Cognates which are too distantly related may not be suitable and there would be little point creating a package for languages which are very closely related. There has been a further suggestion that the program could be used to explain specialist terminology, e.g. legal or medical terminology, within a single language. The capacity to create special character sets within the authoring package has engendered interest in the possibility of using the program to teach palaeography. Others have suggested that students could author texts themselves as grammatical exercises.

Since there is nothing in the program that inherently requires it to be used for cognate language teaching there are clearly many uses to which it could, potentially, be put: it simulates the reading of a textbook by a student and yet gives scope for information to be provided from a variety of sources just as is required in so many different learning situations. It has already been suggested that the word, phrase, clause and sentence help features would be ideally suited to the annotation of literary texts for stylistic and syntactic analysis.

The fact that the program is intended to be suitable for independent use by students implies that, once a course has been authored by an expert, courses in some of the less usual languages could be offered without specialist tutors being available. Students would need to be well-motivated in this situation, which perhaps best lends itself to postgraduate programs and would possibly need to be supplemented by audio-visual materials.

CALL materials would seem to be most successful when they are integrated directly into the teaching program to meet a known need. For class use there must obviously be available a class-size room of microcomputers. There needs to be an easy to use authoring program so that courses can quickly be tailored to the specific needs of a group of students. If these basics can be met, it would seem that most students welcome a change to the normal class situation.

From my experience of teaching Middle High German, both with and without the aid of the CLT package, I believe that any method by which a student can painlessly acquire a reading knowledge of a medieval language has to be welcomed. Perhaps lecturers who teach some of the more esoteric modern languages have fewer problems in motivating students at the outset. Of course it could be argued that a student should not be faced with a compulsory course in a medieval language and its literature at all. However, most students who have persevered with Middle High German have found it a rewarding experience and they often express appreciation at having been encouraged to read the medieval texts in the original language. The new and enjoyable method which the CLT presents helps them along the road to a full appreciation of not only medieval German but, through this, the whole of German literature.

18

The Development of Computer-Based Resources for Teaching Archaeology

S. Rahtz, J. Richards, S. Shennan and B. O'Flaherty

1 Introduction

The love affair of at least some archaeologists with computers now goes back nearly 30 years. The initial interest was in their use as tools for large-scale quantitative data analysis, but since then it has been their use for database management which has become more important. Much of the reason for this lies in the rapid growth of field archaeology, and particularly excavation, on a world-wide scale, in response to industrial development and the provision of appropriate infrastructures for this. It has become increasingly necessary for professional archaeologists to become computer literate in order to do their job properly.

Such pressures were bound to have an impact on the undergraduate education of archaeologists, leading to the inclusion of computing elements in many archaeology degrees. But the trend in this direction has been reinforced for two rather different reasons. In the social and economic climate of the 1980s disciplines such as archaeology have felt obliged to demonstrate the direct relevance of the education they provide to the future careers of their graduates, the majority of whom do not intend to be archaeologists. The provision of courses in statistics and computing has been seen as a means of doing this; these are things students can emphasise on their *curriculum vitae*.

In addition there has been a move in the philosophy of education away from students as consumers of received knowledge to students as active participants in the learning process. In archaeology this trend has become linked with the developments within the discipline already mentioned. It has become less important that archaeologists should know the outline of specific cultural sequences and more important that they should acquire a knowledge of the *methods* by which data are collected and analysed: methods can best be learned by trying them out. While it is fairly easy to arrange such things as training excavations to teach students how to dig or draw plans, this is not a feasible option when it comes to actually being in charge of a site: it would be too expensive in terms of both money and the destruction of rare archaeological resources.

This chapter describes two related projects which attempt to meet the needs just outlined; both of them arise from the Computers in Teaching Initiative (CTI). The first is SYASS (Southampton-York Archaeological Simulation System), which aims to give students experience of excavation management through the medium of a computer-based simulation while at the same time raising the students' level of computer familiarity. The second, ARCH_HELP is a means of providing traditional departmental and course information to students by computerised means, both because this is an efficient way of doing it and because it is a natural way of forcing students to come to terms with computerised information systems.

2 The Problem of Excavation: SYASS

One of the increasingly pressing needs in undergraduate archaeological training is for a way to teach the management of archaeological investigations, and the relationship between resources and results. Before we describe the implications, let us look at a general outline of what happens on an archaeological excavation (for a general introduction, see Barker, 1978, 1986). The process of excavation or other archaeological investigation is a multi-stage process involving (at least):

1. The creation of an initial research design for the investigation;

2. The carrying out of initial work to gather the broad outlines of the problem and how it can be solved;

3. Carrying out detailed investigation and recording in the selected area, in conjunction with continuous assessment of the results;

4. Analysing the full results and writing a report.

All the phases of this process involve a cost, and what we want students to practise is deciding how to allot the money to different parts of the project. We emphasize here that the aim is not to teach them *how* to make the decisions, but to provide a framework within which they can test the skills which they are being taught in other ways. The problem, of course, is that archaeology students (unlike many other science students) cannot try out classic experiments for themselves and test different approaches. So we have to place the student in an archaeological site about which we know everything, and reveal bits to him or her as requested, without necessarily indulging in any 'teaching' by the computer.

It should be stressed that the exploratory stage starts with a completely blank canvas. There is sometimes a misconception about archaeology that the sites (a) make their presence clear in an unequivocal way, and (b) that they are delimited in some clear way, by man-made boundaries like walls, or natural barriers like rivers. In fact, most of the landscape of a highly developed country like Britain is firstly a continuous area of settlement at many periods, and secondly a palimpsest, with no strict temporal boundaries between periods. Excavating anywhere in, say, the

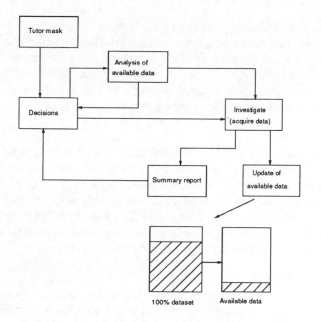

Fig. 18.1: A general model for a resource-based simulation

Thames Valley puts one in the middle of a site with no idea of how close one is to the 'edge,' or any idea of how many periods there might be: deciding where Period 3 ends and Period 4 starts is a matter of interpretation, not an equivalent to recognizing the boundary between the icing and the marzipan on a Christmas cake. Thus the archaeologist will need to spend a large proportion of the resources on non-destructive survey-type analysis before proceeding (if at all) to conventional excavation, and the student excavator must learn these skills.

One way of providing such a 'flight-simulator' is to set up a database of the relevant material and simply ask the student to navigate around it; this passive system is the one being worked on in Southampton and York, which we choose to characterise as a 'resource-based' system (see Fig. 1), as opposed to a structured and active 'computerised tutor,' which leads a student through the investigative process.

After much discussion at many levels it was decided to implement three sets of procedures:

1. Research procedure

2. Excavation procedure

3. Analysis procedure

This was regarded as the easiest way to teach archaeological excavations. As SYASS is essentially a teaching aid it is desirable for the instructor to have some degree of control over the running of the program at any or all stages. This means that SYASS can be run with a direct input from a course tutor to highlight certain points or it can be run free-standing without any direction whatsoever, thereby allowing users with different levels of excavation skill to benefit.

Research Procedure

The research procedure involves all work undertaken before excavation actually begins. Research procedure includes map and archive analysis, reconnaissance methods such as field walking and aerial photography, costing of the project, obtaining funding, etc. Once this reconnaissance has been undertaken the student is in a suitable position to formulate a suitable research design for the project and to decide on realistic (or otherwise) goals for the excavation. At present the SYASS project is concentrating on the excavation and analysis procedures.

Excavation Procedure

Having chosen the excavation procedure module the student is asked to choose how the excavation is to proceed, in terms of Information Recovery levels (Carver, 1985), which are a very important component of SYASS. Recovery is divided into six levels, A–F. Recovery Level A and recovery Level F are not part of the excavation procedure. Level A recording is part of the pre-excavation phase or research procedure and includes such activities as field-walking, the recovery of surface finds, geophysical exploration and the creation of plans on the basis of these. Level F is part of the post-excavation phase (although not always so) and consists of sieving of pit and fill samples under laboratory conditions. Levels B–E are what concern us at the excavation procedure stage; in the field they describe what methods are used to recover data (from a bulldozer to a paintbrush), while in the computer they determine the coarseness of the random sieve used to filter the data before the student gets it.

Defining an Area for Excavation

Once the recovery level is defined the student is then asked to specify where to excavate and to what depth. A set of X and Y coordinates is used to specify the horizontal positions of the south-west corner of the area to be investigated, and the length, width and depth of the area are then requested. Using this system the student can excavate an area of any chosen size based on the square, up to and including the whole site (open area excavation). Similarly small *sondage* trenches can be put in at any point to enable the participant to get a feel for the site and its complexity before commencing larger scale operations across the site. Note that this describes a rather limited method of excavation, which might be inappropriate in practice, but in the current version of SYASS we are content to use anything that forces the student to take management decisions.

Data Access or Excavation

Once all the parameters have been set the program then proceeds to 'excavate' the area specified. Excavate in this context means that the databases are queried and selected information is extracted from them. This data is then stored in the student's log file and tagged as having been excavated and recorded. When this is done the student is told, by means of a simple counter, how many units or archaeological features have been encountered during that particular excavation activity, how much money has been spent and the money remaining in the budget. Control is then passed to the main menu and the participant is free to choose one of the main menu options outlined above.

Analysis Procedure

The analysis procedure forms the core of SYASS. It is here that the student can interpret any or all data that has been accumulated during the course of the excavation and research procedures. This ranges from a simple examination of the contexts and finds descriptions to graphical and statistical analyses of the data. It is important to realize that the *owning* of data is not the same as *understanding* it, so we differentiate in the SYASS system between acquiring data, and actually examining it.

Integrating SYASS into a Course

SYASS received its first exposure to a group of students in November 1988, as part of the archaeological method unit taken by all first year students in the Department of Archaeology at Southampton. This is a half unit of 13 weeks, with lectures and practicals involving 4 contact hours per week. It is designed to introduce the student to some of the basic methods available to the archaeologist in the course of field work. It attempts to explain how the archaeologist knows where to dig, what is involved in the excavation process and how sites and finds can be dated. There is an emphasis on practical work and students receive tuition in selected field and laboratory techniques. Finally the course also involves a week's field survey on Dartmoor, followed by three weeks on an archaeological excavation. Topics covered in the course include remote sensing, geophysical prospecting, and dating techniques, while a large portion of the course is devoted to field survey and excavation techniques.

Within this framework SYASS is timetabled for 7 hours. Three of these hours are formal lectures while the remainder are for practical sessions. As the students did not have any formal computer training other than that which they got before arriving at university, the level of computer literacy was, at best, mixed. Some (very few) had used word processing packages, mainly at school, and this seemed to be the extent of their familiarity with computers. In some respects this lack of familiarity proved a handicap as an introductory session had to be given to the students at a very basic level. There is a good case to be made here for introducing all students of departments which use computing extensively in teaching and practice to basic computing skills in their first weeks at university. This would enable courses where use is made of computers as tools or teaching aids to concentrate on the particular applications rather than worry about basic levels of computer literacy.

During the course of the development of SYASS it was always assumed that students would have some knowledge of the basic mechanics and methodologies of archaeological excavation technique. SYASS was, after all, being designed with strategy and budgetary decisions in mind. However this proved not to be the case; for instance, we encountered ignorance of the single 'context' recording system[1] which is now, in its many guises, the (*de facto*) standard for recording data from archaeological sites. It was clear from the students' use of SYASS that not all of them understood exactly what a context is in the archaeological sense of the word; in this way SYASS can highlight deficiencies in courses in which it is used. These deficiencies may be content related but it is also possible that they are timetable related in that SYASS could have been introduced before the students had a full understanding of archaeological method and its terminology. Perhaps it would be better to use SYASS as an ongoing resource which would be fully integrated into the life of the course and aspects of the software used to illustrate points made in lectures and practical classes.

3 ARCH_HELP

The aim of the next section of this chapter is to describe a rather different aspect of the SYASS project which was undertaken at York University during 1988. The aims, design and implementation of ARCH_HELP, a subject specific online help system, will be described.

One aim of the Computers in Teaching Initiative (CTI) was that computers should infiltrate the curriculum widely, and that their introduction should not be limited to the specific and tangible software packages for which funding is provided. After several years of teaching computing to archaeology students we were also aware that it is sometimes difficult to persuade students to use computers outside the context of the computer course. Whilst some students do go on to undertake computer-related projects, and most may become competent at completing the computer exercises required within the course, they will still not turn to the computer to word process essays required elsewhere, or make use of database management for their dissertations. There may be several factors behind this: residual fear of the computer outside a structured environment, or the way in which computing has been taught; but it is perhaps particularly due to the compartmentalisation of courses by students, and the consequent failure of computers to pervade all aspects of the curriculum. It was clear, therefore, that

---

[1] A context is a unit excavated as an entity, or the boundary between two such units. For example, an archaeologist may excavate the soil now filling an ancient post-hole; that soil will be counted as a context, but the resulting hole (the ancient post-hole) will have its own (different) context number.

the computer was still often regarded as a specific rather than as a general tool and that it was not being exploited to the maximum limit of its potential.

What is ARCH_HELP?

The CTI aim is that students should be taught with computers, not necessarily about them. Techniques of computer-aided learning are therefore adopted to teach areas of a discipline which have hitherto been taught by traditional means. ARCH_HELP takes this to its logical conclusion by providing a computerised guide to all aspects of the university archaeology curriculum. It is designed to accompany students throughout their courses from the first week of their first year until finals examinations. It can also be used by applicants attending interview to answer many of their routine questions, and has already been used as a novel 'information point' at Open Day.

ARCH_HELP, as its name suggests, is analogous to a mainframe HELP system. ARCH_HELP provides information about the archaeology degree in York, ranging from course requirements to seminar handouts and reading lists. In essence it:

- is based on the DEC Help system, using DEC Librarian;

- permits up to 10 levels of information in a hierarchy, in Topics and Subtopics;

- is accessed (read only) via any registered Archaeology user;

- holds data only updateable by authorised usernames;

- contains:

    1. Course outlines;
    2. Booklists;
    3. Seminar timetables and handouts;
    4. Examination details;
    5. Staff profiles; and
    6. Student information (accommodation notices etc).

The information is organised hierarchically within a HELP library. It is accessed interactively from a terminal, and can deal with either general or specific queries. Users can ask, for example, about the fieldwork requirement, and about the departmental training excavations which are available. They can also find out, for instance, what they are likely to be doing in Week Three of the third term of their first year, what the required reading will be, and what essays they will be expected to produce. Since all seminar handouts are held within ARCH_HELP it is intended that the computer will supersede the photocopier. Students are expected to read and/or print out the information as appropriate, and are no longer issued with handouts by the lecturer. A brief outline of the facilities follows (the implementation of the system is described in detail elsewhere: Richards, 1988).

Up to ten levels of information may be stored within a simple text library of unlimited size, divided into Topics and Sub-topics. When a Topic is selected the associated information is displayed, followed by the Sub-topic headings available. Should the user request to view a Sub-topic this information is displayed, followed by the next level headings, and so on, until the bottom of that particular route is reached.

Thus, for example, one of the Level 1 topics is UNDERGRADUATE STUDY. Following some general descriptive information, there are Sub-topics on FIRST YEAR, SECOND YEAR, THIRD YEAR, EXAMINATIONS, FIELDWORK, etc., each of which is further sub-divided, frequently by course, and then by individual week.

The user can enter the system from the top and explore their way down or, if they know what they want to find out about and the route by which it is accessed, they can 'jump into' the library at the Level at which they require help. Movement within the library is controlled by the simple use of '?' and RETURN keys, or by typing in the name (or abbreviated name) of a Topic or Sub-topic. Users can also direct the output for a query to a printer, if required.

The main limitation of the system is the relatively crude software used to implement it, which does not offer the flexibility of a database package. Thus the information hierarchy is built into the system design and there can only be one user-view of the system. Sophisticated queries, such as 'In which courses will I learn about Romans?' cannot be catered for, as the route to all information has to be via the library hierarchy, and course information is organised according to the year in which the course is provided.

Implications of ARCH_HELP

The most significant implication of ARCH_HELP is that all archaeology under-graduates will henceforth have to use the computer every week of their university careers, starting from the first week. It has become normal that new undergrad-uates are given an induction week which includes things such as an introduction to the departmental staff and to the use of the library. Since October 1988 this has also included a session to introduce them to logging on to the VAX and using ARCH_HELP, and to using electronic mail. Until they have used ARCH_HELP they are not able to proceed to print out the handout required for the first seminar in their second week!

It is hoped, of course, that the students find this first encounter with the computer a productive and informative one, and that they will come to regard the computer as a routine tool and source of help. We don't want ARCH_HELP to become an extra member of staff counted in UGC reviews of Archaeology provision, but we do intend that it should free tutors and the departmental secretary (who in most departments is generally regarded as the fount of all knowledge) from the burden of answering such routine queries as: 'When is my excavation application form due in?' or 'How much does this examination count towards my final degree?'

It is too early to say what the long term effects of ARCH_HELP will be, but the system has so far proved to be popular, and we are monitoring its use. A similar development is planned for Southampton to start in 1989, which will be implemented in a slightly different manner. Firstly, the work of setting up the system will be part of the assessment for a group of students doing an M.Sc in Archaeological Computing, thus performing the dual function of providing a working system, and giving students experience in information extraction and provision (by finding out what information lecturers have which they want students to share). Secondly, and partly as an experimental contrast to York, it is intended to mount the details on a free-standing microcomputer, rather than the mainframe (partly also because no-one in their right minds wants to use an IBM mainframe for an introductory system!). If possible, hypertext software will be used to provide the new student with a web of information to explore on the degree and the department.

4 Morals

What are the implications of both the 'main' part of this project, and the secondary aspects, for the undergraduate curriculum? There is no doubt that ARCH_HELP is seen by students and staff alike as a fairly flexible and efficient means of communicating information. It is also hoped that it will encourage students to turn to the computer more widely within their university careers. As an added benefit, by the time students come to do a full course on archaeological computing, generally at the beginning of their second year, it is anticipated that they will have already overcome any fear of computers which they might harbour, and will be ready to go on to learn about more advanced techniques. The greatest strength of this part of the project is in the insidious way the computer is used: it is neither bypassable like an online library catalogue, nor an optional course (which women often do not take), nor a possibly threatening part of a taught course. It is a part of daily life, like the telephone and the photocopier. Whether the use of electronic mail by students will have an impact on their lives it is too early to tell, but there is little doubt that experience in the soul-less and limited world of character-based communication (which some regard as even worse for personal relationships than telephoning!), will be a useful experience.

But is the main SYASS software going to affect either the course or those who teach it? We hope that exposing students to a teaching situation in which they have to manipulate resources will give them tools of wider applicability; it becomes much easier to introduce key commercial concepts, including fairly formal details of data management, by default during what appears to be discussion of archaeology. On the other hand, we feel that the direction taken by this group, compared to other computer teaching projects, has implications for the timetable; and we believe that the introduction of computerised *formal* training in excavation at an early stage could act as a possibly unwelcome check on the rest of the course, since it forces students to come to terms with concepts normally dealt with in the more relaxed atmosphere of the field.

It is important to stress that the same problems will not necessarily apply in all institutions; in York, SYASS is introduced as one element in a course on data analysis. This is a nine week course taught in Term Three of the First Year, involving 7.5 contact hours per week. Students are taught the theoretical aspects of site excavation, context description, the stratigraphic matrix, assemblage sampling, and so forth. For most, their first taste of the practical aspects of these subjects has generally been on the Training Excavation in the first summer vacation. Now they will use SYASS as an integral part of the course to explore for themselves some of the practical aspects of these problems.

It would appear, from the experience so far of using SYASS in a course, that it is easier to develop software that assumes a basic grasp of the underlying principles, methodologies and methods used by excavators. The assumptions which experienced archaeologists and excavators would take for granted cannot be assumed at first year undergraduate training level. SYASS is not an instructional program, however, and is not designed to teach method or terminology; it thus assumes at least some knowledge of the underlying concepts involved. Thus a close liaison will be needed between the formal management training which can be undertaken with SYASS and practical experience in the field.

In this respect, therefore, the teaching burden will actually be greater with the introduction of SYASS, as an extra item is being added to the curriculum. In addition, the not inconsiderable problems to be surmounted in training students to feel at home with IT means that timetable and teacher resources must be expended on basic training even before the formal exercise starts. ARCH_HELP, on the other hand, demonstrates one way in which this necessary training can be put to good use, potentially freeing teaching staff from administration. Thus in an ideal world we would save time by freeing staff to do what they are good at; in practice, it is more likely that the staff will have to work harder, and prepare in more detail, to give the students a better, but not cheaper, education.

Would the widespread use of SYASS concepts have a major impact on teaching archaeology? It certainly means that the curriculum would change: on the positive side, if the ARCH_HELP example is followed up, it would allow more time to teach; on the negative side it would oblige us to allot more time to teaching IT skills; in some departments it would also require rethinking the timing and content of field archaeology classes, since the student needs a good grounding in basic techniques if management skills are to be learnt. It is also possible that the same software could be used for retraining in the field, rather like sending pensioners in for new driving tests every so often after they reach 65. Thus we might see professional standards rise. But it is not clear how the use of passive resources might change the discipline, since the use of large, structured, information stores is already widespread. It is possible that other areas of new technology, like real-time 3D graphics, or expert systems for conducting arguments (see Stutt, 1988, and this volume) might make a huge impact on the practicality of some types of archaeological thinking. But in general it is difficult not to feel that the discipline's greatest agent of change is likely to be not IT but politics.

Bibliography

Adams, J. B. (1985). Probabilistic reasoning and certainty factors. In B. G. Buchanan & E. H. Shortcliffe (Eds.), *Rule-Based Expert Systems*. Reading, MA: Addison Wesley.

Alvarado, S. J., Dyer, M. G. and Flowers, M. (1986). Editorial comprehension in OpEd through argument units. *Proceedings of the Fifth National Conference on Artificial Intelligence* (AAAI-86) (pp. 250–256). Philadelphia, PA: AAAI.

Axelrod, R. (1984). *The Evolution of Cooperation*. New York: Basic Books.

Axelrod, R. (1987). Evolution of strategies in the iterated Prisoners' Dilemma. In L. Davis (Ed.), *Genetic Algorithms and Simulated Annealing* (pp. 32–41). Los Altos, CA: Morgan Kaufmann.

Barker, P. (1978). *Techniques of Archaeological Excavation*. London: Batsford.

Barker, P. (1986). *Understanding Archaeological Excavation*. London: Batsford.

Barthes, R. (1975). *S/Z* (R. Miller, Trans.). London: Cape. (Original work published 1970)

Barwise, J., and Etchemendy, J. (1987). *Tarski's World* [Computer application]. Ventura, CA: Kinko's Academic Courseware Exchange.

Black, M. (1962). *Models and Metaphors*. Ithaca, NY: Cornell University Press.

Bloom, A. (1987). *The Closing of the American Mind: Education and the Crisis of Reason*. New York: Simon & Schuster.

Bloom, Harold (1973). *The Anxiety of Influence: A Theory of Poetry*. New York: Oxford University Press.

Blow, F. (1987). 'A fertile error is more productive than a barren truth:' Computer assisted learning in history. In P. Denley & D. Hopkin (Eds.), *History and Computing* (pp. 285–288). Manchester: Manchester University Press.

Blow, F., and Dickinson, A., Eds. (1986). *New History and New Technology: Present into Future*. London: Historical Association.

Boden, Margaret A. (1987). *Artificial Intelligence and Natural Man*, 2nd Ed. London: MIT Press.

Boden, Margaret (1988). *Computer Models of Mind: Computational Approaches in Theoretical Psychology*. Cambridge: Cambridge University Press.

Bolter, J. David (1984). *Turing's Man: Western Culture in the Computer Age*. Chapel Hill, NC: University of North Carolina Press.

Bolter, J., and Joyce, M. (1989). *Storyspace* [Computer application]. Unpublished.

Booth, S. (1969). *An Essay on Shakespeare's Sonnets*. New Haven, NJ: Yale University Press.

Booth, W. (1967). Introduction. In Crane, R. S., *The Idea of the Humanities and Other Essays Critical and Historical*. Chicago and London: The University of Chicago Press.

Bourne, J. M. (1986). History at the universities. *History*, *71*, 54–60.

Bransford, J. D. (1979). *Human Cognition: Learning, Understanding, and Remembering*. Belmont, CA: Vanderbilt University/Wadsworth Publishing.

Britton, B. W., and Glynn, S. M., Eds. (1989). *Computer Writing Environments: Theory, Research and Design*. Hillsdale, NJ: Laurence Erlbaum Associates.

Britton, R. (1985). Wealthy Scots, 1876–1913. *Bulletin of the Institute of Historical Research*, *58*, 78–94.

Buchan, J. (1940). *Memory Hold the Door*. London: Hodder and Stoughton.

Burrows, J. F. (1987). *Computation into Criticism: A Study of Jane Austen's Novels and an Experiment in Method*. Oxford: Oxford University Press.

Calhoun, J. K. (1989). *Hyper Windows* [Computer software]. Hanover, NH: Dartmouth College.

Calvino, I. (1986). *The Uses of Literature*. San Diego: Harcourt Brace Jovanovich.

Cameron, K. C., Dood, W. S., and Rahtz, S. P. Q., Eds. (1986). *Computers and Modern Language Studies*. London: Ellis Horwood.

Campbell, J. (1982). *Grammatical Man*. New York: Simon and Schuster.

Carver, M. O. H. (1985). The friendly user. In M. A. Cooper & J. D. Richards (Eds.), *Current Issues in Archaeological Computing* (pp. 47–61). Oxford: British Archaeological Reports, International Series 271.

Charniak, E. and McDermott, D. (1985). *Introduction to Artificial Intelligence.* Reading, MA: Addison Wesley.

Chesters, G., and Gardner, N., Eds. (1988). *The Use of Computers in the Teaching of Language and Languages.* Bath: CTISS Publications.

Churchland, P.S. (1986). *Neurophilosophy.* Cambridge, MA: MIT Press.

Cohen, R. (1987). Analyzing the structure of argumentative discourse. *Computational Linguistics, 13*, 11–24.

Cooper, N. L. C. (1981). *The Diversity of Moral Thinking.* Oxford: Clarendon Press.

Council for Science and Society (1989). *Benefits and Risks of Knowledge Based Systems.* Oxford: Oxford University Press.

Covey, P., & Roberts, S. (1988). *A Right to Die?: The Case of Dax Cowart* [Computer controlled interactive video]. Akron, OH: The ALIVE Center.

Dartmouth Dante Project. (1989). *DDP Database* [Electronic Text Database]. Hanover, NH: Author.

Descartes, R. (1911). *Discourse on the Method.* In E. S. Haldane & G. T. R. Ross (Eds. and Trans), *The Philosophical Works of Descartes* (pp. 115–117). Cambridge: Cambridge University Press. (Original publication 1637)

Diagnostic Research, Inc. (1988). *Macintosh or MS-DOS?* Author.

Dreyfus, H. L. and Dreyfus, S. E. (1986). *Mind Over Machine.* Oxford: Basil Blackwell.

Eco, U. (1985). *Reflections on the Name of the Rose.* London: Secker and Warburg.

Eliot, T. S. (1928). Tradition and the individual talent. In *The Sacred Wood: Essays on Poetry and Criticism*, 2nd edition. London: Methuen. (Original essay published 1919)

Elton, G. R. (1969a). *The Practice of History.* London: Fontana.

Elton, G. R. (1969b). Second thoughts on history at the universities. *History, 44*, 60–67.

Ennals, R., et al., Eds. (1986). *Information Technology and Education: The Changing School*. Chichester: Ellis Horwood.

Flowers, M., McGuire, R. and Birnbaum, L. (1982). Adversary arguments and the logic of personal attacks. In W. G. Lehnert & M. G. Ringle (Eds.), *Strategies for Natural Language Understanding*. Hillsdale, NJ: Lawrence Erlbaum Associates.

Fothergill, R. (1987). The Director's view. *British Journal of Educational Technology*, *18*, 181–193.

Freund, E. (1987). *The Return of the Reader*. London: Methuen.

Frye, Northrop (1957). *Anatomy of Criticism: Four Essays*. Princeton, NJ: Princeton University Press.

Galloway, P. (1979). Producing narrative maps with multidimensional scaling techniques. *Computers and the Humanities*, *13*, 207–222.

Gardin, J-C. (1980). *Archaeological Constructs*. Cambridge: Cambridge University Press.

Gardin, J-C. (1987b). The future influence of computers on the interplay between research and teaching in the Humanities. *Humanities Communication Newsletter*, *9*.

Gardin, J-C., et al. (1987a). *Systemes experts et sciences humaines: Le cas de l'archeologie*. Paris: Eyrolles.

Gardin, J-C., and Ennals, R., Eds. (1989). *Exploring the Foundations of Interpretation in the Humanities: The Role of Artificial Intelligence*. London: British Library.

Genette, Gerard (1982). *Palimpsestes: La litterature au second degre*. Paris: Editions de seuil.

Gombrich, E. (1961). *Art and Illusion: A Study in the Psychology of Pictorial Representation*. New York: Pantheon.

Gould, J., and Grischkowsky, N. (1984). Doing the same work with hard-copy and CRT terminals. *Human Factors*, *26*, 323–337.

Hainline, D., Ed. (1987). *New Developments in Computer-Assisted Language Learning*. London: Croom Helm.

Hansen, W. J., and Haas, C. (1988). Reading and writing with computers: A framework for explaining differences in performance. *Communications of the ACM*, *31*, 1080–1089.

Harker, W. John (1989). Information processing and the reading of literary texts. *New Literary History*, *20*, 465–481.

Harrison, B. H. (1968). History at the universities 1968: A commentary. *History*, *53*, 357–380.

Havelock, Eric A. (1962). *Preface to Plato*. Cambridge, MA: Harvard University Press.

Hewson, R. (1987). *Typographic design: One practitioner's view of old meets new*. Internal working paper written for FRI Group, Intelligent Systems Laboratory, Xerox PARC.

Hirsch, E. D., Jr. (1987). *Cultural Literacy: What Every American Needs to Know*. Boston: Houghton Mifflin.

Hirscheim, R. A., Smithson, S. C., and Whitehouse, D. E. (1987). *A Survey of Microcomputer Use in the Humanities and Social Sciences: A U.K. University Study*. London: London School of Economics.

Hockey, S. (1987). An historical perspective. In S. Rahtz (Ed.), *Information Technology in the Humanities: Tools, Techniques and Applications*. Chichester, UK: Ellis Horwood.

Hofstadter, Douglas R. (1985). *Metamagical Themas: Questing for the Essence of Mind and Pattern*. New York: Bantam Books.

Holland, J. H., Holyoake, K. J., Nisbett, R. E., and Thagard, P. R. (1986). *Induction*. Cambridge, MA: MIT Press.

Humanities Computing (1988). *Mnemosyne* [Computer application]. Hanover, NH: Dartmouth College.

Humanities Computing (1989). *Hanzi Assistant* [Computer application]. Hanover, NH: Dartmouth College.

Ide, Nancy M. (1987). Computers and the humanities courses: philological bases and approach. *Computers and the Humanities*, *21*, 209–215.

Illich, I. (1973). *Tools for Conviviality*. London: Calder and Boyars.

Iser, W. (1978). *The Act of Reading: A Theory of Aesthetic Response*. Baltimore: John Hopkins University Press.

Johnson-Laird, P. N. (1983). *Mental Models: Toward a Cognitive Science of Language*. Cambridge: Cambridge University Press.

Jones, J. C. (1981). *Design Methods* (1980 Edition). Chichester: Wiley.

Jordan, Chris (1986). MIDI, what's wrong with it. *Sound on Sound, 1*, (6 April).

Joyce, Michael (1988). Siren-shapes: exploratory and constructive hypertexts. *Academic computing, 3*, 10–14, 37–42.

Kant, I. (1838). *Kritik der reinen Vernunft*. In *Sammtliche Werke*, Vol. 2. Leipzig: Voss.

Katzen, M. (1988). Exchanging ideas. *Times Higher Education Supplement*, 18 November 1988.

Klaeber, F., Ed. (1950). *Beowulf*. Lexington, MA: D. C. Heath.

Kosslyn, S. (1981). *Image and Mind*. Cambridge, MA: Harvard University Press.

Kremer, R., and Chadowitz, A. (1988). *Heavenly Mac* [Computer Application]. Ventura, CA: Kinko's Academic Courseware Exchange.

Kristeva, Julia (1969). *Semiotike: Recherches pour une semanalyse*. Paris: Editions de seuil.

Lancashire, I., and McCarty, W., Eds. (1988). *The Humanities Computing Yearbook 1988*. Oxford: Oxford University Press.

Lanham, Richard A. (1989). The electronic word: Literary study and the digital revolution. *New Literary History, 20*, 265–290.

Laurillard, D. (1988). Evaluating the contribution of information technology to student learning. In D. S. Miall (Ed.), *Evaluating Information Technology in the Arts and Humanities*. Bath: CTISS Publications.

Lenat, D. B., Borning, A., McDonald, D., Taylor, C. and Weyer, S. (1983). Knoesphere: Building expert systems with encyclopedic knowledge. *Proceedings of the International Joint Conference on AI* (IJCAI-83). Los Altos, CA: William Kaufmann.

Lillie, J. A. (1970). *Tradition and Environment*. Aberdeen: Aberdeen University Press.

Lougee, C. (1987). *The Would-Be Gentleman* [Computer application]. Ventura, CA: Kinko's Academic Courseware Exchange.

Mackie, G. (1988). Designing for an enlightened publisher. *Matrix, 8*, 158–163.

Makkuni, R. (1987, December). A gestural representation of the process of composing Chinese temples. *IEEE Computer Graphics & Applications*, 45–61.

Martlew, R. (1988). Optical disc storage: Another can of WORMS? In C. L. N. Ruggles & S. P. Q. Rahtz (Eds.), *Computer and Quantitative Methods in Archaeology 1987* (pp. 265–268). Oxford: British Archaeological Reports, International Series, 393.

Meehan, J. R. (1977). TALE-SPIN, an interactive program that writes stories. *Proceedings of the International Joint Conference on Artificial Intelligence* (IJCAI-77). Los Altos, CA: William Kaufmann.

Miall, D. S. (1989a). Beyond the schema given: Affective comprehension of literary narratives. *Cognition and Emotion, 2,* 55–78.

Miall, D. S. (1989b). An expert system approach to the interpretation of literary structure. In J-C. Gardin & R. Ennals (Eds.), *Exploring the Foundations of Interpretation in the Humanities: The Role of Artificial Intelligence.* London: British Library.

Miall, D. S. (1989c). *A Survey of Information Technology in the Arts and Humanities: Current Practice in Polytechnics and Colleges in the U.K.* London: Council for National Academic Awards.

Miller Rubin, M. (1985). Spatial context as an aid to page layout: A system for planning and sketching. *Visible Language, 19,* 243–250.

Miller, A. (1987). *Imagery in Scientific Thought.* Cambridge, MA: MIT Press.

Minsky, M. L. (1975). A framework for representing knowledge. In P. H. Winston (Ed.), *Psychology of Computer Vision* (pp. 211–277). New York: W. H. Freeman.

Moore, Richard F. (1988). The dysfunctions of MIDI. *Computer Music Journal, 12,* (No 1, Spring).

Morgan, N. J. (1987). Sources and resources: the DISH Project at Glasgow. In P. Denley & D. Hopkin (Eds.), *History and Computing* (pp. 302–308). Manchester: Manchester University Press.

Morgan, N. J., and Moss, M. S. (1986). Listing the wealthy in Scotland. *Bulletin of the Institute of Historical Research, 59,* 189–195.

Morgan, N. J., and Moss, M. S. (1989). Urban wealthholding and the computer. In P. Denley, et al. (Eds.), *History and Computing II* (pp. 181–192). Manchester: Manchester University Press.

Morgan, N. J., and Trainor, R. H. (1990). The dominant classes. In H. Fraser & R. J. Morris (Eds.), *People and Society in Scotland: Vol.2, 1830–1914.* Forthcoming.

Nelson, Theodor Holm (1987). *Literary Machines*. San Antonio, TX: Theodor Holm Nelson.

O'Flaherty, B. (1988a). The Southampton-York Archaeological Simulation System. In S. Rahtz (Ed.), *Computer and Quantitative Methods in Archaeology* (pp. 491–498). Oxford: British Archaeological Reports, International Series 446.

O'Flaherty, B. (1988b). Teaching of archaeological excavations—a new initiative. *Archaeological Computing Newsletter, 15*, 4–8.

Ong, Walter J. (1982). *Orality and Literacy: The Technologizing of the Word*. London and New York: Methuen.

Peat Marwick, Inc. (1987). *Market News* (Fall 1987, Number 2). MacWeek.

Pestalozzi, J. H. (1946). *How Gertrude Teaches her Children* (L. Holland & F. Turner, Trans). Syracuse, NY: Bardeen. (Original publication 1820)

Pinker, S. (1980). Explanations in theories of language and of imagery. *Behavioural and Brain Sciences, 3*, 147–148.

Plato (1959). *Timaeus* (F. Cornford, Trans). New York: Bobbs-Merrill.

Porush, David (1989). Cybernetic fiction and postmodern science. *New Literary History, 20*, 373–96.

Powicke, F. M. (1955). *Modern Historians and the Study of History*. London: Odhams Press.

Presutti, L., and Lancashire, I. (1986). *MTAS: MicroText Analysis System* [Computer program]. Toronto: University of Toronto, Centre for Computing in the Humanities.

Pylyshyn, Z. W. (1984). *Computation and Cognition*. Cambridge, MA: MIT Press.

Rahtz, S. (1988). A resource-based archaeological simulation. In S. Rahtz (Ed.), *Computer and Quantitative Methods in Archaeology* (pp. 473–490). Oxford: British Archaeological Reports, International Series 446.

Rahtz, S., Ed. (1987). *Information Technology in the Humanities: Tools, Techniques and Applications*. London: Ellis Horwood.

Randell K., Ed. (1984). *The Use of the Computer in the Study and Teaching of History*. London: Historical Association.

Reichman-Adar, R. (1984). Extended person-machine interface. *Artificial Intelligence, 22*, 157–218.

Reimer, S. (1988). *Litstats* [Computer program]. Edmonton, Canada: University of Alberta, Department of English.

Richards, I. A. (1936). *The Philosophy of Rhetoric*. New York: Oxford University Press.

Richards, J. (1988). ARCH_HELP: Computer-aided help for archaeology students. *Archaeological Computing Newsletter, 15*, 9–13.

Roszak, Theodore (1988). *The Cult of Information: The Folklore of Computers and the True Art of Learning*. London: Paladin.

Rubinstein, W. D. (1981). *Men of Property*. London: Croom Helm.

Russell, B. (1960). *The Philosophy of Logical Atomism*. In R. C. Marsh (Ed.), *Bertrand Russell: Logic and Knowledge* (pp. 175–281). London: George Allen and Unwin. (Original publication 1918)

Rust, R. D. (1988). *Litterms: A tutorial for understanding literature* [Computer program]. San Diego, CA: Harcourt Brace Jovanovich.

Searle, J.R. (1980). Minds, brains, and programs. *The Behavioral and Brain Sciences, 3*, 417–457.

Shennan, S. (1989). Why should we believe archaeological interpretation? In J-C. Gardin & R. Ennals (Eds.), *Exploring the Foundations of Interpretation in the Humanities: The Role of Artificial Intelligence*. London: British Library.

Shneiderman, B. (1983). Direct Manipulation: A step beyond programming languages. *Computer*, 57–69.

Shneiderman, Ben (1986). *Designing the User Interface: Strategies for Effective Human-Computer Interaction*. Reading, MA: Addison-Wesley.

Simon, H. (1977). *Models of Discovery*. Boston & Dordrecht: Reidel.

Slatin, John M. (in press). *Reading hypertext: Order and coherence in a new medium*. In G. Landow & P. Delany (Eds.), *Hypermedia and Literary Studies*.

Smout, C. (1969). *A History of the Scottish People 1560–1830*. Glasgow: William Collins & Sons.

Stevens, V., Sussex, R., and Tuman, W. V. (1988). *New Technologies in Language Learning*. London: Pergamon Press

Stutt, A. (1988). Expert systems, explanations, arguments and archaeology. In
    S. Rahtz (Ed.), *Computer and Quantitative Methods in Archaeology* (pp.
    353–364). Oxford: British Archaeological Reports, International Series
    446.

Tannenbaum, R. S. (1987). How should we teach computing to humanists?
    Computers and the Humanities, 21, 217–225.

Thagard, P. R. (1988). *Computational Philosophy of Science.* Cambridge, MA:
    MIT Press.

Thomas, Keith (1988). The past in clearer light, a beacon on our future. *The
    Times Higher Education Supplement,* 2 December 1988.

Thorne, M. (1987). The legacy of MEP. *British Journal of Educational
    Technology, 18,* 165–181.

Toulmin, S. (1958). *The Uses of Argument.* Cambridge: Cambridge University
    Press.

Toulmin, S., Rieke, R. and Janik, A. (1979). *An Introduction to Reasoning.*
    New York: Macmillan.

Trainor, R. H. (1987). An experiment in computer based teaching and research:
    the DISH Project at Glasgow. In P. Denley & D. Hopkin (Eds.), *History
    and Computing* (pp. 297–301). Manchester: Manchester University Press.

Trainor, R. H. (1987). The role of the computer in university teaching. In S.
    Rahtz (Ed.), *Information Technology in the Humanities: Tools, Techniques
    and Applications* (pp. 31–40). Chichester: Ellis Horwood.

Trainor, R. H. (1989). History, computing and higher education. In P. Denley,
    et al. (Eds.), *History and Computing II* (pp. 35–42). Manchester:
    Manchester University Press.

Trigg, R. and Weiser, M. (1986). TEXTNET: A network-based approach to text
    handling. *ACM Trans. Office Information Systems, 4,* 1–23.

Tschichold, J. (1932). *Typografische Entwurfstechnik.* Stuttgart: Wedekind.

Turing, A. M. (1950). Computing machinery and intelligence. *Mind, 49* (No.
    236), 433–460.

Wardley, P. (1988). Evaluation of IT in Arts & Humanities at Bristol
    Polytechnic. In D. S. Miall (Ed.), *Evaluating Information Technology in
    the Arts and Humanities.* Bath: CTISS Publications.

Wild, M. (1987). Information handling, history and learning: The role of the computer in the historical process. In P. Denley & D. Hopkin (Eds.), *History and Computing* (pp. 289–296). Manchester: Manchester University Press.

Wild, M. (1989). History and new technology in schools: Problems, possibilities and the way forward. In P. Denley, et al. (Eds.), *History and Computing II* (pp. 20–34). Manchester: Manchester University Press.

Wilkes, J., Ed. (1985). *Exploring History with Microcomputers*. London: Council for Educational Technology.

Williams, William Carlos (1970). *Spring and All*. Rpt. in W. Schott (Ed.), *Imaginations*. New York: New Directions. (Original publication 1923)

Winograd, T. and Flores, F. (1986). *Understanding Computers and Cognition*. Norwood, NJ: Ablex.

Wittgenstein, L. (1953). *Philosophical Investigations*. Oxford: Blackwells.

Wright, P. (1988). Personal communication.

Yankelovich, N., Haan, B. J., Meyrowitz, N. K., and Drucker, S. M. (1988, January). Intermedia: the concept and the construction of a seamless information environment. *Computer*, 81–96.

Young, R. A. (1988). Expert systems and expert opinion. In S. Moralee (Ed.), *Research and Development in Expert Systems IV* (pp. 153–161). Cambridge: Cambridge University Press.

Young, R. A. (1990). Genetic algorithms and scientific method. In J. Tiles (Ed.), *Evolving Knowledge*. London: Pitman.

Index